'You also were included'

Ephesians

Harold J Booth

You also were included Ephesians
Copyright © Harold J Booth 2009

All Rights Reserved

No part of this book may be reproduced in any form,
by photocopying or by any electronic or mechanical means,
including information storage or retrieval systems,
without permission in writing from both the copyright
owner and the publisher of this book.

ISBN 978-1-910693-07-0

First Published 2009 by
Berforts Group Limited

Printed and bound in Great Britain by
Print2Demand Ltd
Westoning

'You also were included'

Contents

- Dedication

- About this book

- Foreword by Dr Derek Stringer

- Introduction to Paul's Letters & The Author's Notes

- Abbreviations used in this Book

- Understanding The Bible, God's Word.

- Acts Chapters 19 & 20

- Ephesians

- About the author

- Acknowledgements and Notices

- Other books by the author

Dedication

The author wishes to dedicate this book to Joan and John Pickbourne, his sister and brother-in-law, recently retired missionaries in France, for their help in proof-reading this book, their helpful comments on the text, and for their love and care over many years.

I remain responsible for any errors and for the views expressed in this book.

Harold J Booth

About This Book

Readers of this book fall into one of two categories:

1. Believers: They have repented of their sin and accepted The Lord Jesus Christ as their Saviour.

2. Unbelievers: They have neither repented of their sin nor accepted The Lord Jesus Christ as their Saviour.

There is no third category.

Paul wrote his letter to believers who lived in and around Ephesus. It contained many truths about Christianity.

What distinguished the believing Ephesians from the unbelieving Ephesians is that the Ephesian believers had:

- repented of their sin and turned their backs on their old sinful way of life.

- put their trust in The Lord Jesus Christ and accepted Him as their personal Saviour.

Before the Ephesians became believers, they pleased themselves how they lived. After they became believers, they lived to please God.

You will get the most benefit from studying Ephesians if you keep these vital spiritual distinctions between believers and unbelievers in mind.

Foreword By Dr Derek Stringer

Harold Booth's profession was that of a Lawyer. Without knowing this it would probably become apparent as you read his commentary of Paul's Epistle to the Ephesians.

I have often found that commentaries are rather dull. Sometimes they seem to focus on detail (much of it not immediately relevant) and to miss the sweep of the biblical book and lose its excitement. This commentary draws upon many years of study and reflection on the eternal riches of the Gospel. This is revealed with encouragement and guidance to reach for and grasp our full spiritual potential. It shows what Christ made possible by introducing life-changing principles leading to a truly blessed life.

The style is analytical and comprehensive leaving the reader in no doubt that there is a difference between a believer and unbeliever in Christ and the consequences. It is a challenging presentation of the message of salvation.

Reading this book gives insights into the Word, ourselves, and the Lord.

Dr Derek Stringer

An Introduction to Paul's Letters

Paul's letters encouraged believers to stand firm in their personal faith. Paul also required local churches to teach the doctrines he taught. As we study Paul's letters, we realise that it was necessary for him to teach believers how they ought to behave as well as to correct false doctrines that were being taught by false teachers. These evil men were causing havoc in the local churches.

Even a cursory reading of the letters in The New Testament will confirm that James, John, Peter and the author of Hebrews had to do what Paul did in their letters that were also written to believers. Paul's Ephesian letter is unique in that there is no personal criticism of the believers or their beliefs. His letter encouraged the Ephesian believers to continue to behave as God's special people should behave.

We recommend that you read Ephesians before beginning your detailed study of Chapter 1.

'You also were included'

The title of this book is a quotation from Ephesians 1:13. If you are a believer, you are included in God's eternal plan. You will be thrilled, and you will praise God when you realise that because Jesus is your Saviour, you have received from God, 'every spiritual blessing in Christ.' The LNT emphasises how blessed believers are and why they praise God.

> 'How we praise God, the Father of our Lord Jesus Christ, who has blessed us with every blessing in heaven because we belong to Christ.'   Ephesians 1:3.

What Paul wrote so many centuries ago was not only vital for believers then, it is vital for believers today. If what you read in Ephesians does not thrill you and make you grateful for all that God has done for you and given you (even though you only deserved His eternal judgment for your sin) you must ask yourself if you are saved.

As you read Ephesians you will discover how God requires believers to live. You might think that the way you live is good enough for God and it ought to earn you a place in Heaven. But, if the way you live now is the same as you have always lived, even though it is as good as most people live, you must ask yourself if you have been saved.

An Important Note - God Detests Sin

The blessings mentioned in Ephesians are only for believers. Repentance means so much more than just saying, "Sorry." God detests sin. Repentance involves turning your back on your sinful way of life and living to please God. You cannot accept Jesus as your Saviour and then please yourself how you live. Hence the need to stress the meaning of repentance and what it means to accept Jesus as Saviour.

The Ephesian Believers - A Word of Caution

Do not assume that the Ephesian believers found living a godly life easy. Paul was in prison when he wrote this letter. His faithfulness to God cost him his liberty. Be clear about this. Unbelievers hearing The Gospel in Paul's day had to make a choice. They could accept The Gospel. They could:

- repent of their sin and accept Jesus as their Saviour.
- live as God would have believers live.

Alternatively, they could reject The Gospel, remain unbelievers, and live as they pleased. Those who decided to accept The Gospel made their decision in the knowledge that they would be persecuted if not executed. There was a choice then. There is a choice now:

- You can reject The Gospel and God's Salvation.
- You can refuse to accept Jesus as your Saviour.
- You can remain unsaved and live as the majority live.

We ask two questions:

Question 1: How do the majority live?

Answer: They live to please themselves.

Question 2: How should believers live?

Paul's answer is:

> 'I urge you to live a life worthy of the calling you have received.' Ephesians 4:1. NIV.

We read in Ephesians what this 'worthy life' is and why believers must live it. Paul's teaching applied to all believers whether newly saved or saved for many years. Unsurprisingly, no allowances or excuses are made for those who by nature are dominant and overbearing.

Unity in 'The Godhead'

There is unity in 'The Godhead.' All believers have experienced the involvement of 'The Godhead' in their lives. Believers can and must live together in unity. Unity might be impossible among unbelievers who have man-made divisions that have no place among believers who:

- 'are blessed with every spiritual blessing in Christ.'
- 'are chosen in Christ before the foundation of the world.'
- 'are forgiven and made holy and blameless in His sight.'

Believers Were Once Unbelievers

When believers were unbelievers, they were the objects of God's wrath. But they have now been individually saved, yet all have been saved on the same basis. And all are undeserving of the blessings they have freely received.

There came a time in every believer's life when they heard The Gospel, also called 'the words of truth' and 'the gospel of your salvation.' They believed it and were there and then 'marked in Christ with a seal, the Holy Spirit.'

Believing The Gospel and receiving The Holy Spirit distinguishes believers from unbelievers. Believers come from the many and varied classes of unbelievers who live in the world. As all believers have accepted the same Gospel and received the same Holy Spirit, they are united in a way that cannot be copied by unbelievers.

Paul Teaches Candid Truths in Ephesians:

1. You cannot be saved without believing The Gospel.

2. Those who are saved are indwelt by The Holy Spirit.

Many consider that they are good enough for God and they meet His divine requirements for entrance into Heaven when they die. Experience teaches that many rely upon the fact that they were born in a country with a Christian heritage. In consequence, they were baptised as infants. Many consider that doing their best to be good entitles them to a place in Heaven when they die. Experience teaches that few hear The Gospel preached when they attend places of worship. We ask two questions:

1: Does faithfully preaching The Gospel make preachers popular?

Answer: The New Testament teaches that the faithful preaching of The Gospel produces hostility.

2: Why is The Gospel unpopular?

Answer: A Holy God must punish sinners. The Gospel must include mentioning sin, repentance and judgment. Sinners love sinning, so preaching about sin, repentance and judgment empties churches faster than fire alarms.

The Bible

Read God's Word to find out what it teaches. Obey what you read. The Bible will always be relevant to you as God will speak to you through His Word. We would not be surprised to hear that most Ephesians had little, if any, interest in The Gospel that Paul preached in Ephesus.

Question: Why do we reach the above conclusion?

Answer: Because the tenor of The Bible is that the majority like sinning and pleasing themselves how they live. Few think that God will hold them to account for their sin.

Paul Wrote Only to Believers

Paul used pronouns like, 'I,' 'you,' 'we' and 'us.' To get the most benefit from reading Ephesians, as you read, ask yourself whether what you read includes you.

Acceptance of The Divine

The Bible is not an encyclopaedia. God does not reveal all that we might want to know. However, there is enough for unbelievers to know, 'The Way Of Salvation,' and for believers to know what God expects of them. We will only waste time speculating about things that God does not tell us. For example, some want to know where Heaven is. The Bible does not tell us. But we know how we can avoid eternal punishment in Hell and live eternally in Heaven.

In Ephesians, you will find such expressions as, 'in the heavenly realms.' Rather than deal with such expressions as they occur, we write about them in Chapter 6.

THE AUTHOR'S NOTES

Parts of this book will be published separately, so some matters may be repeated. This is especially so where the text refers to God's Salvation or warns us about the consequences that ensue when The Gospel is rejected.

Capital Letters

In this book capital letters have meaning and are used for references to God, The Lord Jesus Christ and The Holy Spirit. The Gospel and Salvation are capitalised because they are vital to an understanding of God's message for us. We also use capitals to emphasise the importance of the matter mentioned.

Quotations from God's Word, The Bible

To remind us that The Bible is God's Word, and especially that it is God's Word for us today, we often refer to The Bible as God's Word. Do not confuse 'God's Word,' with the translation of the Bible entitled GOD'S WORD. We use the abbreviation GW to refer to this helpful translation.

Unless otherwise stated, quotations from The Bible in this book are from the NIV. For copyright reasons, we use the spelling and punctuation of The Bible that we quote from.

The Names of Jesus

God never asks us to understand eternal truths, but, as they are contained in His Word, He does require us to believe them. We do not exaggerate when we state that much of the false doctrine taught by the various religions and cults that we come across today, relates to their teaching about Jesus. If you have wrong beliefs about Jesus, you are not a believer.

We refer to The Lord Jesus Christ as Jesus to remind us that Jesus means Saviour. Jesus always was and always will be God the Son and The Son of God. Jesus was also the Jew's Messiah, the One that God promised in The Old Testament that He would send to the Jews.

The Gospels and The Gospel

Matthew, Mark, Luke, and John, the first four books in The New Testament, tell us about Jesus' birth, life, death, burial, resurrection and ascension. They also tell us some of the things that Jesus did and taught. They are commonly known as, 'The Gospels.'

The word 'Gospel' means good news. The Gospel is about God's Salvation, the Salvation that we can have if we repent and believe it.

To save confusion, we refer to the four written Gospels as 'The Gospels.' As, 'The Gospel,' also refers to the message about Jesus and how, though sinners, we can have Salvation, we use the words 'The Gospel' to refer to this message.

Hell, The Lake of Fire and Heaven

Unbelievers will spend eternity in the Lake of Fire.

> And death and hell were cast into the lake of fire. This is the second death. Revelation 20:14-15. NIV.

For the sake of simplicity, we refer to God's home that He has prepared for believers as Heaven and the place where the Devil and unbelievers will spend eternity suffering the punishment of God for their sin, as Hell.

When Unbelievers Become Believers

There are many ways of describing what happens when unbelievers become believers. We could refer to them being saved, converted, born again and redeemed. There are many words that could be used to describe believers.

We could refer to them as Christians, saints, and the redeemed. Some of these names, although correct, are misunderstood. For the sake of clarity, we refer to those who accept Jesus as their Saviour as believers.

ABBREVIATIONS USED IN THIS BOOK

- Acts: The Acts of the Apostles
- ERV: Easy-to-Read Version
- CEV: Contemporary English Version
- GW: GOD'S WORD
- GNB: Good News Bible:
- KJV: King James or Authorised Version
- NLT: New Living Translation
- NIV: New International Version
- NIrV: New International Reader's Version
- WUEST: Wuest Expanded Translation

UNDERSTANDING THE BIBLE

A Word of Caution

Each word in The Bible is there for a purpose. It is there to be read and that means read accurately. We illustrate this point by reference to pronouns. There are many pronouns in Ephesians. We have limited space so we refer only to the pronoun, 'our,' in Ephesians 1: 3.

> Praise be to the God and Father of our Lord Jesus Christ, who has blessed us in the heavenly realms with every spiritual blessing in Christ.   Ephesians 1: 3. NIV.

Question: Does 'our' refer to everyone?

Answer: "No." 'Our' can only apply to believers as 'Christ' is their Saviour. Only believers can truthfully say that Christ belongs to them. We know from Acts how Paul and the Ephesian believers were saved. 'Our' clearly applies to them. If you have been saved, 'our' applies to you. But it does not apply to you if you are not yet saved.

The Importance of Personal Bible Study

Read God's Word, The Bible. You might know what others say about it, or you might have read about it in books. If you read God's Word, God will speak to you.

Read God's Word Accurately

Read God's Word as if you were reading it for the first time. Take time to read it accurately. Whether Paul's letter to the Ephesians is new to you or not, you will receive more blessing from reading what Paul wrote than you will from reading this or any other book about Ephesians. This truth applies to The Bible in general. We know from experience that God will teach you His Word but only if you are prepared to read it. There are obvious dangers in thinking that what you have been taught, or others have told you, is true. Experience teaches that the results of incorrect Bible teaching have been spiritually disastrous. Bibles are available. You have no excuse for believing false teaching. So, check that what you have read or heard is correct.

Our Intentions

This book is not about 'religion, human rules or traditions.' It was written to encourage you to read Ephesians and learn about the wonderful things that God has done, is doing, and will do eternally for believers.

We use the word, 'believers' in this book to distinguish believers from unbelievers. We do not use the word, 'Christians.' So many are deceived into believing that they are Christians. The truth is that because they have not been saved, they are not Christians.

Beliefs and a Lifestyle Change

If you think that the difference between believers and unbelievers relates only to their beliefs, you have either been misled, or you have misled yourself. Ephesians will teach you that believers and unbelievers should be distinguishable by their day-to-day conduct. Why? There must be a lifestyle change when an unbeliever becomes a believer. Believers have repented of their sin and their old sinful way of life. Hence, Salvation involves a lifestyle change. Believers have 'turned their backs' on their sin and their old sinful way of life. You cannot repent, receive God's Salvation and not change your way of life. God's Salvation saves from the:

- Penalty of sin: Only unbelievers will experience a sin-hating God's eternal judgment for their sin in Hell.
- Power of sin: Believers can resist the temptation to sin. They are redeemed. They are no longer sin's slaves. Unbelievers are sin's slaves and cannot stop sinning.
- Presence of sin: When believers die, they will spend eternity in Heaven where there is no sin.

The Indwelling of The Holy Spirit

When unbelievers become believers, The Holy Spirit immediately indwells them. Because He is holy, He changes believers. They stop pleasing themselves how they live and seek to live to please God.

Without the divine intervention of The Holy Spirit in their lives, humans could never please God.

A Warning Regarding A Lifestyle Change

If there is no lifestyle change when an unbeliever claims to have been saved, they deceive themselves and those who believe them. Regrettably, this sad problem exists. When some believers pass on The Gospel, the need to repent is either omitted or quickly passed over. One reason is that preaching repentance causes embarrassment, especially when those listening are educated and live good lives.

Surprisingly, those who omit to mention repentance expect it to be included when The Gospel is preached in prisons and in disadvantaged areas. Experience also teaches that some genuinely consider that preaching about sin, repentance and judgment empties churches. Their view is that no one, 'attends church,' to be told that they are Hell-deserving sinners.

Many churchgoers may never hear that The Gospel requires repentance.

Question: Can The Gospel be faithfully proclaimed without reference to sin and repentance? Paul's answer is, "No." In his farewell message to the Ephesians, he said:

> Acts 20:20-21. NIV. "You know that I have not hesitated to preach anything that would be helpful to you but have taught you publicly and from house to house. I have declared to both Jews and Greeks that they must turn to God in repentance and have faith in our Lord Jesus."

Paul stated that whether he preached publicly or privately, the same Gospel, 'turning to God in repentance and having faith in our Lord Jesus,' was for all. He preached it to both Jew and Gentile even though they worshipped so differently. The Jews worshipped God and the Gentiles worshipped idols. The Gospel that could save a religious Jew could also save an idol-worshipping Gentile.

The Must of The Gospel

Paul said, 'They **must** turn to God in repentance and have faith in our Lord Jesus.' Paul was not too embarrassed to emphasise that without repentance there can be no Salvation. Repentance precedes faith. You cannot be saved and indwelt by The Holy Spirit without repenting of your sin. Although believers only deserved God's eternal punishment for their sin, they have received all God's spiritual blessings.

It should cause you no surprise that believers willingly praise God for The Lord Jesus Christ. His willingness to die so that sinners can be forgiven has made it possible for a holy, sin-hating God to bestow His Salvation on sinners. God's Salvation is available to all, but only those who turn to God in repentance and have faith in The Lord Jesus will receive it and be saved.

If you have no desire to praise God for what Jesus has done to save you, you are not yet a believer. But we trust that as you read Ephesians, you will realise that you desperately need God's Salvation to deal with the problem of your sin. Jesus is the only Saviour of sinners.

Those responsible for this book commend their Saviour to you. If you are a believer, reading Ephesians will confirm to you how special you are to God and what He has done to ensure that your eternal future could not be better.

Acts Chapters 19 & 20

Read these two chapters. They tell us about the time that Paul spent in Ephesus as an itinerant preacher and teacher. You will be surprised at some of the events that are recorded and reading these chapters will assist you in your study of Ephesians. These two chapters are quoted for your convenience.

Acts19 & 20. NIV.

> While Apollos was at Corinth, Paul took the road through the interior and arrived at Ephesus. There he found some disciples and asked them, "Did you receive

the Holy Spirit when you believed?" They answered, "No, we have not even heard that there is a Holy Spirit." So Paul asked, "Then what baptism did you receive?" "John's baptism," they replied. Paul said, "John's baptism was a baptism of repentance. He told the people to believe in the one coming after him, that is, in Jesus." On hearing this, they were baptized in the name of the Lord Jesus. When Paul placed his hands on them, the Holy Spirit came on them, and they spoke in tongues and prophesied. There were about twelve men in all. Paul entered the synagogue and spoke boldly there for three months, arguing persuasively about the kingdom of God. But some of them became obstinate; they refused to believe and publicly maligned the Way. So Paul left them. He took the disciples with him and had discussions daily in the lecture hall of Tyrannus. This went on for two years, so that all the Jews and Greeks who lived in the province of Asia heard the word of the Lord.

God did extraordinary miracles through Paul, so that even handkerchiefs and aprons that had touched him were taken to the sick, and their illnesses were cured and the evil spirits left them. Some Jews who went around driving out evil spirits tried to invoke the name of the Lord Jesus over those who were demon-possessed. They would say, "In the name of the Jesus whom Paul preaches, I command you to come out." Seven sons of Sceva, a Jewish chief priest, were doing this. One day the evil spirit answered them, "Jesus I know, and Paul I know about, but who are you?" Then the man who had the evil spirit jumped on them and overpowered them all. He gave them such a beating that they ran out of the house naked and bleeding. When this became known to the Jews and Greeks living in Ephesus, they were all seized with fear, and the name of the Lord Jesus was held in high honor. Many of those who believed now came and openly confessed what they had done. A number who had practiced sorcery brought their scrolls together and burned them publicly. When they calculated the value of the scrolls, the total came to fifty thousand drachmas. In this way the word of the Lord spread widely and grew in power.

After all this had happened, Paul decided to go to Jerusalem, passing through Macedonia and Achaia. "After I have been there," he said, "I must visit Rome also." He sent two of his helpers, Timothy and Erastus, to Macedonia, while he stayed in the province of Asia a little longer. About that time there arose a great disturbance about the Way. A silversmith named Demetrius, who made silver shrines of Artemis, brought in a lot of business for the craftsmen there. He called them together, along with the workers in related trades, and said: "You know, my friends, that we receive a good income from this business. And you see and hear how this fellow Paul has convinced and led astray large numbers of people here in Ephesus and in practically the whole province of Asia. He says that gods made by human hands are no gods at all. There is danger not only that our trade will lose its good name, but also that the temple of the great goddess Artemis will be discredited; and the goddess herself, who is worshiped throughout the province of Asia and the world, will be robbed of her divine majesty." When they heard this, they were furious and began shouting: "Great is Artemis of the Ephesians!" Soon the whole city was in an uproar. The people seized Gaius and Aristarchus, Paul's traveling companions from Macedonia, and all of them rushed into the theater together. Paul wanted to appear before the crowd, but the disciples would not let him. Even some of the officials of the province, friends of Paul, sent him a message begging him not to venture into the theater. The assembly was in confusion: Some were shouting one thing, some another. Most of the people did not even know why they were there. The Jews in the crowd pushed Alexander to the front, and they shouted instructions to him. He motioned for silence in order to make a defense before the people. But when they realized he was a Jew, they all shouted in unison for about two hours: "Great is Artemis of the Ephesians!" The city clerk quieted the crowd and said: "Fellow Ephesians, doesn't all the world know that the city of Ephesus is the guardian of the temple of the great Artemis and of her image, which fell from heaven? Therefore, since these facts are undeniable, you ought to calm down and not do anything rash. You have brought these men here, though they have neither robbed temples nor blasphemed our goddess. If, then, Demetrius and his fellow craftsmen have a grievance against anybody, the courts are open and there are proconsuls. They can press charges. If there is anything further you want to bring up, it must be settled in a legal assembly. As it is, we are in danger of being charged with rioting because of what happened today. In that case we would not be able to account for this commotion, since there is no reason for it." After he had said this, he dismissed the assembly.   Acts 19. NIV.

Acts 20. NIV. When the uproar had ended, Paul sent for the disciples and, after encouraging them, said goodbye and set out for Macedonia. He traveled through that area, speaking many words of encouragement to the people, and finally arrived in Greece, where he stayed three months. Because some Jews had plotted against him just as he was about to sail for Syria, he decided to go back through Macedonia. He was accompanied by Sopater son of Pyrrhus from Berea, Aristarchus and Secundus from Thessalonica, Gaius from Derbe, Timothy also, and Tychicus and Trophimus from the province of Asia. These men went on ahead and waited for us at Troas. But we sailed from Philippi after the Festival of Unleavened Bread, and five days later joined the others at Troas, where we stayed seven days.

On the first day of the week we came together to break bread. Paul spoke to the people and, because he intended to leave the next day, kept on talking until midnight. There were many lamps in the upstairs room where we were meeting. Seated in a window was a young man named Eutychus, who was sinking into a deep sleep as Paul talked on and on. When he was sound asleep, he fell to the ground from the third story and was picked up dead. Paul went down, threw himself on the young man and put his arms around him. "Don't be alarmed," he said. "He's alive!" Then he went upstairs again and broke bread and ate. After talking until daylight, he left. The people took the young man home alive and were greatly comforted. We went on ahead to the ship and sailed for Assos, where we were going to take Paul aboard. He had made this arrangement because he was going there on foot. When he met us at Assos, we took him aboard and went on to Mitylene. The next day we set sail from there and arrived off Chios. The day after that we crossed over to Samos, and on the following day arrived at Miletus. Paul had decided to sail past Ephesus to avoid spending time in the province of Asia, for he was in a hurry to reach Jerusalem, if possible, by the day of Pentecost.

From Miletus, Paul sent to Ephesus for the elders of the

church. When they arrived, he said to them: "You know how I lived the whole time I was with you, from the first day I came into the province of Asia. I served the Lord with great humility and with tears and in the midst of severe testing by the plots of my Jewish opponents. You know that I have not hesitated to preach anything that would be helpful to you but have taught you publicly and from house to house. I have declared to both Jews and Greeks that they must turn to God in repentance and have faith in our Lord Jesus. "And now, compelled by the Spirit, I am going to Jerusalem, not knowing what will happen to me there. I only know that in every city the Holy Spirit warns me that prison and hardships are facing me. However, I consider my life worth nothing to me; my only aim is to finish the race and complete the task the Lord Jesus has given me—the task of testifying to the good news of God's grace. "Now I know that none of you among whom I have gone about preaching the kingdom will ever see me again. Therefore, I declare to you today that I am innocent of the blood of any of you. For I have not hesitated to proclaim to you the whole will of God. Keep watch over yourselves and all the flock of which the Holy Spirit has made you overseers. Be shepherds of the church of God, which he bought with his own blood. I know that after I leave, savage wolves will come in among you and will not spare the flock. Even from your own number men will arise and distort the truth in order to draw away disciples after them. So be on your guard! Remember that for three years I never stopped warning each of you night and day with tears. "Now I commit you to God and to the word of his grace, which can build you up and give you an inheritance among all those who are sanctified. I have not coveted anyone's silver or gold or clothing. You yourselves know that these hands of mine have supplied my own needs and the needs of my companions. In everything I did, I showed you that by this kind of hard work we must help the weak, remembering the words the Lord Jesus himself said: 'It is more blessed to give than to receive.'" When Paul had finished speaking, he knelt down with all of them and prayed. They all wept as they embraced him and kissed him. What grieved them most was his statement that they would never see his face again. Then they accompanied him to the ship.   Acts 20. NIV.

Ephesians 1. NIV.

'1. Paul, an apostle of Christ Jesus by the will of God, To God's holy people in Ephesus, the faithful in Christ Jesus: 2. Grace and peace to you from God our Father and the Lord Jesus Christ. 3. Praise be to the God and Father of our Lord Jesus Christ, who has blessed us in the heavenly realms with every spiritual blessing in Christ. 4. For he chose us in him before the creation of the world to be holy and blameless in his sight. In love 5. he predestined us for adoption to sonship through Jesus Christ, in accordance with his pleasure and will—6. to the praise of his glorious grace, which he has freely given us in the One he loves. 7. In him we have redemption through his blood, the forgiveness of sins, in accordance with the riches of God's grace 8. that he lavished on us. With all wisdom and understanding, 9. he made known to us the mystery of his will according to his good pleasure, which he purposed in Christ, 10. to be put into effect when the times reach their fulfillment--to bring unity to all things in heaven and on earth under Christ. 11. In him we were also chosen, having been predestined according to the plan of him who works out everything in conformity with the purpose of his will, 12. in order that we, who were the first to put our hope in Christ, might be for the praise of his glory. 13. And you also were included in Christ when you heard the message of truth, the gospel of your salvation. When you believed, you were marked in him with a seal, the promised Holy Spirit, 14. who is a deposit guaranteeing our inheritance until the redemption of those who are God's possession--to the praise of his glory. 15. For this reason, ever since I heard about your faith in the Lord Jesus and your love for all God's people, 16. I have not stopped giving

> thanks for you, remembering you in my prayers. 17. I keep asking that the God of our Lord Jesus Christ, the glorious Father, may give you the Spirit of wisdom and revelation, so that you may know him better. 18. I pray that the eyes of your heart may be enlightened in order that you may know the hope to which he has called you, the riches of his glorious inheritance in his holy people, 19. and his incomparably great power for us who believe. That power is the same as the mighty strength 20. he exerted when he raised Christ from the dead and seated him at his right hand in the heavenly realms, 21. far above all rule and authority, power and dominion, and every name that is invoked, not only in the present age but also in the one to come. 22. And God placed all things under his feet and appointed him to be head over everything for the church, 23. which is his body, the fullness of him who fills everything in every way.' Ephesians 1. NIV.

COMMENTARY ON EPHESIANS 1

Ephesians 1:1-2

> Paul, an apostle of Christ Jesus by the will of God, To God's holy people in Ephesus, the faithful in Christ Jesus. 2. Grace and peace to you from God our Father and the Lord Jesus Christ.   Ephesians 1:1-2.

Commentary Ephesians 1:1-2.

Paul wrote his name at the beginning of the letter. In Paul's day, letter writers did the opposite of what we do today. The Ephesian believers knew Paul. He spent over three years in Ephesus when he was an itinerant preacher and teacher. Through his efforts, the local church at Ephesus was established. At this stage, you should read, or reread, Acts Chapters 19 and 20. Throughout this book we refer to various verses in those two chapters. You will be fascinated by the events that occurred during the time Paul spent in Ephesus. He was a specially commissioned apostle of Christ Jesus. 'Apostle' simply means 'special messenger.' It refers to one who passes on the message of another like present-day ambassadors that many governments appoint. They pass on messages from their governments. Apostles, like ambassadors, did not add to the message. Paul's task was to deliver the message exactly as he had received it. It is important to note that Paul did not vary the message he had been given.

As Paul referred to Jesus three times in the first two verses of his letter, you cannot but realise that the connection between Jesus and believers could not be more important. Paul refers to Jesus as 'Christ Jesus' twice in verse 1 and the 'Lord Jesus Christ' in verse 2. We do not have the space to discuss the various Names given to Jesus in Ephesians and elsewhere in The Bible, but you will note as you read Ephesians that there is a repeated emphasis on the relationship between Jesus and believers.

Do not miss the truth stated in verse 1 because it is so easy to bring current thinking, and personal ambitions into local churches. Paul did not choose to be an apostle. He was chosen by God. He was obedient to 'the will of God.' There is a view among believers today that they can please themselves what they do for The Church. Some think they are suitable for missionary work. Others see themselves as pastors. These examples will suffice to illustrate how erroneous this 'self-selection' process is.

We must add that those who have read all Paul's letters will confirm that if he ever expressed his personal view, he clearly indicated it. Despite this, some believers have the silly notion that Paul's letters contained only his own views and the even sillier notion that their views are better than his. Some believers think that the instructions in Paul's letters apply only to the local churches they were addressed to and only applied to circumstances existing at the time they were written. Some think that if Paul wrote his letters today, his teaching would be different. Experience teaches that those who express these views have their own agendas. They want to promote their own views of what a local church is and what it should be doing. Many want to make Christianity acceptable to the community. But The Church and the local churches belong to God. The local church does not belong to its members and they cannot do what they please with it.

Experience also teaches that some believers have an unusual attitude to The Bible because they choose to ignore verses they do not like. But they have a problem. Paul wrote more about The Church and the local churches than any other New Testament writer. If those who state that Paul's teaching is irrelevant today tore out of The New Testament every page that contained something they considered irrelevant, how many pages would remain?

Some think that a local church belongs to its members and that each member has one vote. Even a cursory reading of The New Testament will confirm that local churches have not been established and cannot be organised on the same basis as political, social or sports clubs. Such clubs:

- never had apostles and prophets who established them and passed on to them divine knowledge.
- do not desire to know 'the will of God.'
- do not have a membership that is composed of, 'God's holy people …. the faithful in Christ Jesus.'

But you will read these things in Ephesians 1:1 and they refer to believers who must acknowledge that God's Will prevails over their own wills. It should not only be in a believer's private prayers that they pray that, 'God's Will be done.' They should seek God's Will for the local church.

The Believers' Spiritual and Practical Status

Because Jesus shed His blood for believers, God sees them as blameless. Paul referred to the Ephesian believers as 'God's holy people.' That was their spiritual status. There is no criticism in Ephesians of the believer's beliefs or conduct. Paul's other letters chastises those he wrote to. The Ephesian believers' spiritual status was also their practical status. Hence, Paul called them 'the faithful in Christ Jesus.'

Holy and Faithful

The Ephesian believers were 'holy' and 'faithful.' All believers have the spiritual status of being 'holy'; but how many are 'faithful?' 'Faithful' means far more than regular attendance at a local church. Before being saved the Ephesians pleased themselves how they lived. Salvation changed their lives. Being faithful to Jesus was their priority.

Ephesians 1:2

> Grace and peace to you from God our Father and the Lord Jesus Christ.   Ephesians 1:2. NIV.

If we read these words quickly we will miss so much. In our comments on verse 1 we stressed that if we want the spiritual blessings that are available to all believers, we must live as the Ephesian believers lived. They acknowledged that God's Will must prevail in everything and hence, they lived as God's holy people should live.

Are we prepared to stop pleasing ourselves and be counted among 'the faithful in Christ Jesus?' We will not change unless we acknowledge that God's Word is for us today. Hence, we warn against those who 'dilute' it.

Paul desired that the believers should have 'grace and peace.' 'Grace' was a Greek greeting and 'peace' a Jewish greeting. But Paul did not use 'grace and peace' as a greeting. He referred to 'grace and peace from God'. We cannot easily substitute another single word for 'grace.' From the context of the verses we can see that 'grace' is something that God freely gives believers. No one has ever deserved the blessings that God gives to those who repent and accept Jesus as their Saviour. We ask you to carefully consider grace, God's undeserved favour to those who believe in Jesus.

Grace

This acronym has helped many to appreciate God grace.

Great **R**iches **A**t **C**hrist's **E**xpense.

But there is more. Believers have also received God's peace.

Peace

'Peace' often refers to the end of hostilities, but Paul wanted the Ephesian believers to:
- have God's peace in their hearts.
- be at peace with God.

Sinners are Rebels

Sin is rebellion against God. Unbelievers cannot have God's peace in their hearts or be at peace with God. They are rebels and hostile to God. Read Romans 5:10.

> 'Once we were God's enemies. But we have been brought back to him because his Son has died for us.'

Many unbelievers do not know God's view of them. God is not the Father of mankind. He is only the Father of His children. Hence Paul stated that the grace and peace that the Ephesian believers enjoyed was from 'God our Father' and The Lord Jesus Christ. The word, 'our,' can only refer to Paul and the Ephesian believers. Many unbelievers use the expression 'our Father' not realising that God is not, and never has been, their Father. Regrettably, they are taught, by religious people, that God is their father from cradle to grave. Many have the idea that God is the universal Father but only believers can truly address God as Father because only they are His children.

If you have been misled about your relationship to God, you have an opportunity now of repenting of your sin and accepting The Lord Jesus Christ as your Saviour.

Question 1: Why in verse 2 does Paul mention both God and The Lord Jesus Christ?

Answer: We quote Colossians 1:13-22 so that you can read the answer for yourself. Reading these verses will also assist you to answer our next question. It relates to both verses 3 and 17. Both refer to 'the God and Father of our Lord Jesus Christ.' Please read these verses carefully as on first reading you could have the false impression that Jesus was inferior to God the Father.

> For he has rescued us from the dominion of darkness and brought us into the kingdom of the Son he loves, in whom we have redemption, the forgiveness of sins. The Son is the image of the invisible God, the firstborn over all creation. For in him all things were created: things in heaven and on earth, visible and invisible, whether thrones or powers or rulers or authorities; all things have been created through him and for him. He is before all things, and in him all things hold together. And he is the head of the body, the church;

> he is the beginning and the firstborn from among the dead, so that in everything he might have the supremacy. For God was pleased to have all his fullness dwell in him, and through him to reconcile to himself all things, whether things on earth or things in heaven, by making peace through his blood, shed on the cross. Once you were alienated from God and were enemies in your minds because of your evil behavior. But now he has reconciled you by Christ's physical body through death to present you holy in his sight, without blemish and free from accusation. Colossians1:13-22 NIV.

Question 2: Why did Paul use the expression 'the God and Father of our Lord Jesus Christ' in Ephesians 1.

Answer: We answer this question when we study verse 17.

Ephesians 1:3-6.

As you read these verses, note that because believers are united to Jesus, God gives them every spiritual blessing. God gives good things to His children. He does not give some good things but not all good things. Believers will never know the extent of God's grace, love and mercy towards them. But whatever befalls them they can praise God for their eternal union with Jesus.

> Praise be to the God and Father of our Lord Jesus Christ, who has blessed us in the heavenly realms with every spiritual blessing in Christ. For he chose us in him before the creation of the world to be holy and blameless in his sight. In love he predestined us for adoption to sonship through Jesus Christ, in accordance with his pleasure and will—to the praise of his glorious grace, which he has freely given us in the One he loves. Ephesians 1:3-6. NIV.

There have been long-standing disagreements among believers about the subjects of predestination and election. Do we choose to accept or decline God's 'Offer of Salvation' or, does God choose those who will be saved? In the author's book, 'The one and only Church,' a book about Acts and his book 'Paul's Letter to the Romans' predestination and election are discussed in depth. Details of these books are provided later.

The New Testament tells us that Paul was chosen by Jesus to reveal to God's newly established Church truth not revealed in The Old Testament. Paul wrote more of The New Testament than any other writer and, in Ephesians, Paul tell us about the special relationship between God and believers that existed before time began. Asking five questions and stating Paul's answers might help us to understand this special relationship. Keep in mind that the eternal God has foreknowledge. He knows the future. He can plan ahead.

1. What did God do? 'He chose us in him.' 'He predestined us for adoption to sonship through Jesus Christ.'

2. When did God chose believers and decide that they would become His family? 'Before creation.'

3. What was God's purpose when He made His choice and decision? God chose believers 'to be holy and blameless in his sight.' They would become His family.

4. On what basis did God make His choices and decisions? Jesus and believers are united. God loved them because of all that Jesus would one day do for them.

5. Did God choose and decide randomly? It was 'in accordance with his pleasure and will.'

So, we know from Paul that God chose believers before creation because of their union with Jesus. God decided that believers would become His family because of all that

Jesus was going to do for them. God has foreknowledge and believers are part of God's eternal plan. All that God did was 'in accordance with his pleasure and will.'

God's Pleasure and Will

Paul's teaching about God's love for Jesus and believers is like the truth stated in John 3. Time spent meditating on John 3 will be time well spent. Space limits us to writing about Ephesians 1:6 and John 3:35-36.

> Ephesians 1:6: 'to the praise of his glorious grace, which he has freely given us in the One he loves.'
> John 3:35-36: 'The Father loves the Son and has placed everything in his hands. Whoever believes in the Son has eternal life, but whoever rejects the Son will not see life, for God's wrath remains on them.'

We cannot read Ephesians 1 without being aware of God's love for both Jesus and believers. The relationship between Jesus and believers, and what Jesus has done for believers is the reason why God chose them 'to be holy and blameless in his sight,' and so He predestined them 'for adoption to sonship.' The easier-to-read style of the NIrV quoted below may assist you to understand this truth that seems to have bewildered so many for centuries.

> Ephesians 1:3-6. NIrV. Give praise to the God and Father of our Lord Jesus Christ. He has blessed us with every spiritual blessing. Those blessings come from the heavenly world. They belong to us because we belong to Christ. God chose us to belong to Christ before the world was created. He chose us to be holy and without blame in his eyes. He loved us. So he decided long ago to adopt us as his children. He did it because of what Jesus Christ has done. It pleased God to do it. All those things bring praise to his glorious grace. God freely

> gave us his grace because of the One he loves.
> Ephesians 1:3-6. NIrV.

You will note from the above that every blessing a believer is given brings praise to God's glorious grace.

God's Glorious Grace

Believers possess no personal qualities that enable God to differentiate between them and unbelievers. Believers are not sinless any more than unbelievers totally sinful. Believers have no grounds to boast, or to seek or receive glory. They have freely received every blessing although they only deserved God's eternal judgment for their sin. 'Grace' in Ephesians 1.6 means 'favour and mercy.' God has not shown believers His glorious favour and mercy to glorify them but that He, and He alone, will receive praise. The tenor of The Bible is that God hates pride. You can take no credit for the fact that you have received all God's spiritual blessings. 'Before the creation of the world' God chose you 'to be holy and blameless in his sight.' God decided you would become one of His family. Your blessings have been given to you because God loves His Son, Jesus. You belong to Jesus and God loves you.

We do not wish to mislead readers. When we write, 'You belong to Jesus and God loves you,' we are only referring to believers. You could become a believer now by repenting of your sin and accepting The Lord Jesus Christ as your Saviour. You will then, and only then, be included.

Ephesians 1:7-8

> In him we have redemption through his blood, the forgiveness of sins, in accordance with the riches of God's grace that he lavished on us. With all wisdom and understanding… Ephesians 1:7-

Redemption

Slavery was common in Paul's day. Slaves were bought and sold. If you were rich and benevolent, you might want to free slaves from their lifelong plight. You could buy them and set them free. They would no longer be slaves as you had paid the redemption price to free them.

Slavery and slaves are equated to sin and sinners in The Bible. We are all born sinners. Unless we repent and accept Jesus as our Saviour, we will die unsaved sinners.

If you are not a believer, sin is your master. It controls you. You might think that you can please yourself what you do but that is not true because you cannot stop sinning. If you disagree, try not sinning for the next seven days. Because we know you will not succeed, we have good news for you.

- The Gospel's good news is that Jesus' blood that He shed on the Cross will both forgive your sin and redeem or free you from sin forever.
- There is more good news because God regards believers as never having sinned.

Believers never deserved to be freed from the slavery of sin or considered sinless. They are the beneficiaries of God's grace. Note how Paul describes God's grace in the context of redemption and forgiveness:

- 'the riches of God's grace.' Ephesians 1:7.
- 'grace that he lavished on us.' Ephesians 1:8.

Paul did not want believers to forget that they never deserved anything from God. Paul did not just refer to God's grace, he stressed that believers have redemption and forgiveness because of the magnitude and the riches of God's grace. Hence, we read that God has lavished His grace on believers.

Experience teaches that people want to discuss 'religion.' Hours are wasted on such discussions. Four matters are worth the time spent discussing them with unbelievers:

1. God's holiness.
2. God's love.
3. God's eternal punishment for sin.
4. God's willingness to forgive.

Ephesians 1:7 tells us:

- why a holy, sin-hating God can receive into Heaven, His eternal home where sin does not exist, saved sinners.
- why sinners who are not saved will suffer a loving and gracious God's eternal judgment for their sin.

Whatever your circumstances, let this thought sink deep into your heart. God is willing to lavish the riches of His grace on those who are willing to accept Jesus as their Saviour. God is a gracious God. We want to emphasise this as we mention God's eternal punishment.

God's Eternal Punishment

Experience teaches that many are hoping to be in Heaven when they die. Many are taught by their churches that God is so loving, everyone will be received into Heaven when they die. We hear it said at funeral services. It might comfort the bereaved, but it is not true. We mention God's judgment in the context of His love and grace and state that if you suffer God's eternal punishment for your sin, you will never be able to say that:

- God's holiness made Him ungracious.
- God never loved sinners or never loved you.
- God never wanted to redeem and forgive you.

The truth can be simply stated. God was always willing to

lavish the riches of His grace upon you but you rejected 'His Offer of Salvation,' and any who suffer God's eternal punishment for their sin will not be able to say that Jesus did not shed His own blood and die so that they could be set free from sin and forgiven.

Those who fail to accept 'God's Offer of Salvation' will suffer God's eternal punishment. We have not decided that this is true. This is not conjecture on our part. Before reading on, we ask you to reread the eight verses we have studied in Ephesians 1. The benefits of being believers are obvious, but the majority choose to remain unbelievers.

We trust you will now understand why we state that God did not exclude unbelievers from His Salvation and His blessings. If you are an unbeliever, we tell you that Salvation is available to you today as Jesus shed His Blood for you on the Cross. But God will never force you to repent and accept Jesus as your Saviour. On the Day of Judgment, you will not be able to say that God refused to choose you to be one of His children. It was you who refused to accept His Salvation.

Today we proclaim The Gospel. Salvation is available to all who heed its message. We proclaim that Jesus shed His blood on the cross and died so that God can forgive all those who repent and accept Jesus as their Saviour.

We trust that we have made it clear that the reason why all unbelievers will suffer God's eternal punishment is that they choose to remain unsaved. Have you chosen to remain unsaved? We have no wish to offend. You might find this question rather blunt. But, if it makes you realise that you have a perilous eternal future, you will be glad that we were frank enough to ask it. And, like the author, you might find that the next verse becomes one of your favourite Bible verses. It refers to Jesus and it is worth memorising.

> In him we have redemption through his blood, the forgiveness of sins, in accordance with the riches of God's grace. Ephesians 1:7. NIV.

Ephesians 1:8-10

> Ephesians 1:8-10. With all wisdom and understanding, he made known to us the mystery of his will according to his good pleasure, which he purposed in Christ, to be put into effect when the times reach their fulfillment--to bring unity to all things in heaven and on earth under Christ. Ephesians 1:8-10. NIV.

It can be difficult to grasp the meaning of these verses at a first reading. Other translations simplify the text. We quote from GOD'S WORD. We start at verse 5 to make verses 8-10 understandable in their context:

> Ephesians 1:5-10. GW. Because of his love he had already decided to adopt us through Jesus Christ. He freely chose to do this so that the kindness he had given us in his dear Son would be praised and given glory. Through the blood of his Son, we are set free from our sins. God forgives our failures because of his overflowing kindness. He poured out his kindness by giving us every kind of wisdom and insight when he revealed the mystery of his plan to us. He had decided to do this through Christ. He planned to bring all of history to its goal in Christ. Then Christ would be the head of everything in heaven and on earth.

Experience teaches that Bible truths that seem crystal clear to believers, seem anything but to unbelievers. The above verses state that only believers have the spiritual ability to understand God's plan. Many years ago, preachers referred to God's plan to save sinners as 'God's Plan of Salvation.' But, as the above verses teach, God's plan involved so much more than saving sinners.

Only in Paul's day did God make His plan known. The word 'mystery' does not refer to something that is sinister or shadowy. It refers to truth that God is now revealing that He has not previously revealed.

- God did not make a new plan to replace a previous plan.
- God's plan existed before creation.
- God has now revealed His plan.
- God's plan involves Jesus and believers.

The New Testament teaches that believers are indwelt by The Holy Spirit immediately they are saved and the verses we are reading tell us that believers have:

- all wisdom and understanding.
- the knowledge of God's Will.

That is not to say that upon being saved, a believer knows all there is to know about spiritual things. But every believer can be taught by The Holy Spirit as they read God's Word. There is no limit to their spiritual knowledge. It is only when you begin to understand the spiritual blessings that believers receive from The Godhead that you appreciate their very privileged position.

The verses we have considered should make unbelievers realise what they are missing. A review of what we have read will prepare us for the verses that follow. A believer:

- is blessed with every spiritual blessing in Christ.
- was chosen in Christ before creation.
- is regarded by God as holy and blameless.
- is loved by God.
- was predestined for adoption into God's family.

- has God's rich and glorious grace lavished upon them.
- has been redeemed and forgiven.
- has wisdom and understanding and knows God's Will.

Has 'God's Plan' been accomplished?

Paul mentioned two periods of time:

1. The first period was in the past - 'before the creation of the world'- Ephesians 1:4.
2. The second period was in the future - 'when the times reach their fulfillment'- Ephesians 1:10.

Question: Is this second period of time still future?

Answer: Until there is 'unity to all things in heaven and on earth under Christ,' God's Plan will not reach its fulfilment.

Today's Good News for Unbelievers

There is still an opportunity for unbelievers to be saved and receive the same blessings that God has bestowed upon all believers. If you are not yet saved, why not repent of your sin and accept Jesus as your Saviour now.

People question why God allows this and that to happen. Few realise that the world today is anything but the perfect world that God created. It is difficult for us to imagine a world without sin. Sin has blighted the whole of creation. Sin is evident everywhere because sinners like sinning. Sin is inherent in us. No one had to teach us how to sin.

Unsurprisingly, those who want God to intervene in various matters and who blame Him for allowing this and that to happen, do not want Him to intervene in their personal lives.

God Has A Plan, and when the time is right, the present sin-ravaged chaotic state of this world will come under the sovereignty of Jesus. We read:

> Ephesians 1:10. GNB. This plan, which God will complete when the time is right, is to bring all creation together, everything in heaven and on earth, with Christ as head. Ephesians 1:10. GNB.

Ephesians 1: 11-14

> Ephesians 1:11-14. NIV. In him we were also chosen, having been predestined according to the plan of him who works out everything in conformity with the purpose of his will, in order that we, who were the first to put our hope in Christ, might be for the praise of his glory. And you also were included in Christ when you heard the message of truth, the gospel of your salvation. When you believed, you were marked in him with a seal, the promised Holy Spirit, who is a deposit guaranteeing our inheritance until the redemption of those who are God's possession—to the praise of his glory. Ephesians 1:11-14. NIV.

We commenced our study of Ephesians by considering how blessed believers are. They have 'every spiritual blessing in Christ.' Can you think of any better than being 'included in Christ?' Being 'included in Christ' has no significance at all for most people. If you ask them what is on their 'wish list,' you would be surprised if anyone mentioned a desire to be 'included in Christ.'

On the other hand, you would not be surprised to hear answers confirming that people are interested in the 'here and now.' Material possessions are likely to head their 'I want it now list.' If they had to limit their wish to just one word it would be either 'money' or 'wealth,' and they mean 'the more the better.' Re-read Ephesians 1:10-14. We quote from GOD'S WORD. Paul's words should thrill you. If they do not, you ought to consider if you are saved.

> Ephesians 1:10-14. GW. He planned to bring all of history to its goal in Christ. Then Christ would be the head of everything in heaven and on earth. God also decided ahead of time to choose us through Christ according to his plan, which makes everything work the way he intends. He planned all of this so that we who had already focused our hope on Christ would praise him and give him glory. You heard and believed the message of truth, the Good News that he has saved you. In him you were sealed with the Holy Spirit whom he promised. This Holy Spirit is the guarantee that we will receive our inheritance. We have this guarantee until we are set free to belong to him. God receives praise and glory for this.'   Ephesians 1:10-14. GW.

The Lord Jesus Christ and Believers

Re-read Ephesians 1:1-14. Count the number of times that Jesus and believers are mentioned. Paul used various Names for Jesus, e.g., Christ Jesus, Lord Jesus, Christ, Jesus Christ. Paul used various pronouns for believers, e.g., you, our, and us. Also note that in these verses Paul repeated two truths, so they must be very important. They teach that Jesus and those who are redeemed by His blood are inseparable for time and eternity. Some teach that believers can lose their Salvation, but Paul did not teach it. Twice he stated the opposite. God's Plan can be known by all believers. There can be no doubt that:

Ephesians 1:4 - 'he' [God] 'chose us [believers] in him' [Christ]

Ephesians 1:5 - 'he' [God] 'predestined us [believers] for adoption to sonship through Jesus Christ.'

Ephesians 1:11 - 'In him' [Christ] 'we were also chosen,

having been predestined according to the plan ....'

God chose believers in Jesus before creation. He predestined them for adoption to sonship through Jesus.

Some ask why God chose some but not others. We have read Paul's answer in Ephesians 1, but it is ignored by those who have misguided views of God's grace, love, and mercy. Did you know that some only preach about God's grace, love, and mercy and remain silent about God's hatred of sin and His punishment for sin? This selective and misleading preaching is as wrong as it is inexcusable.

Why Did God Choose Some But Not Others?

Paul's answer requires us to study several verses. First, we must consider what Paul wrote about believers, their spiritual blessings, and the divine activity relating to them.

We know that some believers are confused about their spiritual welfare because false teaching about Salvation has continued since the days of the early church.

In Ephesians 1, verses 1-9, we read eight truths about believers. Spend time musing upon them:

1. Ephesians 1:1. They are 'God's holy people.'
2. Ephesians 1:1. They are 'in Christ Jesus.'
3. Ephesians 1:2. They know God as 'our Father.'
4. Ephesians 1:4. They know Jesus as 'our Lord Jesus Christ.'
5. Ephesians 1:4. They are 'holy and blameless.'
6. Ephesians 1:7. They are redeemed through Jesus' blood.
7. Ephesians 1:7. Their sins have been forgiven.
8. Ephesians 1:9. They know the mystery of God's Will.

Why did Paul Change The Pronouns?

- Paul initially wrote 'our' and 'us' when he referred to

himself and the Ephesian believers. Ephesians 1:1-10.

- Paul changed the pronouns. He wrote 'we' and 'you' to the same believers. Ephesians 1:11-13.

An Important Difference

Paul's pronouns, 'we,' and 'you,' relate to the historical differences between Jews and Gentiles:

- The Jews worshipped God
- The Gentiles worshipped idols.

This was an important distinction in Old Testament days. It has no relevance in The Church era. We will read this later in Ephesians 2.

Paul was a Jew. The Ephesians were Gentiles. The Gospel was first preached to Jews. Those who were saved were the first believers. They preached The Gospel to Gentiles. Some Gentiles became believers. Paul used 'we,' and 'the first,' in verse 12 to refer to Jewish believers, as they were the first believers, and 'you' in verse 13 to refer to the Gentile believers.

Believers are the Beneficiaries of Divine Activity

Note the divine activity in Ephesians 1:13 that follows the words, 'You also were included.'

- It cannot be ignored.
- It tells us why God chose and predestined believers.

Ephesians 1:13. Part 1.

> Ephesians1:13. NIV. And you also were included in Christ when you heard the message of truth, the gospel of your salvation.   Ephesians1:13. NIV.

Paul stated the history of those chosen by God. Ephesians 1:13 begins with the word 'and' which connects it to the previous verses. The believers had heard and believed 'the message of truth' The Gospel. Their personal belief in The Gospel resulted in their Salvation.

We have read in Ephesians 1 that:

- Believers are very special to God.
- God chose and predestined believers before creation.
- God has blessed believers with every spiritual blessing so that their futures could not be better.

Why God chose those who have come to be believers and not others will become clear as you answer this question.

Question: What did those who were chosen do that those who were not chosen did not do?

Answer: In Ephesians 1:13 Paul wrote two specific facts about those who were chosen. Ephesians 1:13 is so important that we quote it again from the NLT:

> Ephesians 1:13. NLT. And now you Gentiles have also heard the truth, the Good News that God saves you. And when you believed in Christ, He identified you as His own by giving you the Holy Spirit, whom He promised long ago.   Ephesians 1:13. NLT.

Fact 1: The believers, 'the chosen,' had been willing to listen to The Gospel, 'the message of truth.'

Fact 2: The believers, 'the chosen,' had been willing to believe The Gospel, 'the message of truth.'

Facts about Unbelievers: Then and Now

The vast majority of Ephesians had no interest in hearing or believing The Gospel. The vast majority today have no interest in hearing or believing The Gospel. Only a minority of Ephesians chose to do what God required them to do. When they believed The Gospel, God immediately identified them as His own and gave them The Holy Spirit as proof of His eternal plan for them.

Additional Facts

Hearing but taking no notice of The Gospel brings no spiritual benefit to an unbeliever. Hearing and believing The Gospel has three eternal and spiritual benefits:

1. The Gospel becomes The Gospel of the believer's Salvation.
2. God puts His stamp of ownership on the believer.
3. The believer receives God's gift of The Holy Spirit.

Two Facts About Unchosen Unbelievers

1. The unchosen Ephesians unbelievers could have heard and believed The Gospel if they had chosen to do so.
2. The difference between those who were chosen and those who were not chosen had nothing to do with their race, religion or any other difference.

Belief Separates The Chosen and The Unchosen

We either believe or we do not. There is no third option. We are either chosen or not chosen. There is no third group that applies to anyone thinking about becoming a believer. It is obvious from what Paul wrote that God has always known what we would decide. God only chose those who would, of their own freewill, choose to believe.

The Gospel

We have written about The Gospel on several occasions. So that no reader is confused, we need to consider what The Gospel is. If you have not yet read Acts 19 and 20, may we request that you read those two chapters now.

In Acts 20 Paul referred to his time in Ephesus and stated in Acts 20:21 exactly what he preached there. If you are a believer, memorise this verse so that whenever you have the privilege of explaining to an unbeliever what The Gospel is, and what it requires them to do, you will recall this important verse. We quote it from the NLT:

> "I have had one message for Jews and Greeks alike— the necessity of repenting from sin and turning to God, and of having faith in our Lord Jesus." Acts 20:21. NLT.

Acts 20:21: A Vital Gospel Verse

- Believers know that what Paul preached is true because it records their experience when they were saved.
- If what Paul preached in Ephesus comes as a surprise to you, you need to consider if you are saved.

The Gospel's Three Vital Requirements

Paul used the word 'necessity.' So, every time you hear The Gospel proclaimed, you should expect to hear the preacher state these three requirements for Salvation. You should expect to hear sinners must:

1. Repent from their sin.

2. Turn to God.

3. Have faith in our Lord Jesus Christ.

The three vital requirements mentioned in Acts 20:21 sum up what you need to mention if you preach The Gospel. If you omit any part, you will not have preached The Gospel. Whether you preach from a pulpit or share The Gospel with friends and colleagues, you must always tell unbelievers these three vital requirements. There is only one Gospel. Many things have changed in the last two thousand years but not The Gospel. It cannot change or be changed. Hence, even if you are speaking to those who live impeccable lives, you must not avoid mentioning the need to repent and turn to God.

We know from experience that the need to repent is being 'toned down' to make The Gospel more acceptable. Some have foolishly concluded that not mentioning repentance makes The Gospel less embarrassing or confrontational. Those who change, or want to change, The Gospel should consider Acts 20:21. We repeat it:

> "'I have had one message for Jews and Greeks alike—the necessity of repenting from sin and turning to God, and of having faith in our Lord Jesus.'" Acts 20:21. NLT.

Why would Paul refer to 'the necessity of repenting from sin and turning to God,' if it was not necessary? What is the point of people hearing a message that cannot save them? If you did not repent when you thought you had become a believer, we can tell you that you have either misled yourself or been misled. You are an unbeliever. Is that the reason why you do not want preachers to mention sin and repentance or mention them yourself?

Ephesians 1:13 and Acts 20:21

Although we refer to Acts 20:21 several times in this book, our key verse is Ephesians 1:13.

> And you also were included in Christ when you heard the message of truth, the gospel of your salvation. When you believed, you were marked in him with a seal, the promised Holy Spirit ...' Ephesians 1:13. NIV.

It would be foolish to think that God would give The Holy Spirit to unrepentant unbelievers. Preachers who remove repentance from The Gospel, do their hearers a disservice. Without knowing the necessity of repentance, they cannot become believers and receive The Holy Spirit.

'The Second Blessing'

The doctrine known as 'The Second Blessing' needs to be considered and the second part of Ephesians 1:13 is an appropriate time to mention it.

Ephesians 1:13. Part 2

> When you believed, you were marked in him with a seal, the promised Holy Spirit.   Ephesians 1:13. NIV.

Some teach that believers receive The Holy Spirit after they have been saved. They call it 'The Second Blessing.' They think that Salvation is the first blessing and receiving The Holy Spirit some time later is 'The Second Blessing.' We quote two translations, the GNB and the NLT:

> Ephesians 1:13. GNB. 'And you also became God's people when you heard the true message, the Good News that brought you salvation. You believed in Christ, and God put his stamp of ownership on you by giving you the Holy Spirit he had promised.'
>
> Ephesians 1:13. NLT '... now you Gentiles have also heard the truth, the Good News that God saves you. And when you believed in Christ, He identified you as His own by giving you the Holy Spirit, whom He promised long ago.'

We need to be candid. If 'The Second Blessing' teaching is true, Paul was totally unaware of it. He never mentioned a delay between believing and receiving The Holy Spirit.

Question: Why would God want to delay acknowledging that believers belonged to Him?

Experience teaches that false doctrine causes spiritual problems. Paul's teaching in Ephesians 1:13 is consistent with his New Testament teaching. We quote Romans.

> '... if anyone does not have the Spirit of Christ, they do not belong to Christ.'   Romans 8:9. NIV.

IMPORTANT NOTE

You will never identify false doctrine unless you know what The Bible teaches. Hence, we strongly recommend that you read The Bible for yourself. You will receive far more blessing reading The Bible than you will reading this or any other book about The Bible. When you read God's Word, The Holy Spirit will enlighten you. You cannot get this divine experience from books.

But there is a problem that you should be aware of. Experience teaches that the more knowledge believers have about The Bible, the more argumentative they become, and the less gracious they are with those who teach false doctrine, or do not believe The Bible is God's Word, or those who want to discuss 'religion,' rather than God's Salvation.

Bible study should not be to fill your head with knowledge but give you a heart, and hence a life, that responds to what The Holy Spirit teaches you. Becoming a believer is life changing, but Bible study should assist you to become mature in Christ.

Ephesians 1:14

We have cautioned against those who quote verses out of their context to support their false doctrines. Reading The Bible for yourself will assist you to recognise false doctrine.

To assist you to consider the truth in Ephesians 1:14, we quote Ephesians 1:13-14:

> Ephesians 1:13-14. And you also were included in Christ when you heard the message of truth, the gospel of your salvation. When you believed, you were marked in him with a seal, the promised Holy Spirit, who is a deposit guaranteeing our inheritance until the redemption of those who are God's possession--to the praise of his glory. Ephesians 1:13-14. NIV.

Spiritual and Material Blessings

God's blessings for believers are not material blessings. The New Testament warns believers of thinking like unbelievers who desire earthly possessions. But some falsely teach that believers will receive whatever they pray for. 'Name it, Claim it,' is what this false doctrine is sometimes called. If possessing God's Salvation enabled believers to pray for and receive a billionaire's wealth, there would be more unbelievers wanting to become believers than there are people buying lottery tickets.

'When you believed …' Ephesians 1:14

What God has done for believers is beyond human understanding. If you are not yet a believer, continue to read how blessed believers are. We pray that it will encourage you to repent and believe The Gospel.

Ephesians 1:13-14 - The Godhead:

- God The Father
- God The Son
- God The Holy Spirit

Reading Ephesians 1:13-14 will make you realise that each Member of The Godhead, has a personal relationship with every believer. We quote these verses again. Note the emboldened words. Muse upon these verses until they fill you with praise. We deserved nothing but judgment for our sin, but The Godhead is now involved in our eternal Salvation:

> And you also were **included in Christ** when you heard the message of truth, the gospel of your salvation. When you believed, you were marked in him with a seal, **the promised Holy Spirit**, who is a deposit guaranteeing our inheritance until the redemption of **those who are God's possession**-to the praise of his glory. Ephesians 1:13-14. NIV.

The Ephesian believers must have been thrilled to read Paul's words. Note that The Gospel that saved him and them can save you. His words apply to believers today.

A Changed Lifestyle – The Proof of Salvation

- Nothing physical happens when unbelievers become believers. New believers do not become shorter, taller, fatter, or thinner.

- Angels do not descend from Heaven to congratulate new believers because they have repented and received Jesus as their personal Saviour.

Proof that a sinner has repented and become a believer will be obvious by their changed lifestyle. An unchanged lifestyle shows that an unbeliever has not become a believer. Humans cannot grasp the spiritual changes that occur when unbelievers become believers and receive God's Salvation, and The Holy Spirit.

We must make this personal to you:

- When you became a believer, God identified you as His own by giving you The Holy Spirit.

- The evidence that The Holy Spirit lives in you is your

new lifestyle. You will be ashamed of your past lifestyle and thank God for sending Jesus to be your Saviour.

- You are now a member of God's family. The Holy Spirit is God's guarantee to you that He will give you the inheritance He has promised to give His children.

In Ephesians 1:5 we read that before creation, and because of what Jesus would one day accomplish for you personally at the Cross, God chose you to be holy and blameless and for adoption into His family.

Question: What did you do that enabled God before creation to make you a member of His family and give you an inheritance?

Answer: You heard and believed The Gospel. You repented and accepted Jesus as your Saviour.

Jesus' Blood - The Price God Willingly Paid

Please consider these words carefully. God knew before creation that you would believe The Gospel. Because you believed it, it has become 'The Gospel of your Salvation.'

You are redeemed through Jesus' blood. His sacrifice on the Cross, when His blood was shed, was the price God willingly paid so that you could be forgiven, freed from sin's slavery, and Heaven could be your eternal home.

Ephesians 1:14 - God's Promised Holy Spirit

In the first thirteen verses of Ephesians 1, we have read about past events.

Ephesians 1:14 introduces a future tense.

It seems that the translators had difficulties translating Ephesians 1:14 into understandable English. It seems appropriate for us to compare the NIV, GNB and the NLT:

Ephesians 1:14. NIV. GNB. NLT.

NIV: [The Spirit] 'is a deposit guaranteeing our inheritance until the redemption of those who are God's possession--to the praise of his glory.

GNB: 'The Spirit is the guarantee that we shall receive what God has promised his people, and this assures us that God will give complete freedom to those who are his. Let us praise his glory!'

NLT: 'The Spirit is God's guarantee that He will give us the inheritance He promised and that He has purchased us to be His own people. He did this so we would praise and glorify Him.'

We cannot ignore Ephesians 1:14 because it is difficult to translate and understand. It contains truth about The Holy Spirit and those of us who are believers. Clearly, what Paul wrote was understandable to the Ephesian believers. We consider that the NIV correctly translates this verse. To understand what Paul wrote, keep in mind three matters:

1. The Gospel and Salvation cannot be separated.
2. Ephesians 1:13, 'the gospel of your salvation.'
3. A believer's Salvation will not be complete until they are in Heaven. Only then will they be away from the presence of sin. We refer to this matter next.

Saved: This word refers to three periods of time, the past, the present, and the future. Believers can say:

1. Past: I have been saved from God's eternal judgment.
2. Present: I am now being saved from sin's power.
3. Future. I will be saved from sin's presence when I die.

Believers: There are three categories of believers. Those:

1. who have died.
2. who are now alive.
3. who will be living when Jesus returns to take both dead and living believers to Heaven.

Believers look forward to the time when they will be in Heaven, and saved from sin's presence. Only then will their Salvation be complete. We asked you to bear this future aspect of Salvation in mind as you read the words, 'until the redemption of those who are God's possession,' in Ephesians 1:14.

'Until the Redemption of those …'

- 'Until,' clearly refers to a future time or event. Believers will receive their inheritance but not 'until the redemption of those who are God's possession.'
- 'Redemption' has, until Ephesians 1:14, referred to a past event.

To understand Ephesians 1:14, we need to think about the words 'those' and 'until.' We consider they mean:

'Those:' believers redeemed in the future.

'Until:' the moment when the last unbeliever is redeemed because The Gospel will not always be preached.

The Gospel Will Not Always Be Preached

We digress as some might not know that God's Salvation will not always be available.

The New Testament teaches this truth but none of its writers knew when. However, they knew that when this happened, God's judgment would begin. God will now save those who repent and believe The Gospel.

Hence some believers call this present time 'The Day of Grace' to distinguish it from the 'Day of Judgment.'

A Summary of Ephesians 1:1-14

These verses are so vital to a correct understanding of The Gospel and God's Salvation that we summarise them.

Before creation God knew:

- what Jesus would accomplish for sinners when He died.
- those who would repent, believe The Gospel and have a relationship with Jesus by accepting Him as Saviour.
- that there would be a change in the lives of those who became believers. They would be 'His holy people.'

Hence, God did not choose either believers or unbelievers randomly. He had a 'Plan of Salvation.' It involved repentance for sin and believing in Jesus.

It seems that only a minority have acknowledged that they have sinned against God, they cannot save themselves from their sin, and they need Jesus to be their Saviour.

This minority heard The Gospel and it told them that Jesus:

- was willing to be the Saviour they needed.
- was punished for their sin when He was crucified.
- was buried but He had risen from the dead hence, God regards those whom Jesus saves as sinless.

The Gospel told them that to receive God's Salvation:

- they must repent of their sin and believe in what Jesus had accomplished to save them from their sin.
- they must accept Jesus as their Saviour.

This minority obeyed The Gospel and received God's Salvation. Their lives were changed. They became 'God's holy people.' They proclaim The Gospel to others because The Gospel's power to save and totally change lives has not changed in 2000 years.

The lifestyle change that occurs in a believer's life still shows others that they have been saved.

Question: Has your lifestyle change evidenced that you are a believer? If there has been no change in your lifestyle, consider whether you are a true, a real believer. If you are, immediately you believed The Gospel:

- Jesus became your Saviour.
- God included you in Jesus and you became one of God's family.
- God marked you with a seal, His Holy Spirit.

The Holy Spirit Is God's Guarantee

The Holy Spirit is God's guarantee to you and all other believers of His future inheritance for all believers. Believers are His children.

Although God knows those who will become believers, no believers have yet received their inheritance.

Believers must await the redemption of those who will become believers before all believers receive 'God's glorious inheritance.'

To the Praise of His Glory

We consider Ephesians 1:14 again because there is another matter that we must not overlook.

Question: What did Paul want the Ephesian believers to know when he wrote, 'to the praise of his glory?'

A significant word such as 'praise' written by Paul four times in twelve verses, requires our attention. Hence, we quote each verse and we ask you to carefully consider the contexts of the word, 'praise.'

1. Ephesians 1:3. 'Praise be to the God and Father of our Lord Jesus Christ, who has blessed us in the heavenly realms with every spiritual blessing in Christ.'
2. Ephesians 1:6. '... to the praise of his glorious grace, which he has freely given us in the One he loves.'
3. Ephesians 1:12. '... we, who were the first to put our hope in Christ, might be for the praise of his glory.'
4. Ephesians 1:14. '... until the redemption of those who are God's possession--to the praise of his glory.'

Note in the last three verses that 'praise' and 'glorious,' or 'glory,' are linked. We will study the words 'glory' and 'glorious' later. Note also what Paul specifically 'kept asking for,' when he prayed for the Ephesian believers.

> Ephesians 1:17. NIV. '... the God of our Lord Jesus Christ, the glorious Father, may give you the Spirit of wisdom and revelation, so that you may know him better.' Ephesians 1:17. NIV.

Not one single believer will ever have deserved anything from God except His eternal judgment for sin. Every believer reading this will acknowledge that this is true, but because God loved Jesus, and Jesus died for their sins, they have freely received God's glorious grace. If you keep this thought in your mind as you read Ephesians 1:17, and consider the four verses quoted above, you will realise how privileged believers are to be God's children.

Prior to believing The Gospel, the Ephesian believers worshipped idols. What a change had occurred in their lives. They were now children of the true God. Read Acts 19 again. The unbelieving Ephesians admitted they worshipped idols made with their own hands. What a difference The Gospel makes in the lives of those who believe it.

God is The God of Glory

Both The Old and New Testaments confirm that God is 'The God of Glory.' When believers praise God, there are two important aspects to their praise. God is both entitled to be praised and worthy of praise.

If you are a believer, God, your Heavenly Father, wants you to know Him better. You are indwelt by The Holy Spirit. As you read God's Word, open your heart and let what you read enter it. You will not develop spiritually and get to know God better until His Word changes you. Re-read Ephesians 1:17. Consider a question that only you can answer. Do you want for yourself what Paul wanted for the Ephesian believers?

A Prayer for Believers - Ephesians 1:15-18

> Ephesians 1:15-18. NIV. 'For this reason, ever since I heard about your faith in the Lord Jesus and your love for all God's people, I have not stopped giving thanks for you, remembering you in my prayers. I keep asking that the God of our Lord Jesus Christ, the glorious Father, may give you the Spirit of wisdom and revelation, so that you may know him better. I pray that the eyes of your heart may be enlightened in order that you may know the hope to which he has called you, the riches of his glorious inheritance in his holy people ...'

Paul wrote, 'I,' in the following four verses. There are important lessons for believers in them:

1. Ephesians 1:15: 'I heard …'

2. Ephesians 1:16: 'I have not stopped …'

3. Ephesians 1:17: 'I keep asking …'

4. Ephesians 1:18: 'I pray…'

1. Ephesians 1:15. 'I heard …'

Paul heard two facts about the believers. They had:

1. 'faith in the Lord Jesus.'
2. 'love for all God's people.'

The Ephesian believers faced persecution. Paul was in prison for his faith. It must have encouraged him to hear that the Ephesian believers were also standing firm in their faith. His objective at Ephesus had been twofold:

1. To preach The Gospel so that unbelievers would put their faith in Jesus for Salvation.
2. To teach believers divine truth that would encourage and enable them to remain firm in their faith in Jesus.

Paul also heard that the believers had a love for all God's people. Loving others evidences the divine change that has taken place in believers' lives. A lack of love shows a lack of the knowledge of God. The New Testament teaches that loving others is not optional.

2. Ephesians 1:16. 'I have not stopped …'

Paul wrote. 'I have not stopped giving thanks for you, remembering you in my prayers.' Acts 19-20 are printed prior to the commencement of Ephesians. Take time to read these two chapters so you will have the background to Paul's letter to the Ephesians. Paul spent three years preaching and teaching in Ephesus. He thought that when he departed, the local church would be under attack from those putting their own interests above those of the believers. So he warned them of the potential dangers.

Question: Did Paul think that teaching and warning the believers of dangers would suffice to keep them faithful?

Answer: No. Read what he did. He encouraged them by writing that he had not stopped giving thanks to God for them and he remembered them in his prayers. Experience proves that criticism, including well-intentioned criticism, disheartens believers. Remember Paul's example. We can sum it up in three words. 'Encourage and pray.'

3. Ephesians 1:17. 'I keep asking …' Part 1.

'I keep asking that the God of our Lord Jesus Christ, the glorious Father, may give you the Spirit of wisdom and revelation, so that you may know him better.' As in Ephesians 1:13-14, Paul referred to 'The Godhead.'

- 'The God of our Lord Jesus Christ.'
- 'The Glorious Father.'
- 'The Spirit of wisdom.'

Paul addressed his prayer to God the Father. Jesus taught us that prayer should be addressed to, 'the Father.'

> John 15:16. GNB. "… the Father will give you whatever you ask of him in my name.…"
>
> John 16:23. GNB. "… I am telling you the truth: the Father will give you whatever you ask of him in my name."

In Ephesians 1:17, Paul referred to, 'the God of our Lord Jesus Christ, the glorious Father.' In Ephesians 1:2, Paul referred to, 'the God and Father of our Lord Jesus Christ.' When we were commenting on Ephesians 1:2, we stated that we would discuss Paul's words when considering similar words in Ephesians 1:17.

We do not seek to simplify a divine matter that will never be understood by humans. However, we want to state that the above verses in Ephesians do not prove that Paul thought that Jesus was inferior to God The Father. Some teach this error. Limited space allows us only to comment on what Paul wrote in Ephesians. The words, 'the God of our Lord Jesus Christ,' should thrill every believer's heart. Jesus is God's Son and yet believers can refer to Him as, 'our Lord Jesus Christ.' If you are a believer, Jesus is not only your Saviour. He belongs both to God and to you.

'The Glorious Father.' Part 1

Question: Why did Paul mention that God was 'the glorious Father?'

Answer: 'Glory,' 'glorious,' and 'glorify,' were often used by Paul. In Ephesians 1 we read 'glory' or 'glorious' five times. They are significant words. We have commented on verses 6, 12, and 14 that contain them. Read them again in their context. Let the truth in these verses thrill you and fill you with thanks and praise to God:

Ephesians 1:3-6: 'Praise be to the God and Father of our Lord Jesus Christ, who has blessed us in the heavenly realms with every spiritual blessing in Christ. For he chose us in him before the creation of the world to be holy and blameless in his sight. In love he predestined us for adoption to sonship through Jesus Christ, in accordance with his pleasure and will--to the praise of his glorious grace, which he has freely given us in the One he loves.'

Ephesians 1:8-12: 'With all wisdom and understanding, he made known to us the mystery of his will according to his good pleasure, which he purposed in Christ, to be put into effect when the times reach their fulfillment--to bring unity to all things in heaven and on earth under Christ. In him we were also chosen, having been predestined according to the plan of him who works out everything in conformity with the purpose of his will, in order that we, who were the first to put our hope in Christ, might be for the praise of his glory.'

Ephesians 1:13-14: 'And you also were included in Christ when you heard the message of truth, the gospel of your salvation. When you believed, you were marked in him with a seal, the promised Holy Spirit, who is a deposit guaranteeing our inheritance until the redemption of those who are God's possession--to the praise of his glory.'

Do you agree or disagree with this Statement?

Statement

All have sinned. God is holy and righteous and hates sin. God cannot ignore sin. We can do nothing to merit His forgiveness or escape His judgment. But, God's Son Jesus died for our sins and rose again. So, God will forgive those who repent and accept Jesus as their Saviour.

A Word of Caution

Be wary of those who only preach that God is loving and gracious. When they preach, they do not mention God's holiness and righteousness because they would have to concede that a holy and righteous God must punish sin. That would require them to mention God's eternal punishment and Hell. Preachers who want to be popular do not mention God's punishment for sin in Hell.

The truth is that God is loving and gracious. He will forgive those who repent and accept Jesus as their Saviour. But He must punish those who do not. The acronym that so aptly describes God's glorious grace is:

Great Riches At Christ's Expense

The Bible teaches that Jesus bled and died so that those who repent and accept Him as their Saviour can be eternally forgiven and freed from sin's power. Only Jesus' shed blood enables a holy and righteous God to be gracious to repentant sinners who accept Jesus as their Saviour. Ponder the answers to these three questions.

1: Do a small minority or the vast majority glorify

God for all He has graciously done for them?

2: Have you realised that whether or not God's gracious offer of Salvation is accepted rests entirely with those who deserve nothing?

3: Have you accepted God's offer of Salvation?

We ask these three questions as experience teaches that some are misled by their religion into thinking that they are believers. Some mislead themselves.

'The Glorious Father.' Part 2

Question: Why did Paul write 'the glorious Father' in Ephesians 1:17 and not 'our glorious Father?'

Answer: Believers need to grasp a vital truth that Paul changed how he referred to God the Father for emphasis.

We know from Ephesians 1:2 that the Ephesian believers were aware that they belonged to both God the Father and The Lord Jesus Christ. It was unnecessary for Paul to repeat that truth. But it was necessary to emphasise it:

- 'the glorious Father,' is the only source of all divine splendour and perfection.
- all divine splendour and perfection belong only to, 'the glorious Father.'

Ephesus was an idolatrous city. The Ephesians believed that idols made with their own hands were divine. The believers worshipped these idols before they were saved. Paul's words in Ephesians 1:17, 'the glorious Father,' emphasised that God was the only true God and He alone was the source of all divine splendour and perfection. He, 'the glorious Father,' was both able and willing to answer Paul's prayers. Idols could do neither. There was a total contrast between God and idols. Some translators have used the Name, 'the Father of glory,' in Ephesians 1:17 to describe the uniqueness of 'The Father.' Maybe they considered it appropriate to distinguish between Paul's use of the Greek word 'doxa' when he wrote about God's glory in verse 17 and God's attributes or characteristics in verses 6, 12, 14 and 18.

Whether you refer to 'The glorious Father' or The Father of glory never forget that believers should never glorify themselves or each other. We repeat that believers deserved nothing but God's judgment for their sins. The world's religions might glorify individuals who hold high office, but even a cursory reading of these verses shows how dishonouring that is to 'The glorious Father.'

A Word To Readers

If the truth that believers have a prayer-answering Heavenly Father with unlimited power does not thrill you, you ought to consider if you are saved.

A Word To Believers

God's power is described in verse 19 as 'his incomparably great power.' The truth that believers belong to a God who has incomparably great power is wonderful. But, even more wonderful is the fact that God's 'incomparably great power' is for believers. Consider Paul's words. We quote verses 18-20 so that you can read verse 19 in context.

> Ephesians 1:18-20. NLT. I pray that your hearts will be flooded with light so that you can understand the confident hope He has given to those He called—His holy people who are His rich and glorious inheritance. I also pray that you will understand the incredible greatness of God's power for us who believe Him. This is the same mighty power that raised Christ from the dead and seated Him in the place of honor at God's right hand in the heavenly realms.

Because they cannot save themselves, unbelievers need Jesus to save them from God's judgment for their sin. Earlier we indicated that believers **had** been saved, **are** being saved daily, and **will** be saved for all eternity. But, regrettably, some teach that the onus is on believers to 'remain' saved. Some also taught this false doctrine in Paul's day. He did not believe it and we have already read that believers are chosen by God and will belong for eternity to God. In the present time, believers have a prayer-answering God who has incredible great power 'for those who believe.'

The Onus is not on Believers to 'Remain Saved.'

Experience teaches that the false teaching that places the onus on believers to 'remain saved' wrecks their spiritual lives. How can they be 'filled with a glorious joy that can't be put into words' when they can never be sure that they are saved? Put simply, you will not enjoy divine truth if you believe that the onus is upon you to remain saved. Believers are kept by God's power, not their own power.

Those who have read this book from the beginning will agree that we have not asked you to become religious, to change your religion, or to do anything other than consider whether there was a moment in your life when you repented of your sin and asked Jesus to be your Saviour. If there was, Ephesians 1:7 states that you 'have redemption through his blood, the forgiveness of sins.'

3. Ephesians 1:17. 'I keep asking …' Part 2

We have already considered the first part of Ephesians 1:17 and the two specific expressions that would mean so much to the Ephesians believers. They were 'the God of our Lord Jesus Christ' and 'the glorious Father.'

Ephesians 1:17 also states Paul prayed that the believers would have an amazing spiritual blessing.

'The Spirit of Wisdom and Revelation.'

Question: Why did Paul pray that the Ephesians believers would have this particular blessing?

Answer: He wrote 'so that you may know him better.' Note the word 'know.'

Bibles are readily available, but how many believers read them or know their contents? There are no lack of those who can talk about The Bible, but in doing so display their ignorance of what The Bible teaches. Note that:

- 'wisdom' is 'human wisdom in spiritual things.'
- 'revelation' is 'the communication of the knowledge of God to the soul.'

A miracle occurs each time an unbeliever is saved. It is evident by their changed life and their spirit of wisdom and revelation. They behave and think differently.

Believers will Live Eternally

God the Holy Spirit Who indwells believers is eternal. God's Salvation includes God's eternal life. Believers have a guaranteed eternal inheritance. Read and re-read Ephesians 1:13-14 until their truths sink into your heart and the thrill of your Salvation causes you to glorify God. The verses are so important that the time you spend memorising them, will be time well spent

> And you also were included in Christ when you heard the message of truth, the gospel of your salvation. When you believed, you were marked in him with a seal, the promised Holy Spirit, who is a deposit guaranteeing our inheritance until the redemption of those who are God's possession--to the praise of his glory.   Ephesians 1:13-14. NIV.

Believers have God's Word, The Bible, readily available to them. They are indwelt by The Holy Spirit. He will teach them God's Word so that they may know God better. God not only saves and blesses believers in the here and now, He wants them to know Him better day-by-day. The Biblical meaning of 'wisdom' and 'revelation' make it obvious that you will never know God better by human means. The tenor of The Bible is that you will only get to know God better by:

- trusting Him.
- studying His Word.
- obeying what He reveals to you in His Word.

The New Testament had not been compiled in Paul's day. Today, believers, especially those who read English, have many translations of The Bible available to them. So we ask another heart-searching question. Do you know God better now than when you became a believer?

Ephesians 1:18–19

We read in Ephesians 1:17 the first of two wonderful blessings that Paul wanted for every believer. Ephesians 1:18-19 contain the second of the two blessings.

> I pray that the eyes of your heart may be enlightened in order that you may know the hope to which he has called you, the riches of his glorious inheritance in his holy people and his incomparably great power for us who believe. Ephesians 1:18-19. NIV.

'The Eyes of Your Heart may be Enlightened'

In Ephesians 1:18, Paul used the word 'know' once again and what we wrote regarding Ephesians 1:17 also applies to Ephesians 1:18. If we read Ephesians 1:17-19, we learn that Paul wanted believers to have the eyes of their heart enlightened. This was essential if they were to know or increase their knowledge of four specific divine matters. Paul wanted the believers to know:

Ephesians 1:17. 'God better'
Ephesians 1:18. 'the hope to which he has called you'
Ephesians 1:18. 'the riches of his glorious inheritance'
Ephesians 1:19. 'God's incomparably great power'

Paul mentioned 'getting to know God better' first. This knowledge will not be acquired from books. Paul referred to a divine eternal relationship that begins when a sinner receives God's Salvation. You cannot know God better by human means. You will only get to know God better by studying His Word, The Bible, obeying it, and trusting Him.

Paul wanted each Ephesian believer to have the eyes of their heart enlightened. We have deliberately written 'each Ephesian believer.' Paul wrote to the Ephesian church. Hence, he wrote 'your heart.' Paul would later tell the Ephesian believers that they were 'one body.' A body only has one heart. What applied to one applied to all, and what applied to the local church, applied to believers. What Paul wrote so long ago applies today. Believers will not spiritually mature unless they want what Paul wanted for all the believers at Ephesus.

Believers cannot blame the local church for their lack of spiritual growth. The local church will only be as spiritual as the believers are. If they have no desire to have the eyes of their hearts enlightened, the church will not have its heart enlightened.

Question: If a believer's spiritual activity is listening to a weekly sermon, will they get to know God better?

The answer must be obvious. In fact, the answer is so obvious that we wonder why believers never open their

Bibles except on a Sunday in church.

Paul's Three Reasons - An Enlightened Heart

Paul stated three reasons why a believer needs an enlightened heart. Believers need to know:

Ephesians 1:18. 'the hope to which he has called you ....'

Ephesians 1:18. 'the riches of his glorious inheritance ....'

Ephesians 1:19. 'God's incomparably great power ....'

'The Hope to which He has Called You'

Our everyday use of the word 'hope' usually indicates a measure of uncertainty. That is the opposite of the meaning of the word 'hope' in The New Testament. When you read Paul's words you realise why the Greek word for 'hope' indicates 'something anticipated with pleasure.'

The word 'called' has a different meaning today. Paul used 'called' to refer to 'an invitation.' Hence, believers anticipate their future with pleasure because they have responded to God's invitation to accept His Salvation.

'The Riches of His Glorious Inheritance'

This verse is variously translated. The above quotation is from the NIV. The GNB reads:

> 'How rich are the wonderful blessings he promises his people.'   Ephesians 1:18. GNB.

Both the NIV and the GNB are supported by other translations. The difference raises two questions:

1. Are God's holy people God's rich and glorious inheritance as the NIV suggests?
2. Are God's holy people recipients of God's rich and glorious inheritance as the GNB suggests?

The NIV appears correct. In Bible study we must consider words and verses in their context. The tenor of the verses prior to verse 18 is that believers are the beneficiaries of God's rich and glorious inheritance, so Paul did not need to repeat that truth. But there is nothing prior to verse 18 to indicate that God regards His holy people as His inheritance. This amazing truth is taught only in verse 18.

Ephesians 1 contains many amazing truths such as the unique relationship between God and believers and the reason why this relationship can exist between a holy and righteous God who detests sin, and believers who were once Hell-deserving sinners. It is only when we consider what God has done for believers and the standing believers have with God, that we realise why God's Salvation, and only God's Salvation, can change sinners into God's holy people. A question might assist readers to appreciate why only those who respond to God's invitation to accept His Salvation become His holy people.

Question: Why does God regard 'saved sinners' as 'His holy people' and 'His rich and glorious inheritance?'

Answer: There are only two types of sinners:

1. Believers. Their sins are forgiven.

2. Unbelievers. Their sins are not forgiven.

In Ephesians 1 we read eight truths about believers that tell us God's view of them. It is so important to note that Christ is included in all eight truths. Without Him, and what He accomplished for God and believers, there would only have been unforgiven sinners.

God and Believers

1. God blesses them with every spiritual blessing in Christ.

2. God chose them in Christ before the creation of the world and sees them as holy and blameless.

3. Because of Christ, God predestined them to be His family.
4. Because of the riches of God's grace, Christ's blood has bought them redemption and the forgiveness of sins.
5. God freely lavishes upon them His glorious grace in Christ, the One He loves.
6. God has revealed to them His plan to bring unity to all things in Heaven and on Earth under Christ.
7. In Christ God chose them to be His people.
8. Jews and Gentiles were chosen by God but only become 'in Christ' when they believed The Gospel.

The Predestination and Election of Believers

We know that these doctrines cause problems for some who mistakenly think that before creation, God chose to save some sinners and chose not to save other sinners.

The Bible makes four truths clear:

1. God has foreknowledge. God always knew who would repent and accept Jesus as their Saviour.
2. God always knew that only a minority of sinners would willingly repent and accept Jesus as their Saviour.
3. Because God loves His Son Jesus, God adopts saved sinners into His family.
4. Jesus and saved sinners have an eternal personal relationship.

Believers are God's Rich and Glorious Inheritance

Believers throughout eternity will praise and glorify God for Who He is and what He has done. They belong to God.

A Cautionary Note - Misuse of The Bible

It is obvious that all The New Testament writers wrote only

to believers. Despite this, Bible verses are erroneously applied to unbelievers. This very silly, widespread and popular misuse of God's Word only perpetuates the myth that all who die will be in Heaven. You will often hear The Bible read at the funeral services of unbelievers.

Experience teaches that there are problems among believers today. We need to mention three:

1. Believers do not read The Bible often enough for them to know what it teaches.
2. Believers readily accept what they read in books, such as this book, and hear from the pulpit, without checking if it is supported in The Bible.
3. Believers should read The Bible and when we write, 'should read The Bible,' we mean, accurately. This cannot be done at speed. Experience teaches that every word is important, hence, Bible readers should ensure that they read the context of verses, and not verses out of context. The same applies to chapters.

If you do not want to believe error, we can assure you that there is no substitute for Bible study. We have mentioned several errors that contradict the teaching of Ephesians 1 and we now mention another.

The Error of 'Preselected Sinners'

The Bible does not state that Jesus died on behalf of sinners who had no option but to be saved. Only those sinners who chose to accept God's offer of Salvation are special to God. To suggest that God 'preselected' His 'rich and glorious inheritance' from sinners who had no option but to be saved does not honour God.

Our Personal Testimony

Many years' experience proves that God saves those who want to be saved. Salvation is a personal matter between

God and repentant sinners. They have 'their own story' as to how they became aware of The Gospel and why they chose to accept God's Salvation. Some call these stories 'their testimonies.' Others refer to them as 'their Salvation stories.'

Listening to believers' stories of how they were saved is wonderful. We have heard so many stories and never tire of doing so. Many believers are not public speakers but they willingly tell the story of how they were saved. No two stories are alike because no two of us are identical. Hence, God deals with us as individuals. We know that some:

- were saved the first time they heard The Gospel.
- often heard The Gospel before being saved.
- 'struggled' for a while before they realised that God wanted to save them just as they were.
- thought their good life was good enough for God. But when they heard The Gospel, they realised they were sinners who needed God's Salvation.
- read The Bible wanting to know God. When they read about God's offer of Salvation they accepted it.

You may have problems that you think must be resolved before you can be saved. You might need answers to questions. Let us make this clear. Jesus:

- promised that those who seek Him will find Him.
- has never ceased to be 'The Seeking Saviour.'

Salvation: Questions or Excuses

You really do need to ask yourself whether your questions are but excuses because you prefer your sinful lifestyle to God's Salvation. We write this because The New Testament confirms that the majority will prefer their sinful lifestyle to God's Salvation. So, although it might not happen as often as believers would like to see it happen, it is wonderful to witness the moment that a seeking sinner finds the seeking Saviour. This is the amazing miracle of Salvation. Those who experience it never want to return to being unbelievers.

Proof of God's Glorious Grace at Work

- A changed lifestyle.
- A desire to know God better.
- A desire that others be saved.

These are some of the 'tests' that prove that God's glorious grace is at work in believers' lives. If you have no personal knowledge of a 'Salvation Experience,' you can repent and ask Jesus to be your Saviour now. You can be sure that God is gracious and willing to save you. But God will not force you to be saved.

'God's Incomparably Great Power For Us'

There is no other power that can be compared with God's power. This does not surprise us but what does is that the power God used to raise Jesus from the dead is at work in believers. We quote Ephesians 1:18-23 from the ERV.

> Ephesians 1:18-23. ERV. 'I pray that God will open your minds to see his truth. Then …. you will know that God's power is very great for us who believe. It is the same as the mighty power he used to raise Christ from death and put him at his right side in the heavenly places. He put Christ over all rulers, authorities, powers, and kings. He gave him authority over everything that has power in this world or in the next world. God put everything under Christ's power and made him head over everything for the church. The church is Christ's body.

It is filled with him. He makes everything complete in every way.'　　　　　　　　　　Ephesians 1:18-23. ERV.

The Resurrection: 'That Power Is the Same'

Preachers tend to refer to Jesus' death but not to His resurrection. The New Testament writers referred to both. Both are essential to The Gospel and baptism. Paul informed the Ephesians that the power God exerted when He raised Jesus from the dead was the same power that was working in them. If you are a believer, that power is working in you. 'At work in them' tells us that the power is not visible. Only the results are visible.

'The Highest Position in Heaven: 'Far Above All'

Ephesians 1:20 has been variously translated. The NIV and GW translations are at variance over the words 'and seated him at his right hand.' The Greek word, 'Kathizo,' can mean, 'to cause to be seated,' 'set,' and 'appoint.' Translators have used these words and also the word 'sat.'

Some Bible teachers prefer 'seated' or 'sat' as these words indicate that when Jesus returned to Heaven 'He sat down' and this showed that His death and resurrection were sufficient for sinners to be saved and nothing else needed to be done. It is a nice thought and it is true that before returning to Heaven, Jesus did all that God required Him to do to enable sinners to be saved.

However, each verse must be read in its own context. Acts and Revelation refer respectively to Jesus standing and walking. We cannot adjudicate on which translation of Ephesians 1:20 is correct, but we bring three matters about Jesus to your attention:

1. Whether God sat Jesus down at His right hand or whether He put Jesus at His right hand makes no

difference to the fact that as Jesus died and rose again, God can offer Salvation to anyone and everyone.

2. It is not in doubt that Jesus occupies the highest position in Heaven. He will do so for eternity because He will always be 'far above all.'

3. Jesus did not sit Himself down or put Himself at God's right hand. It was God who actively acknowledged that Jesus was worthy to be at His right hand.

Jesus Is 'Far Above All'

Jesus is not just above all, He is 'far above all.' Jesus cannot be compared with anyone. Jesus can only be contrasted with them. That difference is so important when you speak or think about Jesus. Consider carefully these three verses, Ephesians 1:21-23, quoted from the NLT:

> Ephesians 1:21-23. NLT. 'Now He is far above any ruler or authority or power or leader or anything else—not only in this world but also in the world to come. God has put all things under the authority of Christ and has made Him head over all things for the benefit of the church. And the church is His body; it is made full and complete by Christ, who fills all things everywhere with Himself.' Ephesians 1:21-23. NLT.

In these verses we read about 'a head, and a body. As you are aware, the Bible often uses 'picture language' to teach truth. So the expression in the NIV, quoted previously, that God has 'placed all things under his feet' simply means that God has put everything in subjection to Jesus. The NLT makes it quite clear that God has put all things under Jesus' authority. The past tense is used.

Some might look around them and say, 'that is not the way things look to me.'

Question: Is everything under Jesus' authority now? Before answering, we mention two further matters:

1. Ephesians 1:21 confirms that Jesus is above every authority that already exists in this world and will exist in the next.
2. Ephesians 1:22-23 confirm that Jesus is the Head of the Church, His Body. Note that the Church is full and complete and can never be less than full and complete.

Answer: Believers are indwelt by The Holy Spirit, but they remain human. The Eternal God sees everything in the present. He sees the future as having already happened.

God Requires Believers to Trust and Obey Him

Belief does not cease when believers are saved. Believers believe what they read in God's Word. Even though believers cannot see it or prove it, they believe that Jesus is above every authority that exists in this world and The Church is full and complete.

Believers also know that there will come a day when everyone and everything will know and acknowledge that God has already put all things under Jesus' authority for the benefit of The Church. Today, believers willingly acknowledge that, 'Jesus Christ is Lord.'

As we conclude Ephesians 1, if you are not yet a believer, we pray that you will repent and accept Jesus as your personal Saviour.

EPHESIANS 2. NIV.

1 As for you, you were dead in your transgressions and sins, 2 in which you used to live when you followed the ways of this world and of the ruler of the kingdom of the air, the spirit who is now at work in those who are disobedient. 3 All of us also lived among them at one time, gratifying the cravings of our flesh and following its desires and thoughts. Like the rest, we were by nature deserving of wrath. 4 But because of his great love for us, God, who is rich in mercy, 5 made us alive with Christ even when we were dead in transgressions—it is by grace you have been saved. 6 And God raised us up with Christ and seated us with him in the heavenly realms in Christ Jesus, 7 in order that in the coming ages he might show the incomparable riches of his grace, expressed in his kindness to us in Christ Jesus. 8 For it is by grace you have been saved, through faith—and this is not from yourselves, it is the gift of God— 9 not by works, so that no one can boast. 10 For we are God's handiwork, created in Christ Jesus to do good works, which God prepared in advance for us to do. 11 Therefore, remember that formerly you who are Gentiles by birth and called "uncircumcised" by those who call themselves "the circumcision" (which is done in the body by human hands)— 12 remember that at that time you were separate from Christ, excluded from citizenship in Israel and foreigners to the covenants of the promise, without hope and without God in the world. 13 But now in Christ Jesus you who once were far away have been brought near by the blood of Christ. 14 For he himself is our peace, who has made the two groups one and has destroyed the barrier, the dividing wall of hostility, 15 by setting aside in his flesh

the law with its commands and regulations. His purpose was to create in himself one new humanity out of the two, thus making peace, 16 and in one body to reconcile both of them to God through the cross, by which he put to death their hostility. 17 He came and preached peace to you who were far away and peace to those who were near. 18 For through him we both have access to the Father by one Spirit. 19 Consequently, you are no longer foreigners and strangers, but fellow citizens with God's people and also members of his household, 20 built on the foundation of the apostles and prophets, with Christ Jesus himself as the chief cornerstone. 21 In him the whole building is joined together and rises to become a holy temple in the Lord. 22 And in him you too are being built together to become a dwelling in which God lives by his Spirit. Ephesians 2. NIV.

COMMENTARY ON EPHESIANS 2

Ephesians 2:1-3.

> 'As for you, you were dead in your transgressions and sins, in which you used to live when you followed the ways of this world and of the ruler of the kingdom of the air, the spirit who is now at work in those who are disobedient. All of us also lived among them at one time, gratifying the cravings of our flesh and following its desires and thoughts. Like the rest, we were by nature deserving of wrath.' Ephesians 2:1-3. NIV.

Question: Who are the 'you' cited in Ephesians 2:1?

Answer: The believers that are referred to as 'you' in Ephesians 1:13. The title of this book is 'You also were included.' Note the opening words of Ephesians 1:13.

> 'And you also were included in Christ when you heard the message of truth, the gospel of your salvation. When you believed, you were marked in him with a seal, the promised Holy Spirit ...' Ephesians 1:13. NIV.

Paul wrote the pronouns 'you' and 'your' five times in Ephesians 1:13. The importance of the pronouns is this. They only apply to believers.

In Ephesians 1:18-23 we read Paul's prayer and amazing truths about God and believers. Paul's use of 'you,' 'your,' and 'us,' in those verses tell us that the good things mentioned by Paul are only for believers.

It is obvious from Ephesians 2:1 that the believers were not born believers. As far as God was concerned, they were spiritually dead from birth. We write, 'spiritually dead,' because they were very much alive when they sinned. Paul was totally candid as to their behaviour before they became believers. The words 'were' and 'used to' in verse 1 and verses 2-3 need to be carefully considered:

There came a time when the Ephesians changed the way they lived. Their behaviour changed.

Question: When was that time?

Answer: It was when they believed the message of truth, the 'Gospel of their Salvation.'

Prior to believing The Gospel, the Ephesian believers were spiritually dead. They:

- disobeyed God and sinned.
- lived as though God did not exist.
- thought they could do as they pleased.

Paul reminded them that they behaved as unbelievers behaved. They might have thought that they were 'doing their own thing' but they simply followed the world's evil way. They disobeyed God but obeyed 'the evil ruler.'

Question 1: Who is this 'ruler' whom all unbelievers obey?

Answer: The Ephesian believers knew who Paul meant even though Paul only wrote the ruler's 'job description.'

Question 2: What does this 'ruler' do?

Answer: He 'rules the kingdom of the air' and he 'works in those who are disobedient.'

Some might have assumed that God rules everywhere but Ephesians 1:20-23 teaches the sphere of God's rule and Jesus' authority. We have italicised the relevant words.

> Ephesians 1:20. NIV. '.... he raised Christ from the dead and seated him at his right hand *in the heavenly realms ...*' Ephesians 1:20. NIV.

'In The Heavenly Realms'

God the Father and Jesus are presently 'in the heavenly realms.' In Ephesians 6 we refer to this again.

Contrast the Area of Authority of The Evil Ruler

The evil ruler is only permitted by God to rule 'the kingdom of the air.' He, unlike Jesus, is not the supreme ruler 'in the heavenly realms.' He is a spirit who is 'now at work' unseen in the disobedient. His rule is only temporary.

Two Vital Contrasts in Ephesians 1 and 2

1. Believers: controlled by The Holy Spirit. He teaches them how to please God.

2. Unbelievers: controlled by, 'the evil ruler.' He makes them, 'gratify the cravings of their flesh and follow fleshly desires and thoughts.'

Their Eternal Destiny:

Believers: Paul stated their eternal blessings.

> 'the .... Holy Spirit .... is a deposit guaranteeing our inheritance until the redemption of those who are God's possession,'   Ephesians 1:13-14. NIV.(Edited)

Unbelievers: Paul stated their awful fate.

> 'deserving of wrath.'   Ephesians 2:3. NIV.

The Eternal Destiny Of 'The Evil Ruler'

The evil ruler who elsewhere in The Bible is called the Devil and Satan, will spend eternity with unbelievers in the Lake of Fire. These verses need no comment from us.

> Extract from Revelation 20: 'The devil, who fooled them, was thrown into the lake of burning sulfur. That is where the beast and the false prophet had been thrown. They will all suffer day and night for ever and ever. Then Death and Hell were thrown into the lake of fire. The lake of fire is the second death. Anyone whose name was not written in the Book of Life was thrown into the lake of fire.'   Extract from Revelation 20. NIV.

Ephesians 2:3 - 'All of Us' - 'Like the Rest'

- Some respectable unbelievers think that that their upright lives are, or ought to be, 'good enough for God.'
- Some unbelievers commit heinous sins.

The Bible teaches that because all have sinned, all need God's Salvation. The Bible does not separate sinners into good sinners and bad sinners or into any other category of sinners. If you are an unbeliever, please consider carefully what you are about to read. These are not our opinions. They are quotations from The Bible.

Ephesians 2:3 tells us how the Ephesian believers once lived. It is uncomplimentary to unbelievers. 'All of us,' coupled with, 'like the rest,' clearly excludes nobody.

> 'All of us also lived among them at one time, gratifying the cravings of our flesh and following its desires and thoughts. Like the rest, we were by nature deserving of wrath.'   Ephesians 2:3. NIV.

'We Were By Nature Deserving Of Wrath'

Some unwisely think that God has scales similar to those shopkeepers once used to use to weigh their products. They expect that when they die, God will put their good deeds on one side of the scales and their sins on the other side to see if they have done more good than bad. God will then pass judgment upon their lives. The scales do not exist. They are a foolish figment of man's imagination.

The Bible teaches that God detests sin. He will eternally punish unforgiven sinners. Unbelievers have not been forgiven. God will eternally punish them.

Unbelievers will suffer the same fate as 'The Evil Ruler.'

Believers readily admit that Ephesians 2:3 accurately describes their behaviour before they were saved:

- Unbelievers should be troubled at the consequences of being one of 'the rest' who deserve God's wrath.
- Ephesians 2:3 includes all of us. We have all sinned since birth. Hence Paul wrote 'we were by nature.'

This teaching offends many. But, until unbelievers are prepared to accept God's view of them, they can never be saved. There are only believers and unbelievers and Ephesians 2:3 could not make that clearer:

'All of Us' or 'Us and Them'

As Paul referred to believers and himself, he used the word, 'us.' Paul and the Ephesian believers once lived the sinful life that unbelievers live. Paul wrote bluntly about it:

- 'Like the rest.' Paul referred to unbelievers and the awful future they face if they remain as they are.
- 'Us' and 'them.' 'All of us also lived among them at one time.' 'Us' refers to believers 'them,' to unbelievers.

We will shortly consider God's grace. Some erroneously preach that as God is gracious, He will not punish sinners.

We quote Ephesians 2:3 from the GMB.

> Ephesians 2:3. GMB. 'Actually all of us were like them and lived according to our natural desires, doing whatever suited the wishes of our own bodies and minds. In our natural condition we, like everyone else, were destined to suffer God's anger.'

Ephesians 2:4-9 - Preliminary Considerations

There are preliminary matters that we must consider in these verses before studying them individually.

God's Wrath and God's Grace

Ephesians 2:4 begins with that important word, 'but.' It tells us that there is a contrast with what we are about to read with what we have read. Can you think of two more contrasting subjects than God's wrath, and God's grace? If what many preach, and what many more want to hear was true, it would not have been necessary for Paul to have emphasised this contrast.

It really is hard to understand why those who accurately read and understand books, newspapers and the like, and enjoy crosswords, become 'confused' when they read The Bible. Even words that people have used since childhood, like 'us,' are misused and misunderstood when they appear in The Bible. As we consider Ephesians 2:4-9, we ask readers to concentrate on the pronouns.

Ephesians 2:4-9

> Ephesians 2:4-9. 'But because of his great love for us, God, who is rich in mercy, made us alive with Christ even when we were dead in transgressions--it is by grace you have been saved. And God raised us up with Christ and seated us with him in the heavenly realms in

> Christ Jesus, in order that in the coming ages he might show the incomparable riches of his grace, expressed in his kindness to us in Christ Jesus. For it is by grace you have been saved, through faith--and this is not from yourselves, it is the gift of God -- not by works, so that no one can boast.' Ephesians 2:4-9. NIV.

Reading this book cannot be pleasant for some readers, but our desire is that unbelievers become believers and believers learn spiritual truths. Consider what Paul wanted the Ephesian believers to know.

God's Love, Mercy and Grace

- God has a 'great love for us.'
- God, 'is rich in mercy.'
- God will, 'show the incomparable riches of His grace expressed in his kindness to us in Christ Jesus.'

Four Questions about Ephesians 2:4-9.

1. If you ignore references to God, how many pronouns appear in Ephesians 2:4-9.

   Answer: 9 (us 5, we 1, you 2, yourselves 1)

2. How many references are there to Christ?

   Answer: There are four references to Christ.

3. Which eight words in verse 5 could Paul have omitted without altering the truth in Ephesians 2:4 & 5-6? Clue: The eight words are repeated in Ephesians 2: 8.

   Answer: 'it is by grace you have been saved'

4. Why did Paul repeat the words 'it is by grace you have been saved?'

   Answer: The words were written following the

statements of what God had done for believers:
1) 'God .... made us alive with Christ ...'
2) 'God .... raised us up with Christ ...'

God's Wrath and Our Trust

- Those who trust in their own goodness or trust in their religion will not be saved from God's wrath.
- Those who trust in what God has done for them will be saved from God's wrath.

Readers who studied the above four questions and answers will have realised that in just six verses, Paul used nine pronouns that refer only to believers. 'Christ' is mentioned four times. Additionally, twice in four verses Paul wrote 'it is by grace you have been saved.'

Whether you are a believer or an unbeliever, the significance of the repeated references to 'believers and Christ' and the repetition of the words 'it is by grace you have been saved' must have been intended to stress that without God's involvement and Jesus, we would all be unsaved sinners who only deserve God's wrath. We repeat the statement above. 'Those who trust in what God has done for them will be saved from God's wrath.' Only believers have taken advantage of God's love, mercy and grace. A miraculous change occurs when sinners repent and accept Jesus as their Saviour. They become 'alive with Christ' and 'raised up with Christ.' 'God changes them.' After you have read these four verses, we shall consider them individually.

> But because of his great love for us, God, who is rich in mercy, made us alive with Christ even when we were dead in transgressions--it is by grace you have been saved. And God raised us up with Christ and seated us with him in the heavenly realms in Christ Jesus, in

> order that in the coming ages he might show the incomparable riches of his grace, expressed in his kindness to us in Christ Jesus. Ephesians 2:4-7. NIV.

Ephesians 2:4. God's Great Love and Mercy

> 'But because of his great love for us, God, who is rich in mercy …' Ephesians 2:4. NIV.

God does not just love us, He has a 'great love for us.' God is not just merciful, He is 'rich in mercy.' God had a great love for us, and He was rich in mercy toward us, even when we only merited His wrath. Do not forget that we were sinners from the moment we were born.

Ephesians 2:5 - Alive with Christ - Saved by Grace

> [God] made us alive with Christ even when we were dead in transgressions--it is by grace you have been saved. Ephesians 2:5. NIV.

We repeat what we wrote above. 'Only believers have taken advantage of God's love, mercy and grace.' Hence, only believers are spiritually alive with Christ.

Ephesians 2:6. Raised up - Seated with Christ

> 'God raised us up with Christ and seated us with him in the heavenly realms in Christ.' Ephesians 2:6. NIV.

In Ephesians 2:6 Paul used the Name 'Christ.' He emphasised that believers occupy His exalted position, the highest place in Heaven. They were 'with Christ' and 'in Christ.' God wanted them eternally associated with His exalted Son. They had no personal virtues that entitled them to be in this exalted position. They were only there because at some point in their lives, they acknowledged they were sinners who were willing to repent and accept Jesus as their Saviour. As we shall read, the next verse also emphasises that believers owe every divine blessing they have, and will have, to Jesus. He has saved them, and God will use them in a coming day to show 'the incomparable riches of his grace.'

Ephesians 2:7. 'in order that .... he might show ...'

> 'in order that in the coming ages he might show the incomparable riches of his grace, expressed in his kindness to us in Christ Jesus.'   Ephesians 2:7. NIV.

Note that the believers' exalted position in Heaven is not to exalt them. It is to show 'the incomparable riches of God's grace, expressed in his kindness to us in Christ Jesus.' Space limits our comments but note that:

- Paul's emphasis in Ephesians 2:6 is the blessings associated with being 'with Christ' and 'in Christ.'
- Paul used the Name 'Christ Jesus' in Ephesians 2:7.

In Ephesians 2:7 Paul wrote that believers were the recipients of the 'incomparable riches of his grace, expressed in his kindness to us in Christ Jesus.' We suggest that Paul added Jesus to Christ and wrote 'Christ Jesus' because all he had written about the future of believers could only have been possible because Jesus came into this world to save sinners.

Ephesians 2:8-9. Salvation: The Gift of God

> Ephesians 2:8-9. For it is by grace you have been saved, through faith--and this is not from yourselves, it is the gift of God—not by works, so that no one can boast.   Ephesians 2:8-9. NIV.

These verses are worth memorising. They ought to divert proud believers' attention from themselves to God who gave them His undeserved and free gift of Salvation.

We previously stated why we consider Paul repeated the words in Ephesians 2:5 'it is by grace you have been saved' in Ephesians 2:8. We also suggest this word for word repetition should emphasise that we have not, and cannot, contribute to God's Salvation or save ourselves.

We also read in Ephesians 2:8 'This is not from yourselves. It is the gift of God.' The expressions 'not from ourselves' and 'the gift of God' are in sharp contrast. This emphasises our inability and God's grace. Although it is expressed differently, Ephesians 2:9 confirms the truth in Ephesians 2:8 'not by works.' The reason for this emphasis is so that no one can boast. The Bible emphasises that God hates pride. Experience teaches that proud believers are 'bad advertisements' for The Gospel and Salvation.

'It is by Grace You Have Been Saved through faith'

We cannot leave Ephesians 2:8-9 without considering again the words that we first read in Ephesians 2:5. When Paul repeated them in Ephesians 2:8 he added 'through faith.' So, we must now consider ten important words that state the two sides of Salvation, God's side and our side.

1. God's Side of Salvation

If you are an unbeliever and you desire to be saved, you can be sure that God wants you to be saved:

- God has done all that is necessary for you to be saved, even though, as an unforgiven sinner you are spiritually dead and deserve nothing but God's wrath for your sin.

- God hates your sin, but He has a great love for you. He is rich in mercy and He will be gracious to you.

2. A Believer's Side of Salvation

Consider the two extra words, 'through faith.' We need to clarify these two words because some teach doctrinal error about God's Salvation. You recall that we asked you to count the number of pronouns in Ephesians 2:4-9 and the number of times that Christ was mentioned. We did this to emphasise the personal relationship that exists between Christ and believers. It is vital that you know five truths:

1. Unbelievers are saved individually.
2. Unbelievers must individually repent of their sins and put their faith in Jesus to save them from their sins.
3. There is only one Saviour. Jesus died for our sins. He was buried and on the third day He rose again.
4. Those who do not or will not repent and put their trust in Jesus cannot be saved.
5. Those who are not saved will receive God's wrath.

We appreciate that these words might upset some, but what we write must be honest. It is utterly futile for you to have faith in your own ability to be saved. Performing religious observances, going on pilgrimages, doing good works, being a good neighbour, providing charitable support and the like is the 'religion' of many and although you will hear it preached, it did not come from God. This might be the first time that you have read this. Regrettably, it is very popular, and we could call it, 'Christianity without Christ.' But, preaching it, and listening to it, has awful consequences. Many assume that they:

- are Christians.
- will spend eternity in Heaven.

They are mistaken because they are not saved. But there is another problem.

Many religions promise God's forgiveness to those who obey their man-made rules. These rules vary from religion to religion, and church to church. We have read that Salvation is based on faith. They teach it is based on 'doing good works.' Further, many churches promote the belief that there is no Hell, but we have read that God's forgiveness for sins is based only on repentance and faith in Jesus. It comes as no surprise that many churchgoers do not give Jesus the honour that is due to Him.

'It is the Gift of God'

As these six words begin with the word 'it' many are unsure as to exactly what 'the gift of God' is. The word 'it' refers to the word 'saved.' Not all translations make this clear. We quote from GOD'S WORD that does.

> 'God saved you through faith as an act of kindness. You had nothing to do with it. Being saved is a gift from God.' Ephesians 2:8. GW.

Excuses

Some educated unbelievers have suggested that 'faith' is not a universal ability. However, The Bible refers to sins, sinners, Salvation and 'whosoever' over one hundred and eighty times. So we stress to readers that:

- The Gospel can be preached both anywhere and everywhere.
- anyone and everyone can repent and believe that Jesus died for their sins and rose again to be their Saviour.

Salvation-God's Gift to You

If you are not yet a believer, you can accept God's Salvation as His personal gift to you. But you cannot work for it. You either accept God's Salvation as a gift or you reject it. It cannot be a reward for anything you have done.

Ephesians 2:8-10

We need to explain the difference between 'works' that is common to Ephesians 2:9-10. We commence at verse 8 so that you can read these verses in their context:

> Ephesians 2:8-10. NIV. For it is by grace you have been saved, through faith--and this is not from yourselves, it is the gift of God--not by works, so that no one can boast. For we are God's handiwork, created in Christ Jesus to do good works, which God prepared in advance for us to do. Ephesians 2:8-10.

We also quote Ephesians 2:10 from the NLT. It translates Ephesians 2:10 so simply. As you read it, seek to grasp just how wonderful God's Salvation is.

> For we are God's masterpiece. He has created us anew in Christ Jesus, so we can do the good things He planned for us long ago. Ephesians 2:10. NLT.

Works

Note the negative in Ephesians 2:9 and the positive in Ephesians 2:10.

- Verse 9, 'not by works.'
- Verse 10, 'to do good works.'

Verse 9: We cannot be saved by what we do.

Verse 10: God's Plan for us once we become believers is that we do the good things He planned for us long ago.

Some are surprised when informed that God has always actively worked. Both Old and New Testaments state that God not only works, but that everything God does is perfect, holy and righteous. In Ephesians 2:10 we read that believers are 'God's handiwork' or, in the words of the NLT 'God's masterpiece.' They are created anew in Christ Jesus. An important matter needs to be considered.

Question: Can God change every unbeliever into His masterpiece, no matter how wicked they were before being saved?

The Answer is, "Yes." All believers are 'created' or 'created anew in Christ Jesus to do good works.' We need to have Paul's confidence in 'The Gospel.' He wrote about The Gospel to the Roman believers and confidently stated:

> 'For I am not ashamed of the gospel, because it is the power of God that brings salvation to everyone who believes …' Romans 1:16. NIV.

Note on Ephesians 2:10.

Believers should not 'do their own thing.' They should only do 'the good works' that God has planned for them.

Salvation - Us or God

Salvation does not 'begin and end with us' and 'what we can do for God.' Salvation begins and ends with what God has done and can do for us. However, God does not expect those He has created in Christ Jesus to live like the people they once were who gratified the cravings of their flesh and followed its desires and thoughts.

God's Work

When sinners who deserve nothing but God's wrath receive God's gift of Salvation, the evidence that they have been saved and changed by God's grace should be visible to both believers and unbelievers.

Are you thrilled when someone tells the story of how they became a believer? You know that they will mention their former life and how it changed when they became a believer. There must be a change because believers are 'created anew' in Christ Jesus by God. He, not believers, does this unique work. He does it so that they can do the good things He planned for them long ago.

Salvation - Repentance and Faith

To receive God's Salvation, a sinner must repent and have faith in the Lord Jesus. Those reading this book from the beginning will recall Paul's words in Acts 20:21.

> I have declared to both Jews and Greeks that they must turn to God in repentance and have faith in our Lord Jesus. Acts 20:21. NIV.

Salvation is God's unique work. Hence, it can be distinguished from all 'self-help' methods of improvement such as:

- Turning over a new leaf.
- New Year resolutions and the like.
- Learning good manners and etiquette.

God's Salvation is also not connected with church attendance or membership, baptism or confirmation, confession or any other religious act or observance. If you are relying on what you do for a home in Heaven, as many are, you need God's gift of Salvation now. Read and re-read Acts 21:20, quoted above, and do what it says.

Important Lessons from History

When The Church was established, the Gospel was first preached to the Jews. Paul, himself a Jew, journeyed miles to preach The Gospel to both Jews and Gentiles.

Some Jewish believers mistakenly thought that only Jews could be saved. Others, who were also mistaken, thought that Gentiles could be saved, but only if they adopted The Jewish Faith. Paul correctly believed that The Gospel could be preached to everyone so that anyone who repented and believed it could be saved.

Ephesians 2:11-22

Paul was a Jew. He wrote to the Gentile Ephesian believers. In these verses, 'you' refers only to Gentiles and 'us' or 'we' refers to both Jews and Gentiles.

> Ephesians 2:11-22. NIV. 'Therefore, remember that formerly you who are Gentiles by birth and called "uncircumcised" by those who call themselves "the circumcision" (which is done in the body by human hands) -- remember that at that time you were separate from Christ, excluded from citizenship in Israel and foreigners to the covenants of the promise, without hope and without God in the world. But now in Christ Jesus you who once were far away have been brought near by the blood of Christ. For he himself is our peace, who has made the two groups one and has destroyed the barrier, the dividing wall of hostility, by setting aside in his flesh the law with its commands and regulations. His purpose was to create in himself one new humanity out of the two, thus making peace, and in one body to reconcile both of them to God through the cross, by which he put to death their hostility. He came and preached peace to you who were far away and peace to those who were near. For through him we both have access to the Father by one Spirit. Consequently, you are no longer foreigners and strangers, but fellow citizens with God's people and also members of his household, built on the foundation of the apostles and prophets, with Christ Jesus himself as the chief

> cornerstone. In him the whole building is joined together and rises to become a holy temple in the Lord. And in him you too are being built together to become a dwelling in which God lives by his Spirit.'

Remember

Twice in these verses Paul asked the Ephesian believers to 'remember.' Significant problems between the Jewish and Gentile believers would have been on his mind and be relevant to the Gentile Ephesian believers. We are not aware of this problem today. It seems that the majority of Jews have rejected The Gospel and although it would be wrong to say that the Gentiles have embraced it, it seems that the majority of believers in the last 2000 years have been Gentiles. Although these problems no longer exist, Paul's teaching is a wonderful insight into 'God's Plan of Salvation.' This is not a Biblical term but it does help us to understand that God planned the Salvation of believers before creation. And, day by day, as unbelievers become believers, 'God's Plan of Salvation' is being worked out. If you are a believer, you are part of this 'Plan of Salvation.'

Ephesians 2:11-16

> Ephesians 2:11-16. NIV. 'remember that formerly you who are Gentiles by birth and called "uncircumcised" by those who call themselves "the circumcision" (which is done in the body by human hands)--remember that at that time you were separate from Christ, excluded from citizenship in Israel and foreigners to the covenants of the promise, without hope and without God in the world. But now in Christ Jesus you who once were far away have been brought near by the blood of Christ. For he

> himself is our peace, who has made the two groups one and has destroyed the barrier, the dividing wall of hostility, by setting aside in his flesh the law with its commands and regulations. His purpose was to create in himself one new humanity out of the two, thus making peace, and in one body to reconcile both of them to God through the cross, by which he put to death their hostility.' Ephesians 2:11-16. NIV.

We ask two questions:

1: Why did Paul add 'by birth' in verse 11?'

2: If the Ephesian believers were 'Gentiles by birth,' why not simply call them Gentiles?

The Answers are found in verses 14-16. The Church is composed of believers. They were either Jews or Gentiles prior to being saved. Thereafter, the distinction associated with their birth was irrelevant.

Circumcision Contrasted With God's Salvation.

Before Jesus death, God required Jewish males to be circumcised. It was proof of the Jew's special relationship with Him. In error, the Jews thought that all other nations were inferior to them as they did not circumcise the males. But they overlooked one aspect of circumcision. It was performed with human hands. Hence, it could only be contrasted with God's Salvation.

Salvation is from first to last God's divine work. It does not require sinners to do anything except repent and believe The Gospel.

Circumcision is like the many religious practices that so many people rely on for Salvation and Heaven today. They refuse to repent and believe. They want to do something to earn God's Salvation. They refuse to accept Salvation as a gift from God.

Ephesians 2:11-12 - Importance Lessons

The Jews thought that they were superior to the Gentiles. They were proud of their ancestry and nationality. This is like many who think that their Christian heritage, church membership and the like, guarantees them Salvation and Heaven. They overlook the truth that God saves sinners who repent and believe in Jesus individually.

It does not amaze those who read their Bibles how misguided and mistaken the general public are about God, Heaven and Salvation. Many must be misled by what they hear and sing in churches at Christmas and Easter and what they hear from the clergy at funerals.

The Jews, but not the Gentiles, had the advantage of being in a covenant or contractual relationship with God. The Jews also possessed God's Word, The Old Testament.

The Jews

The Old Testament history of the Jews is a history of spiritual decline. The Gospels prove this. Read what Jesus said to the religious people of His day. You will realise that religion is no substitute for Salvation. In Jesus' day, like today, organised religion keeps people from hearing God's Word and in consequence, 'God's Truth.'

The Gentiles

They were idolaters. Paul stated their awful plight. The ERV translates Ephesians 2:12 so simply.

> Ephesians 2:12. ERV. '.... you were without Christ. You were not citizens of Israel, and you did not know about the agreements with the promises that God made to his people. You had no hope, and you did not know God.'

Ephesians 2:12 states five truths about the Gentiles. They:

1. were 'without Christ.'
2. 'were not citizens of Israel.'
3. did not know God's promises to the Jews.
4. 'had no hope.'
5. 'did not know God.'

1: The Gentiles were 'without Christ'

The Old Testament taught the Jews that one day their Christ or Messiah would come to them. They were so nationalistic that they mistakenly thought that when He came, He would organise an army that would defeat their Roman enemies. They presumably expected that their Messiah would have the same ungodly attitude to the Gentiles that they had.

The Jews misunderstood The Old Testament. They heard it read regularly. It is clearly taught that God had blessings for the Gentiles as well. The Jews should have evangelised them by introducing them to God but the Jews appalling attitude to them ensured this never happened.

We know from Acts 15:13-18 that James quoted from The Old Testament to prove to Jewish believers that God had always intended to bless the Gentiles. But like so many so-called Christian Churches today, they ignored those parts of The Scriptures that they did not like.

A Note and a Question

Note: Believers must have a godly attitude to unbelievers.

Question: Do we 'misunderstand' The Bible because we only read it when we want it to support our views?

2: The Gentiles, 'were not citizens of Israel'

Before Jesus' death, if Gentiles wanted to worship with the Jews, they had to convert to The Jewish Faith and males had to be circumcised. However, converted Gentiles only obtained some of God's privileges for the Jews.

What a difference now exists because Jesus was willing to bear God's punishment for sin and be crucified. If you want to be saved, if you will repent and believe The Gospel, you can be saved. Let us make this as simple as we can.

Whoever you are, and whatever you might have done that has angered a holy God, there are no limitations and no limits on the forgiveness and the blessings that can be yours. A holy God can forgive you and give you His Salvation and every spiritual blessing because, and only because, Jesus took the punishment you deserved when He was crucified for you.

A holy God will not demand that you be punished if Jesus is your Saviour. Whether you are young or old, whether you have lived a respectable life or you have sinned without regret and remorse, God desires to give you all His Heavenly blessings. But He will not force you to be saved.

3: The Gentiles 'did not know God's promises'

A covenant existed between God and the Jews. Only if they obeyed Him did they get the covenant's promises:

- Whenever the Jews disobeyed God, He punished them. But, when they repented, God blessed them.
- When the Jews disobeyed God, He allowed foreign armies to invade Israel. Many Jews were captured and taken to foreign countries.
- As proof that God does punish sin, we know that before Jesus was born, as many Jews did not return home, there were more Jews living outside Israel than in it.

It is not just the Jews who have incorrect views about God's holiness and righteousness, His hatred of sin and His judgment. Many today have the silly notion that a loving and gracious God will not punish sinners. Even a cursory reading of The Old Testament shows that this notion is wrong. God severely punished the Jews when they sinned. God is holy and righteous and He does what He says He will do. God would not be holy and righteous if He ignored sin and did not keep His Word.

A Caution: God Must Judge Sin

It might be a popular view and what people want to hear, but to preach that God will forgive everyone and accept everyone into Heaven dishonours God. God does not lie.

Such preaching offends God's holiness and insults God. It is wrong and foolish to preach it.

4: The Gentiles 'had no hope'

'Hope' in The New Testament does not have its present English meaning that implies an element of chance. 'Hope' in The New Testament means 'a confident expectation of something pleasurable' and 'without hope' means the opposite.

God wants believers to have this 'confident expectation of something pleasurable' when they think about their future.

5: The Gentiles 'did not know God'

The Gentiles were idolaters. Paul simply stated that they 'did not know God.' As many of us live in countries with a Christian heritage, we must distinguish between factual knowledge about God and knowledge that comes from knowing God personally. You will appreciate the contrast.

Unbelievers may know some facts about God, but, as they do not have a personal relationship with God, they can only know about God. Only believers can have a personal relationship with God.

You will realise why it is vital to distinguish between those who know about God and those who know God. Put simply, it is the difference between 'head knowledge,' and 'heart knowledge.' Only you know which you have.

Ephesians 2:13-16.

To read these verses in context we quote from verse 12:

> Ephesians 2:12-16. NIV. 'remember that at that time you were separate from Christ, excluded from citizenship in Israel and foreigners to the covenants of the promise, without hope and without God in the world. 13. But now in Christ Jesus you who once were far away have been brought near by the blood of Christ. For he himself is our peace, who has made the two groups one and has destroyed the barrier, the dividing wall of hostility, by setting aside in his flesh the law with its commands and regulations. His purpose was to create in himself one new humanity out of the two, thus making peace, and in one body to reconcile both of them to God through the cross, by which he put to death their hostility. Ephesians 2:12-16. NIV.

Ephesians 2:13 commences with the word, 'But.' So we know that Paul intended to contrast what he had already written with what he was about to write. Ephesians 2:12 refers to the Gentiles' historical plight. We have separated these words from our commentary so that you can consider them and ask yourself if they apply to you.

'Without hope and without God in the world'

These words from Ephesians 2:12 tell us quite succinctly, why, in over 60 years, we have never met a believer who would prefer to be an unbeliever. Ephesians 2:13 refers to a spiritual change. As we have emphasised, this change is not about what we have done or can do. It is about what Jesus has done for believers. Hence, we read His name twice in the verse. We refer to the various contrasts in Ephesians 2 later. In the meantime consider the contrasts in Ephesians 2:12-16.

<u>Verses 12-13</u>:

The Past: 'separate from Christ.'

The Present: 'in Christ Jesus.'

<u>Verse 13</u>:

The Past: 'far away.'

The Present: 'brought near.'

<u>Verses 14-15</u>:

The Past: 'two groups,' - 'hostility.'

The Present: 'one new humanity,' - 'peace.'

<u>Verse 16</u>:

The Past: 'both,' - 'hostility.'

The Present: 'one,' - 'to reconcile both.'

A Summary – The Jews and the Gentiles

The Jews and the Gentiles were hostile to each other:

- God made an agreement with the Jews that He would bless them if they obeyed Him, but few did.
- God made no agreement with the Gentiles but He blessed those who obeyed Him.

The vast majority of both Jews and Gentiles were far away from God. We would not be exaggerating if we said that they both preferred their sin and sinning.

God has foreknowledge. His 'Plan of Salvation' was in place before creation. He wanted both Jews and Gentiles who repented and believed The Gospel to have His gift of Salvation. God planned that believing Jews and Gentiles would be reconciled and formed into a body called 'The Church.' We read later why 'The Church' did not begin until Jesus had died, risen, and ascended to Heaven.

The Stark Contrasts in Ephesians 2

This chapter is so important to a correct understanding of:

1. God's Salvation.
2. The Church of God. The Church is referred to as 'The Church of God' seven times in The New Testament.

We have been reading from the NIV but for this review of Ephesians 2:1-16, we switch to the NLT as it uses words that English readers can more easily understand and it is vital that readers understand these verses.

We ask you to re-read Ephesians 2 from verse 1 because in Ephesians 2:1-10, Paul reminded the Ephesian believers of what they once were and what God's Salvation had accomplished for them. Every believer should know and enjoy these truths:

> Once you were dead because of your disobedience and your many sins. You used to live in sin, just like the rest of the world, obeying the devil—the commander of the powers in the unseen world. He is the spirit at work in the hearts of those who refuse to obey God. All of us used to live that way, following the passionate desires and inclinations of our sinful nature. By our very nature we were subject to God's anger, just like everyone else. But God is so rich in mercy, and He loved us so much, that even though we were dead because of our sins, He gave us life when He raised Christ from the dead. (It is only by God's grace that you have been saved!) For He raised us from the dead along with Christ and seated us with Him in the heavenly realms because we are united with Christ Jesus. So God can point to us in all future ages as examples of the incredible wealth of His grace and kindness toward us, as shown in all He has done for us who are united with Christ Jesus. God

> saved you by His grace when you believed. And you can't take credit for this; it is a gift from God. Salvation is not a reward for the good things we have done, so none of us can boast about it. For we are God's masterpiece. He has created us anew in Christ Jesus, so we can do the good things He planned for us long ago. Don't forget that you Gentiles used to be outsiders. You were called "uncircumcised heathens" by the Jews, who were proud of their circumcision, even though it affected only their bodies and not their hearts. In those days you were living apart from Christ. You were excluded from citizenship among the people of Israel, and you did not know the covenant promises God had made to them. You lived in this world without God and without hope. But now you have been united with Christ Jesus. Once you were far away from God, but now you have been brought near to Him through the blood of Christ. For Christ Himself has brought peace to us. He united Jews and Gentiles into one people when, in His own body on the cross, He broke down the wall of hostility that separated us. He did this by ending the system of law with its commandments and regulations. He made peace between Jews and Gentiles by creating in Himself one new people from the two groups. Together as one body, Christ reconciled both groups to God by means of His death on the cross, and our hostility toward each other was put to death.   Ephesians 2:1-16. NLT.

What God did for Hell-deserving sinners, He did because:

- He 'is so rich in mercy' Ephesians 2:4.
- He 'loved us so much' Ephesians 2:4.

There was nothing good in any one of us that merited such mercy and love. If you doubt this, re-read the first three verses of Ephesians 2. If you doubt that God will punish unbelievers, consider the last 14 words of Ephesians 2:3. Because there is no lack of widespread misinformation about God's judgment, we quote them.

> 'By our very nature we were subject to God's anger, just like everyone else.' Ephesians 2:3. NIV.

Ephesians 2:7

Many will be familiar with Ephesians 2:8-9. We need to consider the previous verse for three reasons. We want:

1. 'to set the scene' for verses 8-9.
2. believers to realise how wonderfully blessed they are to be united with Christ Jesus.
3. unbelievers to realise what they will never experience if they reject God's Salvation.

> '... the incredible wealth of His grace and kindness toward us, as shown in all He has done for us who are united with Christ Jesus.' Ephesians 2:7. NLT.

'The Incredible Wealth of His Grace and Kindness'

Are you thrilled to read about God's grace that will last throughout eternity? Paul stated how unique:

- believers are to God.
- believers always will be to God.

Paul also emphasised:

- 'the incredible wealth of God's grace and kindness.'
- 'the boundlessness of God's mercy and love.'

God is not just gracious and kind. The incredible wealth of

His grace and kindness is shown in all He has done for those who are united with Christ Jesus. God is not just merciful. He is 'so rich in mercy.' God is not just loving. He 'loved us so much.' These truths seem even more amazing when, to quote the words of Ephesians 2:2, believers used to 'live in sin, just like the rest …'

We must ask two questions.

1. A Question for believers: Are you rejoicing day by day in the knowledge that you are an eternal beneficiary of God's mercy, love and grace? If God's Salvation and the wonderful blessings that God has for you do not make you rejoice, you should ask yourself whether you have deceived yourself or you have been deceived into thinking that you are a believer.

2. A Question for unbelievers: Is it your desire to stay 'like the rest' which stops you accepting God's Salvation?

Ephesians 2:8-9 - Two Familiar Verses

Do not let familiarity cause you to miss the truth in these verses. Read them as if you had never read them before:

> Ephesians 2:8-9. NLT. 'God saved you by His grace when you believed. And you can't take credit for this; it is a gift from God. Salvation is not a reward for the good things we have done, so none of us can boast about it.'

Believers: Salvation is God's gift. Believers must not behave as though they deserved it or had earned it.

Unbelievers: Salvation will never be a reward for good works. Salvation can only ever be a gift from God.

The Crucifixion

Paul did not use the word 'death' when referring to the crucifixion in the first fifteen verses of Ephesians 2, although he often used it in his other letters. In the NLT 'death' is only mentioned in Ephesians 2:16. Other translations use words such as 'slain.' We consider Ephesians 2:16 later.

'The Blood of Christ'

'His Own Body on the Cross'

We now comment on these two important expressions:

1. Ephesians 2:13: 'the blood of Christ'

2. Ephesians 2:14: 'in His own body on the cross'

Ephesians 2:13. 'The Blood of Christ'

Paul used the word 'you' three times in Ephesians 2:13 and on each occasion, he referred to Gentile believers.

> Ephesians 2:13. NLT. But now you have been united with Christ Jesus. Once you were far away from God, but now you have been brought near to Him through the blood of Christ. Ephesians 2:13. NLT.

Paul wanted his readers to know that because they were Gentiles, they were once far away from God. But, the blood of Christ had now brought them near to God.

Question: Did the blood of Christ not also bring Jewish believers near to God? We answer this question in two separate parts. It is important for readers to know the spiritual position of both the Jews and the Gentiles before and after the death of Jesus.

Answer. Part 1: Paul was specifically writing to Gentile believers about their past and present spiritual condition. He had already written about the Jews and their spiritual condition prior to Jesus' death, because he wanted to contrast their spiritual condition with that of the Gentiles. Hence, he had no need to repeat what the blood of Christ had accomplished for the Jews. It is the opening words of Ephesians: 2:11 that give us a clue as to Paul's thoughts as he wrote to these Gentile believers.

> Ephesians 2:11. NLT. 'Don't forget that you Gentiles used to be outsiders. You were called "uncircumcised heathens" by the Jews …' Ephesians 2:11. NLT.

Paul's four contrasts between Jews and Gentiles:

1. Prior to Jesus' death there was a distinction between Jews and Gentiles.
2. It was a divine, not a 'man-made' distinction.
3. Although God gave His Laws to the Jews, some Laws applied to any Gentiles that lived with the Jews.
4. The Gentiles that lived with the Jews are called 'foreigners' as in Leviticus 17:13:

> 'And if any native Israelite or foreigner living among you goes hunting and kills an animal or bird that is approved for eating, he must drain its blood and cover it with earth.' Leviticus 17:13. NLT.

Answer. Part 2: We repeat Paul's words in Ephesians 1:7.

'He is so rich in kindness and grace that He purchased our freedom with the blood of His Son and forgave our sins.'

Note that Paul used the word 'our' twice in Ephesians 1:7. He was a Jew. They were Gentiles. 'Our' included both of them. So, prior to Ephesians 2:13, Paul had already stated, and hence the Ephesian believers knew, that Jesus' blood had brought redemption and the forgiveness of sins to both Jews and Gentiles.

A Sincere Request

We ask you not to read on until you have considered what

it cost God to do what we could never have done.

- Believer: It was Jesus' blood that paid the price for your redemption and enabled God to forgive your sins.
- Unbeliever:
  - Do you want to be released from sin's power over you, Satan's dreadful lifelong slavery?
  - Do you want to serve God and not Satan?
- Only Jesus' blood can enable God to forgive your sins and set you free from Satan's slavery.
- Only Jesus' blood can reconcile Hell-deserving sinners and a holy and righteous God.

Only God can forgive sins. He will forgive you if you repent and accept Jesus as your Saviour.

Ephesians 2:14: 'In His Own Body on The Cross'

It was only Jesus' death that brought peace and reconciled believing Jews and Gentiles. This verse it is so important:

> For Christ Himself has brought peace to us. He united Jews and Gentiles into one people when, in His own body on the cross, He broke down the wall of hostility that separated us.   Ephesians 2:14. NLT.

It is common knowledge that for thousands of years there has been hostility, even war, between Jews and Gentiles. But Ephesians 2 teaches us that when Jews and Gentiles become believers, there is peace between them. Hence, in Ephesians 2:14, we read the word 'us' twice. Believing Jews and Gentiles become 'one body.' They can be at peace with each other because they are united in Jesus.

Question: What price did Jesus pay so that peace could replace the hostility between Jew and Gentile?

Answer: Jesus was crucified so that believing Jews and Gentiles could be at peace with each other. 'In His own body on the cross' describes Jesus' cruel death by crucifixion. Note that Paul also used the word 'body' metaphorically in Ephesians, as elsewhere in his letters, to refer to the mystic Body of Christ. He did this whether he wrote about The Church or individual local churches. In the following verses, note how he emphasised this truth regarding Christ's body and The Church.

> Ephesians 1:23. NLT. 'And the church is His body; it is made full and complete by Christ, who fills all things everywhere with Himself.'
>
> Ephesians 4:12. NLT. 'Their responsibility is to equip God's people to do His work and build up the church, the body of Christ.'

Paul wrote that Jesus had broken down the wall of hostility that separated Jews and Gentiles. Many Jewish believers rejected Paul's teaching. They wrongly thought that 'Christianity' was part of their Jewish Faith. In Acts we read how Paul dealt with these misguided believers.

Consider again Ephesians 2:15-16 quoted from the NLT. If you think you can acquire God's Salvation by keeping 'The Ten Commandments' as The Law of Moses is often called, or any other religious rules, these verses ought to change your mind. We quote from Ephesians 2:14 so that you can read verses 15-16 in context.

> Ephesians 2:14-16. NLT. 'For Christ Himself has brought peace to us. He united Jews and Gentiles into one people when, in His own body on the cross, He broke down the wall of hostility that separated us. He did this by ending the system of law with its commandments and regulations. He made peace

> between Jews and Gentiles by creating in Himself one new people from the two groups. Together as one body, Christ reconciled both groups to God by means of His death on the cross, and our hostility toward each other was put to death.'   Ephesians 2:14-16. NLT.

Time spent considering these verses will be time well spent, because despite what is so often preached today, The Law of Moses, known today as 'The Ten Commandments' never applied to Gentiles unless they lived in Jewish households.

Ephesians 2:15 confirms that it was Jesus' death that made The Law of Moses, 'The Ten Commandments,' ineffectual, so that Jews and Gentiles could be at peace with each other and formed into one new body. But, because they are not aware of what The Bible teaches, many religious Gentiles today take pride in 'keeping The Ten Commandments.' It is only when you grasp the truth that God's Salvation is a gift and not a reward for good living that you realise the futility of relying on living a good life for Salvation. This 'living a good life' might be keeping the Ten Commandments. It might be keeping any other 'church rules.' It is good to aspire to live as God would have us live, but it will never result in our Salvation. If you had lived 100 years ago, and you wanted to possess God's Salvation, you would have been told 'it is not try but trust.' You might not hear those words today, but they do summarise our next paragraph.

We must reject 'self-help' or 'do-it-yourself' efforts, to obtain God's Salvation. No one can earn God's Salvation. It can never be a reward. It is a gift from God that we will only receive when we repent and accept Jesus as our Saviour. Consider this next question carefully. If keeping 'The Ten Commandments' or any other self-help method could have provided us with Salvation, why did Jesus suffer the agonising death of crucifixion?

Ephesians 2:17-22. Jesus Came

> Ephesians 2:17-22. NIV. 'He came and preached peace to you who were far away and peace to those who were near. For through him we both have access to the Father by one Spirit. Consequently, you are no longer foreigners and strangers, but fellow citizens with God's people and also members of his household, built on the foundation of the apostles and prophets, with Christ Jesus himself as the chief cornerstone. In him the whole building is joined together and rises to become a holy temple in the Lord. And in him you too are being built together to become a dwelling in which God lives by his Spirit.'   Ephesians 2:17-22. NIV.

There are five references to Jesus in the last six verses of Ephesians 2. We read why Jesus is unique. Paul mentioned historical facts and their spiritual implications.

Historical Fact - 'He came' - Spiritual Implications

Ephesians 2:17. Paul abridged into just two words 'He came' 'The Christmas Story.' It was unnecessary in this letter for Paul to detail the reason for Jesus coming into the world. He did this in other New Testament letters. His admission to Timothy, recorded in 1Timothy 1:15-16, is probably his most well-known reason.

> Here is a trustworthy saying that deserves full acceptance: Christ Jesus came into the world to save sinners--of whom I am the worst. But for that very reason I was shown mercy so that in me, the worst of sinners, Christ Jesus might display his immense patience as an example for those who would believe in him and receive eternal life.'   1Timothy 1:15-16. NIV.

It is a historical fact that Jesus came into the world. Few seem to know why and, for so many, it has made absolutely no difference to their life or their eternal future. We do not exaggerate when we write that for so many, it was an irrelevant event, remembered only at Christmas.

In Ephesians 2:17 we read Paul's words that Jesus preached peace to 'those who were far away' and 'those who were near.' He referred to Gentiles and Jews. Before proceeding, we want to consider how Paul referred to the Gentiles. We ask a thought-provoking question:

Question: Who would choose to be far away from God? Readers must answer for themselves. Is it only because we were saved when we were young that to be far away from God seems so dreadful to us believers?

Peter was the first apostle to preach The Gospel to the Gentiles. He preached the same truth that Paul wrote and you have read in Ephesians 2:17. As you read Acts 10:36-43, note what Peter said about Jesus and The Gospel. He called it 'the good news of peace through Jesus Christ.'

> Acts 10:36-43. NIV. "'You know the message God sent to the people of Israel, announcing the good news of peace through Jesus Christ, who is Lord of all. You know what has happened throughout the province of Judea, beginning in Galilee after the baptism that John preached—how God anointed Jesus of Nazareth with the Holy Spirit and power, and how he went around doing good and healing all who were under the power of the devil, because God was with him. "We are witnesses of everything he did in the country of the Jews and in Jerusalem. They killed him by hanging him on a cross, but God raised him from the dead on the third day and caused him to be seen. He was not seen by all the people, but by witnesses whom God had

> already chosen--by us who ate and drank with him after he rose from the dead. He commanded us to preach to the people and to testify that he is the one whom God appointed as judge of the living and the dead. All the prophets testify about him that everyone who believes in him receives forgiveness of sins through his name.'" Acts 10:36-43. NIV.

People generally know more about what Jesus did than what He said. Both Paul and Peter confirmed that Jesus preached 'The Gospel.' It is 'the good news of peace.'

Re-read the above verses because it is fascinating to read Peter's first Gospel message to a Gentile audience. Luke records in Acts that Peter preached four times. A study of his Gospel messages will both educate and fascinate you because, unlike Jews, Gentiles had no knowledge of The Old Testament. But, if you read Acts, you will note that the essential content of Peter's Gospel messages to both Jews and Gentiles is the same.

An Important Truth - Access to God

Prior to Jesus' death, the Jews had access to God but only at The Temple in Jerusalem where priests conducted specific sacrifices. After Jesus' death, and despite what many teach, no special buildings or priests are required for believers to have access to God. Believers, those who have repented and accepted Jesus as their Saviour have immediate access to God wherever they are. This is because they possess The Holy Spirit. There is no reason for you or anyone else who wants to be 'included in Christ Jesus' to be and remain far away from God.

Ephesians 2:18-22

We commence our quotation from Ephesians 2:16 so that you can read Ephesians 2:18-22 in context.

> Ephesians 2:16-22. NIV. '... to reconcile both of them to God through the cross, by which he put to death their hostility. He came and preached peace to you who were far away and peace to those who were near. For through him we both have access to the Father by one Spirit. Consequently, you are no longer foreigners and strangers, but fellow citizens with God's people and also members of his household, built on the foundation of the apostles and prophets, with Christ Jesus himself as the chief cornerstone. In him the whole building is joined together and rises to become a holy temple in the Lord. And in him you too are being built together to become a dwelling in which God lives by his Spirit.'

The word 'Trinity' which we use to refer to God The Father, God The Son, and God The Holy Spirit, is not a Bible word but, it is so well-known that we also use it. Some so-called Christian Churches and cults deny the existence of 'The Trinity.' They claim that it does not make sense that three separate and distinct divine Persons are 'One God.' God does not expect us humans to understand divine truths. Whether these truths make sense to us or not is irrelevant. God expects us to believe what He has written in His Word, The Bible.

Ephesians 2:18

We cannot go into details but, if you are a believer, God The Father, God The Son, and God The Holy Spirit, were involved in your personal Salvation and 'The Trinity' is still involved with your daily spiritual welfare.

If the Ephesian believers thought that 'The Trinity' dealt with Jewish and Gentile believers differently, Paul told them that because of Jesus' death, Jewish and Gentile believers had identical access to God. But sadly, 2000 years after The New Testament was written, some so-called Christian Churches are still unaware of how God is or should be approached.

'Access to The Father by One Spirit'

Unlike Old Testament days, believers do not need:

- special buildings.
- anyone to approach God on their behalf.
- formalities that must be observed.

Be wary of any claiming that access to God requires a special building, a human intermediary or payment. It really is a privilege to be able to tell believers that access to God is free because Jesus' blood paid the price of their access to God.

Jesus shed His blood so that you could be redeemed from the slave market of sin. If you are a believer, your sins are forgiven and no longer separate you from God.

- All believers have immediate access to God.
- Unbelievers have no access to God.

These truths are condensed into Ephesians 2:18. We repeat it because of its vital importance.

> Ephesians 2:18. NLT. Now all of us can come to the Father through the same Holy Spirit because of what Christ has done for us.   Ephesians 2:18. NLT.

When Paul wrote 'all of us' he was not referring to 'all and sundry.' He referred only to the Jewish and Gentile believers mentioned in Ephesians 2:17.

It is only believers that are indwelt by The Holy Spirit. He helps believers make their prayers to God. It is important that readers know this truth because all sorts of unscriptural beliefs, customs and practices have found acceptance with religious people and churchgoers. The reason that these 'religious errors' persist is that few read The Bible for themselves. Few know what it teaches.

Ephesians 2:19-22

> 'So now you Gentiles are no longer strangers and foreigners. You are citizens along with all of God's holy people. You are members of God's family. Together, we are His house, built on the foundation of the apostles and the prophets. And the cornerstone is Christ Jesus Himself. We are carefully joined together in Him, becoming a holy temple for the Lord. Through Him you Gentiles are also being made part of this dwelling where God lives by His Spirit.'   Ephesians 2:19-22. NLT.

These verses need our careful consideration. Re-read them from the standpoint of Gentile believers who might have thought that they were inferior to Jewish believers.

Question: Who would not wish to be included in the good things we read about in Ephesians 2:19-22?

Strangers and Foreigners

None of us like being viewed as strangers or foreigners but that is how the Jews viewed Gentiles. Since Jesus' death it has been possible for anyone who, although, because of their sin, deserved nothing but God's wrath, to repent and accept Jesus as their Saviour. If they do this, they become:

- citizens along with all of God's holy people.
- members of God's family.

Is there a greater spiritual contrast than deserving God's wrath and being a member of His family? But, there is even more. However, we first need to correct some false doctrine that could so easily ruin a believer's enjoyment of their very privileged spiritual status.

When we read Ephesians, it seems that Paul anticipated that some would contradict his teaching about The Gospel and God's eternal Salvation. Some erroneously teach that Salvation is only a temporary gift from God and that believers can lose it. They have ignored Ephesians 2:19-22 and other verses teaching the same truth. We ask you to study these four verses:

> Ephesians 2:19-22. NIV. 'So now you Gentiles are no longer strangers and foreigners. You are citizens along with all of God's holy people. You are members of God's family. Together, we are His house, built on the foundation of the apostles and the prophets. And the cornerstone is Christ Jesus Himself. We are carefully joined together in Him, becoming a holy temple for the Lord. Through Him you Gentiles are also being made part of this dwelling where God lives by His Spirit.'

Paul wrote divine truth in words that we can understand:

- We know what 'strangers' and 'foreigners' are.
- We realise the problems of those who are marginalised.
- We understand 'citizenship' and what it means to be part of a community where we are accepted and live on equal terms with others.

'All of God's Holy People'

Because we read, 'citizens along with all of God's holy people,' there must also be unholy people. They do not belong to God. They are not citizens.

'Members of God's Family'

Because we read, 'members of God's family,' there must also be people who do not belong to God's family.

When we read Ephesians 2:19-22 we are taught that:

1. A named body of people, 'Gentiles who have become

believers,' are no longer strangers and foreigners. They are now citizens along with all of God's holy people and members of God's family.

2. The cornerstone of God's house is Christ Jesus and it is built on the foundation of the apostles and prophets.
   1) Jewish and Gentile believers are part of God's house. They are carefully joined together in Christ Jesus, becoming a holy temple for God.
   2) Through Christ Jesus, Gentile believers are also being made part of God's house, a dwelling where God lives by His Spirit.'

Questions might assist us to explain to you why believers cannot lose God's Salvation:

Question 1: If we had not referred to the false teaching that believers can lose their Salvation, would reading Ephesians 2:19-22 have made you aware that God's Salvation was only temporary and not eternal? We are sure your answer will be, "No." That is our answer.

Before we ask our next question, we think you will agree with our next comment:

In Ephesians 2:19-22, Paul mentioned:

1. 'God's holy people,' 'God's family,' and 'God's house.'

2. 'a holy temple for the Lord.'

3. 'a dwelling where God lives by His Spirit.'

Question 2: In what part of the construction of this 'dwelling, where God lives,' are believers involved?

Answer: Believers take no part in the construction of this, 'dwelling where God lives by His Spirit.' Paul confirmed this. He wrote:

'Through Him you Gentiles are also being made part of this dwelling where God lives by His Spirit.'

Because of what Jesus has done, believers are being made part of this divine building.

Do not read on until this important truth about Jesus has sunk deep into your heart. It will help you to ignore the doctrine that has caused havoc in the lives of believers.

Read the verses again. Note the four words, 'being made part of.' This can only mean that neither Jewish nor Gentile believers had anything to do with the construction of this 'dwelling where God lives by His Spirit.'

Believers are not part of a building made with their own hands. They will never be removed by the Divine Builder.

Question 3: When did the construction of this 'holy temple for the Lord' begin?

Answer: Construction was in progress when Paul wrote about it. For 2000 years believers have been added. If you are a believer, you are part of this wonderful building and we repeat that there is not even a hint, let alone an indication, that you could ever be removed from it.

Question 4: As the 'foundation' and 'cornerstone' are the 'apostles, prophets' and 'Christ Jesus,' was Paul referring to a permanent or a temporary 'dwelling?'

Answer: The dwelling had a solid foundation and a perfect cornerstone. A cornerstone ensured that the sides of a building joined perfectly and permanently together. There is no hint or suggestion that this dwelling that believers are made part of was not also solid and perfect.

Question 5: Do the words 'we are carefully joined together in Him' denote an act that might only be temporary?

Answer: "No." If you are not yet a believer, we can assure you that if you become a believer, Paul's words will be true of you. You will be carefully joined to Christ Jesus and to every other believer for eternity.

Choose to be 'One of the 'Us'

Whenever we can choose to be 'one of the us' or 'one of the them,' we choose to be one of the 'us.' We anticipate that it will be better for us. Divisions and segregation provide winners and losers. No one wants to be on the losing side in life, and yet so many remain on the losing side when it comes to spiritual and eternal matters. You could be one of the spiritual 'us.' You do not need to remain a spiritual stranger or foreigner. You could be a citizen of Heaven and a member of God's family now.

God's House

We all know what a house is and what its function is. We know how vital it is that before construction commences, a complete and accurate plan is prepared and a competent builder employed. Decisions must be taken regarding:

- the foundations.
- the structure.
- the materials to be used.

We would not expect God's house to be anything less than perfect, a house fit for a perfect God and His holy family.

God's House - The Plan and The Builder

We know from Ephesians that 'God's Plan of Salvation' was prepared before creation.

Question: Did Paul state the name of the Builder in these four verses?

Answer: When we first read them, it appears that the answer is, "No." We are not told that Jesus laid the foundations, chose the materials to be used, and the like.

The Good News Bible clarifies two matters:

1. Jesus holds the whole building together.

2. Jesus makes the whole building grow into a sacred temple dedicated to the Lord.

> Ephesians 2:21. GNB. He is the one who holds the whole building together and makes it grow into a sacred temple dedicated to the Lord.   Ephesians 2:21. GNB.

God's House – Its Foundation

God's House is 'built on the foundation of the apostles and the prophets.' We will learn more about these 'gifts' in Ephesians 4. In the meantime, we quote Ephesians 4:11.

> Ephesians 4:11. NIV. 'So Christ himself gave the apostles, the prophets …'

Jesus gave specific gifts to The Church after His ascension including apostles and prophets. The New Testament did not exist and the prophets were believers who spoke for God. It was vital that believers did not rely on The Old Testament for guidance about The Church because, put simply, Jesus' death made The Old Testament way of worshipping God obsolete.

Believers needed to know that a new Church era had begun. The Old Testament does not refer to The Church. It was new to believers. They were its first members. It was God's intention that The Church would bring together into one spiritual body both Jewish and Gentile believers. We now know this because The New Testament teaches it. These prophets needed to pass on new truths to the new members of the new Church.

Like the apostles, the prophets formed a solid foundation. Once the foundation was in place, the special work of the apostles and the prophets ceased. As the apostles and the prophets were a gift to The Church from Jesus Himself,

God's house could not have had a better foundation but it still needed a perfect cornerstone.

God's House – Its Cornerstone

In Paul's day, a cornerstone was used by builders to make stone buildings into solid structures. A cornerstone united and gave strength to the two walls to which it was connected. This refers to the fact that both believing Jews and Gentiles were united by Jesus into one body. God's house could not have had a more perfect 'Cornerstone' than Jesus Himself.

God's House – Its Structure

The structure consists of Jewish and Gentile believers. A perfect plan, foundation and Cornerstone ensured a building could have a perfect structure. If you are a believer, you are part of this perfect structure.

A Believer's Importance to God

All believers are of equal importance to God. We read nothing to suggest that one part of the structure is more important than another. If you are a believer, it was before creation that God chose you to be in this structure. If you consider yourself to be better than, or inferior to, other believers, your view of yourself is not God's view of you. The words of Ephesians 2:22 were written by Paul to Gentile believers so that they would know that they were not inferior to Jewish believers. Nevertheless, what Paul wrote is true of every believer.

Ephesians 2:22 – 'You too'

> Ephesians 2:22. NIV. 'And in him you too are being built together to become a dwelling in which God lives by his Spirit.' Ephesians 2:22. NIV.

A Time to Reflect

We ask a vital question.

Question: Are you one of those that has been built into the dwelling referred to in Ephesians 2:22?

Answer: The tenor of The Bible is that the majority should answer, "No." Each reader will answer for themselves. We asked this question because Ephesians 2:22 refers to a dwelling in which God lives by his Spirit.' Hence, it is comprised of believers. For 2000 years they have been, and still are, in the minority on Earth but we read in Ephesians 2:19 that they are:

- God's holy people.
- God's family.

We have reached the end of Ephesians 2. We have one further question. As you might not have read all that has gone before, we write this short statement.

Statement:

Each of us deserves only God's judgment for our sin, but God wants to show us His grace and kindness. He was willing to pay the price that would enable us to be forgiven for eternity. He sent His own son Jesus to be punished for our sins on the cross. Jesus' shed blood, and only Jesus' shed blood, could enable a holy God to forgive our sins.

Question: Who could deny that God is gracious and kind and has a great love for each one of us?

A Question to those who are not yet believers

Why do you remain without hope and without God? Jesus shed His blood for you. You could receive God's Salvation, be one of His holy people and a member of His family. Repent of your sin now and accept Jesus as your Saviour.

EPHESIANS 3. NIV.

For this reason I, Paul, the prisoner of Christ Jesus for the sake of you Gentiles-- Surely you have heard about the administration of God's grace that was given to me for you, that is, the mystery made known to me by revelation, as I have already written briefly. In reading this, then, you will be able to understand my insight into the mystery of Christ, which was not made known to people in other generations as it has now been revealed by the Spirit to God's holy apostles and prophets. This mystery is that through the gospel the Gentiles are heirs together with Israel, members together of one body, and sharers together in the promise in Christ Jesus. I became a servant of this gospel by the gift of God's grace given me through the working of his power. Although I am less than the least of all the Lord's people, this grace was given me: to preach to the Gentiles the boundless riches of Christ, and to make plain to everyone the administration of this mystery, which for ages past was kept hidden in God, who created all things. His intent was that now, through the church, the manifold wisdom of God should be made known to the rulers and authorities in the heavenly realms, according to his eternal purpose that he accomplished in Christ Jesus our Lord. In him and through faith in him we may approach God with freedom and confidence. I ask you, therefore, not to be discouraged because of my sufferings for you, which are your glory. For this reason I kneel before the Father, from whom every family in heaven and on earth derives its name. I pray that out of his glorious riches he may strengthen you with power through his Spirit in your inner being, so that Christ may dwell in your hearts through faith. And I pray that you, being rooted and

> established in love, may have power, together with all the Lord's holy people, to grasp how wide and long and high and deep is the love of Christ, and to know this love that surpasses knowledge--that you may be filled to the measure of all the fullness of God. all we ask or imagine, according to his power that is at work within us, to him be glory in the church and in Christ Jesus throughout all generations, for ever and ever! Amen.

EPHESIANS 3. COMMENTARY

Ephesians 3:1

This verse begins an interesting and informative chapter.

> 'For this reason I, Paul, the prisoner of Christ Jesus for the sake of you Gentiles …' Ephesians 3:1.

Paul did not write that he was a prisoner of the Roman authorities, although he was imprisoned by them in Rome. Why and how Paul was taken by the Romans from Jerusalem to Rome is a story you can read in Acts. You will find detailed commentary about all Paul's journeys in the author's book, 'The one and only Church.' Details of the author's books are found towards the end of this book.

Paul did not complain that he was in prison. He clearly did not share some preachers' views that receiving God's Salvation will end all unbelievers' problems. That teaching is contrary to The New Testament.

Being faithful to Jesus, living as believers should live, and preaching The Gospel faithfully will never make you popular and your life a 'bed of roses.' If this is not your personal experience, you should question your own spirituality and faithfulness. Paul considered himself a prisoner of Jesus because he had been obedient to Jesus and faithfully preached The Gospel to the Gentiles.

The tenor of Ephesians 3 is that Paul did not want his imprisonment to dismay the Ephesian believers. He did not want them to think that they were responsible for his plight. He wanted them to know that God was in control of His life. So he informed them about His personal work of preaching The Gospel to Gentiles. God's grace and mighty power had enabled him to do God's work. It had been his privilege to serve God.

In Acts we read two conversations about Paul's work for God. The first was between Jesus and Paul, the second between Jesus and Ananias. These two conversations were about Paul's personal salvation and his mission of taking The Gospel to the Gentiles. Doing God's work did not make him, a Jew, popular with either unbelieving Jews who despised Gentiles, or Jewish believers who wrongly thought that Gentiles could not become believers without first accepting the Jewish Faith.

Ephesians 3:2-6. A Word of Caution

Ephesians 3:2 needs careful consideration. The ERV and the NLT translations of Ephesians 3:2-6 are easier to understand than the NIV. Because of the importance of these verses we quote both the ERV and the NLT.

> Ephesians 3:2-6. ERV. 'God let me know his secret plan by showing it to me. I have already written a little about this. And if you read what I wrote, you can see that I understand the secret truth about Christ. People who lived in other times were not told that secret truth. But now, through the Spirit, God has made it known to his holy apostles and prophets. And this is the secret truth: that by hearing the Good News, those who are not Jews will share with the Jews in the blessings God has for his people. They are part of the same body, and

> they share in the promise God made through Christ Jesus. Ephesians 3:2-6. ERV.
>
> Ephesians 3:2-6. NLT. '… assuming, by the way, that you know God gave me the special responsibility of extending His grace to you Gentiles. As I briefly wrote earlier, God Himself revealed His mysterious plan to me. As you read what I have written, you will understand my insight into this plan regarding Christ. God did not reveal it to previous generations, but now by His Spirit He has revealed it to His holy apostles and prophets. And this is God's plan: Both Gentiles and Jews who believe the Good News share equally in the riches inherited by God's children. Both are part of the same body, and both enjoy the promise of blessings because they belong to Christ Jesus.'

On first reading you might wonder why we consider verse 2 to be of considerable importance. It tells us that we might not know that God has given a special task to a specific believer. So, interference with another believer's work for God can never be our prerogative. God decides what work is done and who does it. Believers do not choose who does God's work or the period of their involvement with God's work. When we do God's Work, God must be our Master. We must be God's willing and obedient servants.

This might not be a popular view of evangelism, nor of any other work that believers do for God today. Experience teaches that 'God's Work' is time and again organised like a commercial enterprise. We foolishly apply human wisdom to divine matters. 'God's Work' must be done 'God's way' to achieve 'God's purposes' and 'God's way' may not equate to 'the best use of human resources.' If you read Acts, you will discover that what we have written is true.

Some might challenge what we have written about 'God's Work' today. Many seem to consider that a 'modern-day approach' to evangelism is essential for The Church to survive. They argue that we are not in the days of the early Church and the world has changed in the last 2000 years. They sincerely contend that The Church must change so that it can be relevant to a modern society. They assert that Paul's ministry was unique and relevant only when for many centuries, the Jews had been 'near to God' and the Gentiles had been 'far away from God.'

Ephesians 3:2-6 does indeed confirm the uniqueness of Paul's ministry but we need to consider 'God's Plan' that Paul referred to and the consequences of ignoring the truth made known to him by revelation.

In Ephesians 1:9 we read about 'the mystery of his will,' the truth about The Church previously hidden or unknown. You will search The Old Testament in vain for the truth that Paul revealed. No Old Testament writer knew anything about it. It was hidden from all of them. 'The mystery' that was revealed by Paul was God's plan 'to bring unity to all things in heaven and on earth under Christ.'

Paul received his knowledge of 'God's Plan' by direct revelation from God. We shall read in Ephesians 3:9-11 that Paul referred to 'God's Plan and eternal purposes' when he wrote what God accomplished through Jesus' death and resurrection. When we read about 'God's Plan' we must remember that:

- God devised 'His plan' before Creation.
- 'God's Plan' applies today and it will apply for eternity.

This is our answer to those who think that Paul's views are outdated. When you hear a challenge to Paul's teaching, it is often because the speaker wants to reorganise the local church and have things done 'their way.' Remember that Paul's 'view' of 'what believers should and should not do, was God's eternal view. It was God's eternal view both before Creation and at the time He revealed it to Paul.

Ephesians 3:4-5 also states what God revealed to the other apostles and prophets. We use the word 'other' because Paul was both an apostle and a prophet.

The Apostles and Prophets

We will read in Ephesians 4 that the apostles and prophets were gifts that Jesus gave to The Church after His ascension. They did not have to use their own human resources or ingenuity to lead and teach the new believers who were being added to The Church day by day. Ephesians 3:5 teaches us that The Holy Spirit revealed 'God's Plan' to them.

There are important lessons in Ephesians 3:5. The Holy Spirit distinguishes apostles and prophets from believers who are neither. In days of democracy and equality, some tell us that all believers are equal, all are entitled to their views and all are entitled to vote in local church matters.

- Believers are often surprised to hear that The Church is not a democratic organisation organised on the same basis as a social, political or golf club.
- Even fellowships who proclaim that 'Jesus Christ is Lord' are organised like members' clubs and approve the 'one member, one vote' basis of management.

The Church is dependent on The Holy Spirit for guidance. The apostles are called 'holy.' They spent three years with Jesus when He was an itinerant preacher. No reader had that unique privilege and yet we read that the 'holy apostles' needed to rely on The Holy Spirit for guidance.

The Holy Spirit is mentioned sixty times in Acts. He is involved from first to last in The Church or the local churches, The Gospel and the spiritual welfare of believers. The Holy Spirit:

- indwells every believer immediately they are saved.
- provides divine power to preach The Gospel.
- specifies where The Gospel should be preached.
- chooses who should be involved in missionary work.
- appoints elders in the local churches.

Do not forget who The Church and the local churches belong to. Experience teaches that ambition, desire, prestige, family loyalties and the like have taken their toll on many local churches. Paul's words to the elders at Ephesus are worth memorising. We quote the GNB:

> "'So keep watch over yourselves and over all the flock which the Holy Spirit has placed in your care. Be shepherds of the church of God, which he made his own through the blood of his Son.'"   Acts 20:28. GNB.

Ephesians 3:6. God's Eternal Plan

> Ephesians 3:6. NIV. This mystery is that through the gospel the Gentiles are heirs together with Israel, members together of one body, and sharers together in the promise in Christ Jesus.

Ephesians 3: 6 contains so much truth that we need to deal with it separately. The first matter we must discuss is God's plan to unite all things in Heaven and on Earth with Jesus as the head.

This plan could not come to fruition until Jesus' death, resurrection and ascension to God's Throne. Readers should bear this in mind as they read on.

THE GOSPEL: An Essential Part of God's Plan

We have read in Ephesians three important truths:

1. God chose believers in Christ before creation.
2. God purchased believers' freedom from Satan's power with His Son's blood and God forgave believers' sins.
3. It was God's intention before creation to bring unity to all things in Heaven and on earth under Christ.

Jesus and The Old Testament

The Name 'Jesus' is not in The Old Testament, but there are over 300 prophesies relating to Him. Joseph, Mary's husband was told by an angel to call Him 'Jesus.'

The Gospel and The Old Testament

There are references to The Gospel in The Old Testament. Hence, 'the New Testament preachers,' quoted from The Old Testament when preaching The Gospel.

Question: Is there a difference between The Gospel in The Old and New Testaments?

Answer: "Yes." Jesus came to save sinners. He died for our sins, was buried, rose again, ascended to Heaven, and took His rightful place at God's right hand. The Old Testament was written prior to these events so it looks forward to them. The New Testament was written after these events. It records them as facts.

The Gospel - The Jews and The Gentiles

We need to study Ephesians 3:6. We quote the NLT.

> 'And this is God's plan: Both Gentiles and Jews who believe the Good News share equally in the riches

> inherited by God's children. Both are part of the same body, and both enjoy the promise of blessings because they belong to Christ Jesus.'   Ephesians 3:6. NLT.

We must consider the following important expressions:
- 'this is God's plan'
- 'both Gentiles and Jews'
- 'who believe the Good News'
- 'share equally in the riches inherited by God's children.'
- 'both are part of the same body'
- 'both enjoy the promise of blessings'
- 'because they belong to Christ Jesus.'

'This Is God's Plan'

Paul could not have written a more positive statement. There are no 'ifs,' 'buts,' 'exclusions' or 'exceptions.' At the time, there would have been Jewish believers who thought that Paul was wrong but because it was God's revealed truth, Paul wrote it. God's truth does not belong to us. We must never compromise God's truth because others object to it, it offends them, or makes us unpopular.

'Both Gentiles and Jews'

Paul mentioned Gentiles first. Some Jewish believers considered themselves superior to Gentiles. In a nutshell, the Jewish believers had an opinion of themselves that God did not share. How easy it is to fall into Satan's trap and become proud, arrogant and self-opinionated. If only the Jewish believers had considered God's view.
- The Old Testament did not differentiate between Jewish and Gentile sinners. The Jews had no reason to believe that God would treat Jewish sinners more favourably than Gentile sinners.

- Some Jewish believers resented God saving Gentiles even though The Old Testament clearly taught that God wanted to bless the Gentiles.
- The Gentiles were idolaters. It is clear from The Old Testament that the Jews should have introduced God to them. The Jews' unjustified and sinful hatred of the Gentiles meant that this never happened.

Religious prejudice is anything but a modern-day problem and it is not only unbelievers who have such prejudice. Even a cursory reading of Acts and Paul's letters will show how brave Paul was in taking The Gospel to the Gentiles.

'Who Believe The Good News'

Let us be quite clear about Ephesians 3:6. The wonderful eternal blessings that God has are only for a specified group. It is composed of Jews and Gentiles who 'believe the Good News' The Gospel. Paul also made it clear that Jewish believers do not receive any blessings that Gentile believers do not receive. He wrote that they both:

- 'share equally in the riches inherited by God's children,'
- 'are part of the same body,'
- 'enjoy the promise of blessings.'

'Because They Belong to Christ Jesus'

If you are a believer, Ephesians 3:6 applies to you. It is irrelevant what you were before you were saved. When you are saved, you 'belong to Christ Jesus.'

Earthly status fades into utter insignificance when contrasted with the privilege of belonging to Christ Jesus.

A Question for Believers:

Are you living in the enjoyment of the blessings we have read in Ephesians 3:6?

Two Questions for Unbelievers:

- Question 1: If you are not yet a believer, have you ever heard better good news than The Gospel?
- Question 2: If The Gospel is the best good news you have ever heard, why have you not believed it?

We ask you to spend time considering these questions before reading on.

Ephesians 3:7-12

> 'I became a servant of this gospel by the gift of God's grace given me through the working of his power. Although I am less than the least of all the Lord's people, this grace was given me: to preach to the Gentiles the boundless riches of Christ, and to make plain to everyone the administration of this mystery, which for ages past was kept hidden in God, who created all things. His intent was that now, through the church, the manifold wisdom of God should be made known to the rulers and authorities in the heavenly realms, according to his eternal purpose that he accomplished in Christ Jesus our Lord. In him and through faith in him we may approach God with freedom and confidence.'   Ephesians 3:7-12. NIV.

In Ephesians 3:1 we read about Paul the prisoner. Now we read about Paul the servant. We do not seek to revere Paul, but we do take note of the fact that God chose to reveal to him His eternal plans. We ask two questions:

Question 1: If God had chosen us, would we, like Paul, have endured whatever it took to be obedient to God?

Question 2: Would we have said to God:

- "there is only so much that one person can do?"

- "there are only twenty-four hours in a day?"

We are sure that these popular excuses will not surprise you. Paul regarded it as a privilege to be God's servant. Because of his past crimes against believers, Paul did not rate himself very highly. In fact, as we read in Ephesians 3:8, he thought he was the least important of all believers.

In view of Paul's assessment of himself, how many of us would have considered him suitable for God's Work? Is it not true that in Christian things, as in life generally, we prefer dynamic people who have no lack of confidence in their own abilities?

Note that Paul paid tribute to what God had done for him that enabled him to do God's Work. Paul referred to God's grace and power. Paul was aware that God had withheld no spiritual blessings from him.

Do not gloss over this truth. Because God had given Paul work to do, God had also given him the divine power he needed to do it. Paul was human. Had he relied on his own ability, you would not be reading about him. Paul totally relied on God for the divine ability to do God's Work. We ask two questions about the work you do for God:

1: Did you know what God wanted you to do for Him?

2: Did you decide what work you would do for God?

Has reading about Paul's attitude, and his testimony to God's grace and power, enabled you to appreciate why we have asked these two questions? Do you now understand why a negative answer to the first question and an affirmative answer to the second question will have the greatest impact on your effectiveness in God's Work?

Ephesians 3:8. 'The Boundless Riches of Christ'

Consider Paul's description of The Gospel:

- NIV: 'the boundless riches of Christ.'
- NLT: 'the endless treasures available to them in Christ.'
- ERV: 'The Good News about the riches Christ has.

The ERV adds these words:

'These riches are too great to understand fully.'

So, if like the author, you are overwhelmed with words like 'boundless' and 'endless' you are in good company as even Paul had to admit that despite God's personal revelation to him, he could not quantify 'the good things that God has prepared for those who love Him.'

Many unbelievers think that if they become believers, they will have to give up this or that. They associate God's Salvation with a miserable, unhappy life. Unbelievers might have gained this impression from seeing miserable believers or listening to miserable preachers who fail to mention the wonderful blessings that God has for those who put their trust in Jesus.

Question: If you are a believer, do you live as though 'the boundless riches of Christ' are non-existent?

We must be honest and state that miserable believers and miserable preachers are bad personal advertisements for Christianity. No wonder it never dawns on unbelievers that all believers were once unbelievers, and they would not exchange what they are now for what they once were.

It is difficult to explain to unbelievers who do not possess The Holy Spirit how wonderful the Christian life is. But, even if unbelievers were correct in their view of a believer's earthly life, an eternity in Hell cannot compare with the eternity that God has planned for believers. Even a well-educated and respected lawyer like Paul, who knew God's eternal plan, could not adequately describe how good believers' futures are.

But Ephesians 3:7-12 is not simply about a believer's future blessings. Paul wrote about 'the here and now.' He wrote to living believers who could now 'approach God with freedom and confidence.'

'Freedom and Confidence'

If you are not a believer, would you like the privilege believers have of approaching God with freedom and confidence?

Ephesians 3:10

In this verse Paul referred to 'the church.' We need to consider his words carefully. Paul's words, 'The church' have been badly misused and corrupted in English usage. In The New Testament 'the church:'

- never refers to a building.
- is never associated with a specific country.

In The Bible, 'church' only refers to believers. It refers to:

- all believers.
- believers who meet locally.

We do not know how many unbelievers:

- have become believers since The Holy Spirit indwelt believers and 'the church' was established in Jerusalem 2000 years ago.
- will become believers before Jesus comes again and takes all believers, whether living or dead, to Heaven.

We read that 'the church' is an 'object lesson' to the rulers and authorities in the heavenly realms of God's wisdom in all its different forms.

We read the expression 'the heavenly realms' in

Ephesians 1 and 2. We read it again in Ephesians 3:10. We now mention 'God's wisdom,' but delay our remarks on 'the heavenly realms' until we read Ephesians 6:12.

'God's Wisdom'

Translators have experienced difficulty in translating into understandable English what Paul meant when he wrote about 'God's wisdom.' Hence, they mention:

- 'the manifold wisdom of God.'
- 'the many-sided wisdom of God.'
- 'God's wisdom in all its different forms.'

The Amplified Bible reads, 'the complicated, many-sided wisdom of God in all its infinite variety and innumerable aspects.' One thing is certain. If you are a believer, your present and your eternal welfare are in God's hands. His wisdom is beyond our understanding. Preachers in a day long gone emphasised that believers must 'trust and obey.' We might not understand why this or that happens to us, but we can be certain that everything that does happen is part of a wise God's Plan for us.

Ephesians 3:11-12

For contextual reasons, we quote from verse 9:

> Ephesians 3:9-12. NLT. 'I was chosen to explain to everyone this mysterious plan that God, the Creator of all things, had kept secret from the beginning. God's purpose in all this was to use the church to display His wisdom in its rich variety to all the unseen rulers and authorities in the heavenly places. This was His eternal plan, which He carried out through Christ Jesus our Lord. Because of Christ and our faith in Him, we can now come boldly and confidently into God's presence.'

The Church, that body composed of all believers, displays God's unfathomable wisdom to the rulers and the authorities in the heavenly places. Note that it was always God's eternal plan and Jesus accomplished it. Because you repented and put your trust in Jesus for Salvation, you can enter God's presence boldly and confidently.

Question: What does it mean to enter God's presence boldly and confidently?

Answer: Although you personally have done nothing to earn the right to enter God's presence, yet, because of what Jesus has done for you, and because of your faith in Him, you can enter God's presence fearlessly. The Amplified Bible translates Ephesians 3:12,

'because of our faith in Him, we dare to have the boldness, the courage and confidence of free access, an unreserved approach to God with freedom and without fear.'

A story might illustrate this wonderful blessing that is available to every believer. It is said that a boy stood near the open gates of Buckingham Palace, London. He said he wanted to see Queen Victoria. He was told that it was impossible, but undeterred, he approached the open gates. Guardsmen of The Household Cavalry blocked the boy's path. He repeated his request. He was told that the Queen did not see visitors without prior appointment.

The Palace gates, normally closed, had been opened to allow Prince Albert access to the Palace. He saw the Guardsmen's actions and asked what the boy wanted. He took the boy into the Palace to see Queen Victoria, his wife. Prince Albert had access to Queen Victoria 'with freedom and without fear.' Because of Prince Albert, the boy had access to Queen Victoria. Paul wrote:

'Because of Christ and our faith in Him, we can now come boldly and confidently into God's presence.'

A Question for Unbelievers: You know what Jesus did for you, and that without faith in Him, you will never have access to God. So, if you are not relying upon Jesus for access to God, who or what are you relying on?

Ephesians 3:13.

> Ephesians 3:13. NIV. I ask you, therefore, not to be discouraged because of my sufferings for you, which are your glory.   Ephesians 3:13. NIV.

Paul had a close relationship with the Ephesian believers. He spent three years preaching and teaching at Ephesus, substantially longer than anywhere else. He was now in prison. He knew that the Ephesian believers would be thinking that if he had not been faithful to God in taking The Gospel to them, he would not have been put in prison.

The translators differ as to how they translate Ephesians 3:13. We offer this suggestion. Paul wanted the Ephesian believers to know that they should be encouraged by the fact that he thought so much about them that he was willing to suffer for taking The Gospel to the Gentiles. It is similar to the thought that Jesus must love us so much that He was willing to suffer God's punishment for our sins so that God could forgive us. Hence, instead of the Ephesian believers feeling discouraged because Paul was in prison, they should feel honoured.

Ephesians 3:14-15. Part 1

> Ephesians 3:14-15. NIV. 'For this reason I kneel before the Father, from whom every family in heaven and on earth derives its name.'   Ephesians 3:14-15.

Some think that God will only answer the prayers of those

who kneel. It is true that in addition to Ephesians 3:14 we read in Acts 9:40 that, 'Peter …. got down on his knees and prayed …' But, other New Testament verses mention prayer but not kneeling. Jesus never mentioned that kneeling was a requirement, and experience teaches us that God answers prayer whenever we pray, wherever we pray and whether we kneel, stand, sit, et cetera.

Question: Why did Paul kneel?

Answer: He wrote, 'For this reason ...' It seems that Paul did not normally kneel to pray but that on this special occasion he did. Many of the translators add the word 'bow' with or without the word 'kneel.' Bowing is indicative of 'an act of reverence.'

When we read the previous verses, we realise the unique task that God gave Paul. He was required to tell every other believer God's eternal plan. This task was not given to Peter or John or any other apostle, it was given to the man who, before he became a believer, wanted to eliminate Christianity. For those unfamiliar with Paul's pre-Christian history, when he was called Saul, we quote these verses from Acts 9.

'… Ananias answered, "Here I am, Lord." The Lord said to him, "Get up and go to the street called Straight Street. Find the house of Judas and ask for a man named Saul from the city of Tarsus. He is there now, praying. He has seen a vision in which a man named Ananias came and laid his hands on him so that he could see again." But Ananias answered, "Lord, many people have told me about this man. They told me about the many bad things he did to your holy people in Jerusalem. Now he has come here to Damascus. The leading priests have given him the power to arrest all people who trust in you." But the Lord Jesus said to Ananias, "Go! I have chosen Saul for an important work. I want him to tell other nations, their rulers, and the people of Israel about me.' Acts 9:10-15. ERV.

This is what Paul said about himself:

"'I persecuted the people who followed the Way. Some of them were killed because of me. I arrested men and women and put them in jail.'" Acts 22:4. ERV.

We suggest that Paul bowed in an act of reverence when he considered his past, the privilege of his unique task, and the divine assistance he had received to take The Gospel to Gentile idolaters who lived as far away as Ephesus, in present-day Turkey. It was an amazing achievement 2000 years ago.

'The Father - every family - derives its name'

Did Paul believe in 'The Fatherhood of God' doctrine? Unfortunately, many do. The nineteenth century hymn, 'Dear Lord and Father of Mankind,' has given many the belief that God is the Father of everyone. Even a cursory reading of John's Gospel will prove that this is not true:

- God is the Father of His children. When John mentioned Jesus and God's children, he wrote:

    'But to all who believed Him and accepted Him, He gave the right to become children of God.' John 1:12. NIV.

- The Devil is the father of his children. When John wrote about the Devil's children, he quoted what Jesus said to the Pharisees.

    'For you are the children of your father the devil, and you love to do the evil things he does.' John 8:44. NIV.

So, what do the words '…. the Father, from whom every family in heaven and on earth derives its name' mean?

Regrettably, it seems that no two translators agree as to what the original language means in understandable English. Most translators agree that Paul wrote 'family,' 'name,' and 'heaven and earth,' but agree little else:

- ERV: 'Every family in heaven and on earth gets its true name from him.'
- GNB: 'from whom every family in heaven and on earth receives its true name.'
- GW: 'from whom all the family in heaven and on earth receives its name.'
- NIV: 'from whom every family in heaven and on earth derives its name.'
- NLT: 'the Father, the Creator of everything in heaven and on earth.'

When we are unsure as to what a verse means, 'the golden rule' is to check its context. We ask two questions relating to the verses prior to and following verse 15.

Question 1: What did Paul write prior to Ephesians 3:15?

- Prior to Ephesians 3:10: The Gospel is able to unite Jews and Gentiles in one body so that they can share in God's promised blessings for believers.
- Ephesians 3:10: The Church is composed of believing humans and it displays God's wisdom to those in the heavenly realms who are not human. We comment about 'the heavenly realms' in Ephesians 6.
- Ephesians 3:11-12: Jesus completed what God always planned to do. Because of their faith in Jesus, believers can approach God with freedom and without fear.

Question 2: What did Paul write after Ephesians 3:15?

Answer: In Ephesians 3:16-19 we read Paul's four prayers for the Ephesian believers.

Ephesians 3:16-19. Paul's Four Prayers

First Prayer: 'Ephesians 3:16. GNB. I ask God from the wealth of his glory to give you power through his Spirit to be strong in your inner selves,'

Second Prayer: Ephesians 3:17. GNB. 'I pray that Christ will make his home in your hearts through faith.'

Third Prayer: Ephesians 3:17-18. GNB. 'I pray that you may have your roots and foundation in love, so that you, together with all God's people, may have the power to understand how broad and long, how high and deep, is Christ's love.'

Fourth Prayer: Ephesians 3:19. GNB. '…. may you come to know his love---although it can never be fully known---and so be completely filled with the very nature of God.'

Ephesians 3:14-16. Part 2.

We return to the question asked earlier. What do the words '…. the Father, from whom every family in heaven and on earth derives its name' in Ephesians 3:15 mean?

It seems to us that Paul is stressing to the Ephesian believers that although they are human, because they have accepted Jesus, God's Son, as their Saviour, they now have an eternal divine relationship with God. They now belong to God's family, He is their Heavenly Father, and they are His children. It is common knowledge that:

- humans have families.
- families have a distinct name that identifies them and sets them apart from other families.
- the children have a name that identifies who their father and family are and sets them apart from other children.

If you ask children their names, you learn the identity of their fathers and family. God regards believers as His children as He is their Heavenly Father. They have access to Him. When unbelievers become believers, they quickly grasp that they now belong to God's family, and as He is now their Heavenly Father, He wants a dialogue with them.

Paul's Four Prayers: Ephesians 3:17-19.

We mentioned the four prayers when we read Ephesians 3:15. We now want to consider what Paul prayed for. We quote the NLT from Ephesians 3:16 so that we can read the four prayers in Ephesians 3:17-19 in context.

> Ephesians 3:16-19. NLT. I pray that from His glorious, unlimited resources He will empower you with inner strength through His Spirit. Then Christ will make His home in your hearts as you trust in Him. Your roots will grow down into God's love and keep you strong. And may you have the power to understand, as all God's people should, how wide, how long, how high, and how deep His love is. May you experience the love of Christ, though it is too great to understand fully. Then you will be made complete with all the fullness of life and power that comes from God.   Ephesians 3:16-19. NLT.

Note the work of God The Holy Spirit in the lives of believers. Maybe you have never realised the potential that God's Salvation can have in your life. You can be empowered with 'inner strength.' This strength comes from God. Note that this does not diminish God's strength as He has 'unlimited resources.'

Some believers look back at their lives before they became believers and feel ashamed. They wrongly conclude that they are unworthy of the blessings they have freely received from God, are inferior to other believers, and God cannot use them. That could have been Paul's attitude in view of his pre-conversion behaviour but note his words:

'as you trust in Him' Ephesians 3:17. NLT.'

Trust is not only required for Salvation, it is a vital part of a believer's life. Experience teaches that some believers trust in themselves and some preachers give the impression that they have discovered the secret of a successful Christian life. Regrettably, they pass on their advice. What Paul wrote in Ephesians 3:16-19 is all a believer needs to know if they want the wonderful blessings that are available to every believer.

Ephesians 3:20-21. To Him Be the Glory- Part 1

> 'Now to him who is able to do immeasurably more than all we ask or imagine, according to his power that is at work within us, to him be glory in the church and in Christ Jesus throughout all generations, for ever and ever! Amen.' Ephesians 3:20-21. NIV.

Paul's confidence in God was total. In Acts we read how he was saved and what subsequently happened to him. We read more about him than any other believer. His experiences make fascinating reading. Almost everything he did had never been done before. He learnt to trust God. His words in Ephesians 3:20-21 are his testimony to:

- God's faithfulness to The Church, His believing people.
- Jesus. His death and resurrection made it possible for believers to have every eternal blessing.

Paul's Testimony to God's Faithfulness

God is able to do immeasurably more than all we ask, and immeasurably more than all we imagine.

We have rewritten Paul's words in Ephesians 3:20 to stress the difference between 'ask' and 'imagine.' Ponder on these words before considering our comments. The word 'we' clearly indicates to us that these blessings apply to all believers.

If, because it accords with His Will, God did what believers asked Him to do, that would be wonderful. The reality is even better because 'able to do immeasurably more' shows that God:

- is already aware of what believers need.
- knows better than believers what they really need.

God's ability to supply is not limited to what believers ask for. God is able and willing to give believers more than they imagined He could give them. As we muse on these words, we realise how special believers are to God. He cares for His children. Unlike human fathers, there is no limit to what He is both able and willing to do for His children. What a contrast there is between human fathers, who have limited abilities and resources, and God.

'According to His Power that is at Work Within Us'

In Ephesians 3:20 the words 'is' and 'us' indicate that God's power is constantly at work in all believers.

You will recall that in Paul's fourth prayer he mentioned that it was The Holy Spirit who supplied God's power to believers.

'According to' in Ephesians 3:20 might indicate that believers could themselves limit God's power. 'According to' in Wuest's Expanded Translation reads, 'in the measure of the power which is operative in us.'

As we have mentioned, believers must 'trust and obey.' So we end our commentary on Ephesians 3:20 by reminding readers of what we read in Ephesians 3:16-17.

> Ephesians 3:16-17. NLT. I pray that from His glorious, unlimited resources He will empower you with inner strength through His Spirit. Then Christ will make His home in your hearts as you trust in Him. Your roots will grow down into God's love and keep you strong.

Ephesians 3:21. In The Church and in Christ Jesus

So that we read this verse in context we quote verse 20.

> Ephesians 3:20-21. NIV. 'Now to him who is able to do immeasurably more than all we ask or imagine, according to his power that is at work within us,' 'to him be glory In The Church and in Christ Jesus throughout all generations, for ever and ever! Amen.'

The words 'to him be glory in the church and in Christ Jesus' are not easily understood unless we read them, appreciating what Paul wrote in the preceding verse, and the wonderful truths about the relationship between Christ Jesus and believers in The Church that we read in Ephesians 1:22-23. These two verses are worth repeating. Referring to Jesus, Paul wrote:

> 'God placed all things under his feet and appointed him to be head over everything for the church, which is his body, the fullness of him who fills everything in every way.' Ephesians 1:22-23. NIV.

In these two verses Paul stated the importance of The Church in 'God's Plan' that many years ago was known and referred to as 'God's Plan of Salvation.' When He appointed Jesus, God could not have chosen a more important Head for The Church. The words 'all things under his feet' and 'him to be head' indicate God's evaluation of Jesus' pre-eminence 'over everything.'

Paul also stated God's reason for appointing Jesus to be 'head over everything.' It was 'for the church.' The above two verses are quoted from the NIV, but the words 'head over everything for the church' have been variously translated to make clear their meaning in understandable English. We quote three popular translations:

1. 'to the church as supreme Lord over all things.' GNB.
2. 'head of everything for the good of the church.' GW.
3. 'head over all things for the benefit of the church.' NLT.

The Praise of God in The Old Testament

We quote Psalm 148. The Old Testament indicated:

- the source of the praise that God receives.
- God's special relationship with 'the people of Israel.'

Psalm 148, like everything in The Old Testament, was written before The Church began and before God revealed that The Church would be comprised of both Jew and Gentile believers. As you read Psalm 148, note verses 13-14 and that the psalmist concluded by mentioning God's Name, glory, nation and people.

As you muse on these words remember that the psalmist did not know, and could not have known, that a day was coming when the words 'His people' would be used by John, Jude, Paul and Peter to refer to those who believed in The Lord Jesus Christ and possessed God's Salvation.

Psalm 148. GNB.

1 Praise the LORD! Praise the LORD from heaven, you that live in the heights above. 2 Praise him, all his angels, all his heavenly armies. 3 Praise him, sun and moon; praise him, shining stars. 4 Praise him, highest heavens, and the waters above the sky. 5 Let them all praise the name of the LORD! He commanded, and they were created; 6 by his command they were fixed in their places forever, and they cannot disobey. 7 Praise the LORD from the earth, sea monsters and all ocean depths; 8 lightning and hail, snow and clouds, strong winds that obey his command. 9 Praise him, hills and mountains, fruit trees

and forests; 10 all animals, tame and wild, reptiles and birds. 11 Praise him, kings and all peoples, princes and all other rulers; 12 young women and young men, old people and children too. 13 Let them all praise the name of the LORD! His name is greater than all others; his glory is above earth and heaven. 14 He made his nation strong, so that all his people praise him—the people of Israel, so dear to him. Praise the LORD! Psalm 148. GNB.

When we later read Ephesians 5, we will learn that the relationship between The Church and Christ Jesus was revealed to Paul. We quote two extracts from Ephesians 5 that might help us to understand Paul's words 'to him be glory in the church and in Christ Jesus,' in Ephesians 3:2:

- Ephesians 5:23. Weymouth. 'Christ also is the Head of the Church, being indeed the Saviour of this His Body.'
- Ephesians 5:29-30. NIV. 'Christ feeds and cherishes the Church …. we are, as it were, parts of His Body.'

Paul referred to 'The Church' six times in Ephesians 5. Perhaps his earlier references to it were to prepare his readers for the truths he intended to mention. We refer to two of them that might help us understand Paul's words, 'to him be glory in the church and in Christ Jesus:'

1. The Church is the body of Christ.
2. Christ is the Head of The Church.

Ephesians tells us how special The Church is to God and what Jesus has done for God and for believers. We are not surprised to read verses like Ephesians 1:22-23:

> 'God placed all things under his feet and appointed him to be head over everything for the church, which is his body, the fullness of him who fills everything in every way.' Ephesians 1:22-23. NIV.

What is surprising are those wonderful verses that tell us how blessed believers are. Ephesians 3:20, that we have already considered and we quote again, is one such verse.

> Ephesians 3:20. NIV. 'Now to him who is able to do immeasurably more than all we ask or imagine, according to his power that is at work within us,'

We now revert to Ephesians 3:21 and the words, 'to him be glory in the church and in Christ Jesus.' We again quote the verse so that we consider the words in their context.

> Ephesians 3:21. NIV. 'to him be glory in the church and in Christ Jesus throughout all generations, for ever and ever! Amen.'   Ephesians 3:21. NIV.

The Church began in Jerusalem 2000 years ago. It is not surprising that believers, the Body of Christ in The Church headed by Christ Jesus, have responded to what God has done for Hell-deserving sinners by glorifying God. There are seven verses in Ephesians 3 that refer to 'God's Secret Eternal Plan.' In this book we usually refer to it as 'God's Plan of Salvation.' We have abridged the verses:

> Ephesians 3:6-12. ERV. (Abridged) '… this is the secret truth: that by hearing the Good News, those who are not Jews will share with the Jews in the blessings God has for his people. They are part of the same body, and they share in the promise God …. 7 … I became a servant to tell that Good News …. 8 … to tell the non-Jewish people the Good News about the riches Christ has. These riches are too great to understand fully. 9 And God gave me the work of telling all people about the plan for his secret truth …. hidden in him since the beginning of time …. 10 His purpose was that all the rulers and powers in the heavenly places will

> now know the many different ways he shows his wisdom. They will know this because of the church. 11 ... He did what he planned, and he did it through Christ Jesus our Lord. 12 In Christ we come before God with freedom and without fear. We can do this because of our faith in Christ.' Ephesians 3:6-12. ERV. (Abridged)

These verses tell us:

- that The Gospel can be preached to everyone.
- about the good things that God has promised for those who belong to Christ Jesus.
- why The Church was part of God's plan.

What God planned The Church would do to display His wisdom was done by Jesus:

'He did what he planned, and he did it through Christ Jesus our Lord.' Ephesians 3:11. ERV.

The Church, comprising Christ Jesus and believers, glorifies God. It will do this 'throughout all generations for ever and ever!'

This seems to us to be the meaning of the words, 'to him be glory in the church and in Christ Jesus.'

A few, although not many, translations of Ephesians 3:21 appear to support our view. We quote examples. Readers of these translations would not have had the problem that the majority of translations seem to cause. For example:

Darby: 'to him be glory in the assembly in Christ Jesus unto all generations of the age of ages. Amen.'

English Majority Text: 'to Him be glory in the church in Christ Jesus to all generations, forever and ever. Amen.'

The Living Bible: 'May he be given glory forever and ever through endless ages because of his master plan of salvation for the Church through Jesus Christ.'

Ephesians 3 has taught us some vital truths that demand to be carefully considered before reading on.

- Believers are in The Church because Christ Jesus, its Head, is their Saviour.
- Christ Jesus is The Church's Head, and believers are The Church's body.
- The Church glorifies God in this generation and it will do so in every generation and forever.

A SHORT GOSPEL MESSAGE TO UNBELIEVERS.

You might belong to one of the churches that were established by men. You do not belong to The Church that we have been considering in Ephesians 3, although you could if you chose to repent and become a believer. Jesus was sent to this world by His Father to save sinners. He saved them by dying for their sins and being resurrected. Paul and John wrote the words we now quote:

- Paul wrote: '"Christ Jesus came into the world to save sinners." This saying is true, and it can be trusted.' 1Timothy 1:15. CEV.
- Paul wrote: 'God gave Jesus to die for our sins, and he raised him to life, so that we would be made acceptable to God.' Romans 4:25. CEV.
- John wrote: 1John 4:14. CEV. 'God sent his Son to be the Savior of the world. We saw his Son and are now telling others about him.'

Paul - God's Secret Plan - God's Plan of Salvation

Paul was a unique believer, but he sought no personal glory. Having read Ephesians 3:7-8 we know his own assessment of his worth. It seems unquestionable that his humility and his achievements for God go hand in hand.

'Throughout All Generations, For Ever and Ever!'

When you first read these words, you wonder how much of 'God's Secret Plan' was disclosed to Paul and whether Paul knew that for several generations Jesus would not return from Heaven and take both living and dead believers back with Him to Heaven. We ask questions:

1. Was Paul aware that God had a timetable?
2. Did Paul know God's future plans that others, including the apostles, were unaware of?

Answers: We consider various matters before answering.

In John 21:18-22 we read Jesus' dialogue with Peter about Peter's and John's deaths. Peter was told that he would die before Jesus returned, but when Peter asked about John, Jesus would not tell him.

In Acts 1:7 we read that Jesus did not answer the apostles' question about the timing of future events:

"The Father sets those dates," he replied, "and they are not for you to know." Acts 1:7. TLB.

Paul wrote two letters to both the Corinthian and the Thessalonian churches. He wrote that he was revealing truths he had only learnt by divine revelation. In some translations, they are called secrets.

1Corinthians 15:3-4. The Gospel

> I passed on to you what was most important *and what had also been passed on to me.* Christ died for our sins, just as the Scriptures said. He was buried, and He was raised from the dead on the third day, just as the Scriptures said.   1Corinthians 15:3-4. NLT.

Paul's words, which we have italicised, indicate that he passed on a message he had personally received. It was not information he heard from a human speaker.

Jesus' Return and Believers who have Died

In 1Corinthians 15:51-53 and 1Thessalonians 4:14-15, we read words of assurance about believers who die. These words are often quoted at their funeral services. In the following quotations, we have italicised words that confirm Paul received what he wrote by direct revelation.

> 1Corinthians 15:51-53. NLT:
>
> '... *let me reveal to you a wonderful secret.* We will not all die, but we will all be transformed! It will happen in a moment, in the blink of an eye, when the last trumpet is blown. For when the trumpet sounds, those who have died will be raised to live forever. And we who are living will also be transformed. For our dying bodies must be transformed into bodies that will never die; our mortal bodies must be transformed into immortal bodies.' 1Corinthians 15:51-53. NLT.
>
> 1Thessalonians 4:14-15. NLT:
>
> '... since we believe that Jesus died and was raised to life again, we also believe that when Jesus returns, God will bring back with Him the believers who have died. *We tell you this directly from the Lord:* We who are still living when the Lord returns will not meet Him ahead of those who have died.' 1Thessalonians 4:14-15. NLT.

Galatians

In the first two chapters of Galatians, Paul recorded what he did after he became a believer and when and why he was chosen to receive direct revelations from God. We recommend that readers study these chapters in the near future because in addition to reading when and why Paul was chosen to receive direct revelations from God, we read what can happen when believers decide to amend or change The Gospel.

Ephesians 3:20-21 Part 2

> Ephesians 3:20-21. NIV. 'Now to him who is able to do immeasurably more than all we ask or imagine, according to his power that is at work within us, to him be glory in the church and in Christ Jesus throughout all generations, for ever and ever! Amen.

Wuest Expanded Translation is excellent for ascertaining the exact English meaning of the original language but, like The Amplified Bible, it is not as easy to read as a translation that intends to make the original language understandable in English.

Hence in Wuest we read in Ephesians 3:21 that Paul desired that The Church should glorify God:

'into all the generations of the age of the ages. Amen.'

We consider that, with the exception of Peter, all believers have always been entitled to look forward to Jesus' return in their lifetimes. Our knowledge of what is happening in the world, that was not available to prior generations, might explain the notions that some believers in previous generations have written. The contents of their books have proved to be erroneous. We have always considered it foolish to regard this or that world event as indisputable proof that Jesus' return is imminent.

During the author's lifetime, sermons have been preached that have predicted Jesus' imminent return. Events that have occurred during the twentieth century have encouraged some believers to engage in the foolish practice of searching The Bible for verses to back up their ill-conceived notions. As was to be expected, when these notions proved to be no better than fairy-tales, some believers' work for God grounded to a permanent halt.

So, we answer the two questions we asked when we first considered the words, 'Throughout All Generations, For Ever and Ever!' If Paul was aware of 'God's timetable' when he wrote to the Ephesian believers, he did not disclose it. And as we have cautioned previously, be wary of those who say that they know God's timetable.

So that you are not misled by silly teaching about the timing of future events, we end Ephesians 3 with the two verses already quoted from Acts 1:6-7.

> Acts 1:6-7. NLT. 'So when the apostles were with Jesus, they kept asking Him, "Lord, has the time come for You to free Israel and restore our kingdom?" He replied, "The Father alone has the authority to set those dates and times, and they are not for you to know."'

EPHESIANS 4. NIV.

As a prisoner for the Lord, then, I urge you to live a life worthy of the calling you have received. Be completely humble and gentle; be patient, bearing with one another in love. Make every effort to keep the unity of the Spirit through the bond of peace. There is one body and one Spirit, just as you were called to one hope when you were called; one Lord, one faith, one baptism; one God and Father of all, who is over all and through all and in all. But to each one of us grace has been given as Christ apportioned it. This is why it says: "When he ascended on high, he took many captives and gave gifts to his people." (What does "he ascended" mean except that he also descended to the lower, earthly regions? He who descended is the very one who ascended higher than all the heavens, in order to fill the whole universe.) So Christ himself gave the apostles, the prophets, the evangelists, the pastors and teachers, to equip his people for works of service, so that the body of Christ may be built up until we all reach unity in the faith and in the knowledge of the Son of God and become mature, attaining to the whole measure of the fullness of Christ. Then we will no longer be infants, tossed back and forth by the waves, and blown here and there by every wind of teaching and by the cunning and craftiness of people in their deceitful scheming. Instead, speaking the truth in love, we will grow to become in every respect the mature body of him who is the head, that is, Christ. From him the whole body, joined and held together by every supporting ligament, grows and builds itself up in love, as each part does its work. So I tell you this, and insist on it in the Lord, that you must no longer live as the Gentiles do, in the futility of their thinking. They are darkened in their understanding and separated from the life of God because of the ignorance that is in them due to the hardening of their hearts. Having lost all sensitivity, they have given themselves over to sensuality so as to indulge in every kind of impurity, and they are full of greed. That, however, is not the way of life you learned when you heard about Christ and were taught in him in accordance with the truth that is in Jesus. You were taught, with regard to your former way of life, to put off your old self, which is being corrupted by its deceitful desires; to be made new in the attitude of your minds; and to put on the new self, created to be like God in true righteousness and holiness. Therefore each of you must put off falsehood and speak truthfully to your neighbor, for we are all members of one body. "In your anger do not sin": Do not let the sun go down while you are still angry, and do not give the devil a foothold. Anyone who has been stealing must steal no longer, but must work, doing something useful with their own hands, that they may have something to share with those in need. Do not let any unwholesome talk come out of your mouths, but only what is helpful for building others up according to their needs, that it may benefit those who listen. And do not grieve the Holy Spirit of God, with whom you were sealed for the day of redemption. Get rid of all bitterness, rage and anger, brawling and slander, along with every form of malice. Be kind and compassionate to one another, forgiving each other, just as in Christ God forgave you.

EPHESIANS 4: COMMENTARY

Ephesians 4:1-3

> Ephesians 4:1-3. NIV. As a prisoner for the Lord, then, I urge you to live a life worthy of the calling you have received. Be completely humble and gentle; be patient, bearing with one another in love. Make every effort to keep the unity of the Spirit through the bond of peace.

'The Calling You Have Received.' Part 1.

Some who preach from Ephesians 4:1 misunderstand the meaning of the words, 'the calling.' The AV translates these words, 'the vocation.' Some who only read and preach from the AV think that Paul wrote about professions. Hence, we have heard this verse preached at meetings of Christian lawyers.

Each Ephesian believer knew that the words applied to them personally whether they were employed or unemployed, educated or uneducated.

There is no indication in Ephesians that the believers were not behaving as believers should behave, but Paul was aware of the spiritual and moral problems that had affected other local churches. It appears that he was warning the Ephesian believers to be on their guard.

The New Testament teaches that believers need to be taught, as well as reminded, of their personal obligations to God. Paul summed them up in Ephesians 1:4:

> Ephesians 1:4. NIV. 'For he chose us in him before the creation of the world to be holy and blameless in his sight.' Ephesians 1:4. NIV.

Paul's Appeal

Paul had a special relationship with the Ephesian believers. They were Gentiles and he was in prison for preaching The Gospel to the Gentiles. He used this reason to appeal to them to live lives that would please God. An appeal from an old and trusted friend might not always be heeded. So Paul reminded the believers of their personal obligations to God who had chosen them to be His family.

'The Calling You Have Received.' Part 2.

What is 'the calling?' In Ephesians 1:18 we read,

> 'I pray that the eyes of your heart may be enlightened in order that you may know the hope to which he has called you …' Ephesians 1:18. NIV.

The believers knew that they had been individually called by God. Are believers left to their own devices to work out how they should behave? We suggest that you memorise Ephesians 4:2-3. We quote the GNB.

> Ephesians 4:2-3. GNB. 'Be always humble, gentle, and patient. Show your love by being tolerant with one another. Do your best to preserve the unity which the Spirit gives by means of the peace that binds you together. Ephesians 4:2-3. GNB.

Unity and Peace

We might instinctively think that all believers would desire unity and peace in the church. The New Testament and experience teach that this is not so. To reinforce what we have written, note that even in a letter where there is no suggestion there are problems in the Ephesian church, Paul mentioned three matters:

1. Why unity must be maintained.
2. How unity can be maintained.
3. How believers should behave towards each other.

Maintain Unity: The Unity of the Spirit

Believers are not required to make unity. They are required to maintain unity.

Question: Do the words 'do your best' provide believers with excuses for ignoring the problems that cannot be resolved by humility, gentleness, patience and love?

Answer: "No." We emphatically state this because of the context of these words. 'Do your best to preserve the unity which the Spirit gives ...' 'Do your best,' is not an excuse, it is an obligation. When it is not possible for believers to maintain the unity of the Spirit, they are required to act.

Holiness and Spiritual Judgements

The unity of the Spirit is based on holiness and spiritual judgements. Some think that believers should make allowances for other believers' sins and weaknesses but this ignores the truth that it is The Spirit who provides the unity that believers must preserve. It is based on holiness, not tolerance. Spiritual judgements do not ignore sin.

The Local Church – The World's Organisations

Believers who do not differentiate between the local church and a members' sports or social club expect the local church to be managed by ballots and the like.

Believers who live a life worthy of their calling and who are 'humble, gentle and patient' would be considered weak, if not 'spineless,' by members of organisations governed by a rulebook, officers and committees.

Holiness and Blamelessness in God's Sight

Holiness and blamelessness in God's sight are not part of the rules that govern clubs and similar organisations but they must be the spiritual objectives of believers. They must not be ignored when believers make every effort to 'maintain the unity of the Spirit.'

'The Bond of Peace'

The word 'bond' in Ephesians 4:3 means 'a binding bond.' Paul did not offer options. You will look in vain for 'unity at any price,' or 'peace at any price.' Believers 'live a life worthy of their calling' or they do not. They 'make every effort' or they do not. Believers maintain unity and peace or they do not. There are no third options.

The recipe for unity and peace among believers was written 2000 years ago. It is in Ephesians 4:1-3. Then, as now, the world was not united. Sin marred God's perfect creation. It brought disorder and conflict. Disunity in the world will not last for ever. Ephesians 1:10 tells us that everything one day will be united in Jesus. Ephesians 4:1-3 tells us that there should be unity among believers now.

Ephesians 4:4-6

Paul has just stated that divine unity already exists among believers. In these three verses, he stated that believers are an integral part of a divine unity. Although these words might be familiar to you, we ask that you consider them as though you were reading them for the first time.

> Ephesians 4:4-6. NIV. 'There is one body and one Spirit, just as you were called to one hope when you were called; one Lord, one faith, one baptism; one God and Father of all, who is over all and through all and in all.' Ephesians 4:4-6. NIV.

One Body

We know how human bodies work. So we are not surprised that the human body is used to illustrate divine truth some one hundred and thirty-eight times in The New Testament. Paul used the human body as an illustration on seventy-two occasions.

'The Church, Which Is His Body'

Twelve times in Ephesians we read the word 'body.' The first time was Ephesians 1:23. Paul stressed the relationship of Jesus and His Church. We quote again three important verses:

> Ephesians 1:21-23. NLT. 'Now He is far above any ruler or authority or power or leader or anything else—not only in this world but also in the world to come. God has put all things under the authority of Christ and has made Him head over all things for the benefit of the church. And the church is His body; it is made full and complete by Christ, who fills all things everywhere with Himself.' Ephesians 1:21-23. NLT.

One Spirit

There is only one Holy Spirit. Immediately unbelievers repent of their sins and accept Jesus as Saviour, they are indwelt by The Holy Spirit. 1Corinthians 12 contains truths like those we read in Ephesians 4. We cannot compare the two chapters now but we must draw your attention to 1Corinthians 12:13.

> 1Corinthians 12:13. NLT. 'Some of us are Jews, some are Gentiles, some are slaves, and some are free. But we have all been baptized into one body by one Spirit, and we all share the same Spirit.'
> Ephesians 4:4-5. NIV. 'There is one body and one

> Spirit, just as you were called to one hope when you were called; one Lord, one faith, one baptism

Spend a few moments considering Paul's words in 1Corinthians 12 and Ephesians 4:4-5. 1Corinthians 12, states how believers become part of the body, The Church. They are baptised into it by The Holy Spirit. Paul adds 'and we all share the same Spirit.' He could add those words because immediately unbelievers become believers, The Holy Spirit indwells them.

Not all believers agree with the doctrine you have just read. Some believe in a doctrine which is called 'The Baptism of The Holy Spirit' or 'The Second Blessing.' This doctrine states that believers are baptised into The Holy Spirit after they become believers.

Those who teach this doctrine consider that at any one time there are believers who are indwelt by The Holy Spirit and believers who are not. You will search Paul's letters in vain for evidence to support the view that there are believers who are not indwelt by The Holy Spirit and therefore not in The Church because they have not yet been baptized into it by The Holy Spirit. In 1Corinthians 12:13 Paul stated two unequivocal truths. We:

1. 'have all been baptized into one body by one Spirit.'

2. 'all share the same Spirit.'

One Hope

Consider the CEV translation of Ephesians 4:4.

> All of you are part of the same body. There is only one Spirit of God, just as you were given one hope when you were chosen to be God's people.' Ephesians 4:4.

We have already explained that the word 'hope' in The New Testament refers to an expectation that is certain and anticipated with pleasure. All believers' futures could not be better. God's eternal plan for The Church and believers separates them from everything human. One day, all that is not already divinely united, will be united in Jesus, and believers will receive and enjoy their eternal inheritance.

Readers might find it confusing that Paul used two different illustrations to teach divine truth. We have read about:

1. God and His family.
2. The Church and God's people.

We know that all believers have:

- been chosen by God to be His children.
- been indwelt by the same Holy Spirit.
- the same expectation of a wonderful eternal future.

We can state with certainty that whatever your present circumstances are, if you are a believer, you will receive all that God has promised you.

God expects us to live a life worthy of our calling. Paul has emphasised that we have an obligation to maintain the 'unity of the spirit' when dealing with believers. However, most of a believer's time will be spent with those who have not been chosen, who have no hope, and no expectation of a wonderful eternal future.

When believers hanker after what they once enjoyed doing before they were saved, they must ask themselves whether what they want, or want to do, is consistent with:

- being one of God's family.
- being indwelt by The Holy Spirit.
- their expectation of a wonderful eternal future.

When we considered Ephesians 4.4 we stated that Paul used two different illustrations to teach divine truth. But, you can see that they produce a threefold test as to how believers must behave.

'One Lord'

Experience teaches that some believers have the view that the local church belongs to its members. They declare that 'Jesus Christ is Lord,' but they control their local church. Their conduct negates their declaration. Bizarrely, some think that Jesus is Lord of their personal life but not their church life. Someone once said,

"If Jesus is not Lord of all, He is not Lord at all."

It is not a scriptural quotation but it must be true. There is no evidence in The Bible that Jesus has delegated His Lordship to individual believers or groups of believers.

'One Faith'

Many translators use the words 'one faith.' At least two use the words 'one belief' or 'one trust.' All three are unequivocal. Believers know that the bond that unites them is their faith in Jesus, their Saviour.

Unbelievers think that they can get to Heaven their own way, but believers know that there is only 'one faith.' Their experience of God's Salvation enables them to agree with Paul's words in Ephesians 2:8-9. We quote from the GNB.

> For it is by God's grace that you have been saved through faith. It is not the result of your own efforts, but God's gift, so that no one can boast about it.

Where the word 'faith' is used in the New Testament, some translators have tried to give extra emphasis by referring to 'the faith' or 'the Christian faith,' for instance. 2 Corinthians 13:5 is a good example.

> NIV. '.... whether you are in the faith ...'
> GW. '.... whether you are still in the Christian faith ...'
> GNB. '.... whether you are living in faith ...'
> Wuest. '.... whether you are in the Faith ...'

However, all the translators agree that 'faith,' 'belief' and 'trust' correctly translate Paul's words in Ephesians 4:5.

> 'one Lord, one faith, one baptism'   Ephesians 4:5. NIV.

Paul referred to the faith that:

- individual believers possess.
- all those who believe in Jesus possess.

There is only 'one faith.' It unites believers to each other because it unites all believers to Jesus.

A WORD TO THOSE NOT YET BELIEVERS

Study the context of the words 'one faith' in Ephesians 4:

- Ephesians 4:1. ERV. 'I beg you to live the way God's people should live, because he chose you to be his.'
- Ephesians 4:3. ERV: 'You are joined together with peace through the Spirit.'
- Ephesians 4:4. ERV: 'There is one body and one Spirit.'
- Ephesians 4:4. ERV: 'God chose you to have one hope.'
- Ephesians 4:5. ERV: 'There is one Lord, one faith, etc.'

We refer to the first five matters that Paul emphasised. He mentioned that there is only 'one body,' 'one Spirit,' 'one hope,' 'one Lord' and one faith.

Today, as in Paul's day, there are many diverse 'religions'

in the world but Paul stressed that there is only 'one Lord.' The Lord Jesus Christ wants to be your Saviour. His Name 'Jesus' means Saviour. Unless you repent and ask Jesus to save you, you:

- are not part of the body of Christ, The Church.
- do not possess The Holy Spirit.
- do not possess the hope that believers eagerly await.

Jesus is neither your Saviour nor your Lord. You might be a member of this or that religion but you are not one of 'God's people.' The truth is that you have not repented and asked Jesus to save you from your sin. If you had, you would possess God's Salvation. You would know that:

- only repentance and faith in Jesus saves from sin.
- those who accept Jesus as their Saviour cannot live the way they once lived or please themselves how they live.

There is only one faith. Before reading on, consider if your faith is in Jesus. If not, why not repent of your sin and accept Jesus as your Saviour now?

One Baptism

The Ephesian believers knew there were two baptisms:

1. They had all been baptised into The Church by The Holy Spirit when they were saved.
2. They had also been publicly immersed in water, openly declaring that their old way of life was dead and buried, and they now lived a new spiritual life.

Paul wrote, 'one baptism,' but did he refer to:

- the baptism of The Holy Spirit?
- water baptism?

Paul spent three years preaching and teaching at Ephesus. The believers would know which baptism he referred to in his letter to ensure that unity was maintained. We consider that Paul referred to the fact that all the Ephesian believers had been baptised into The Church by The Holy Spirit. Note:

- Ephesians 4:3. The believers are being urged to keep the unity of The Holy Spirit.
- Ephesians 4:4. 'the body' and 'the Spirit' are linked.

It is part of God's plan that believers are baptised by The Holy Spirit into The Church. This is a divine transaction. Immediately unbelievers become believers they are united by The Holy Spirit to all believers.

Ephesians 4:6 - 'One God and Father of All'

> 'one God and Father of all, who is over all and through all and in all.' Ephesians 4:6. NIV.

No one will be surprised that Paul referred to one God. God is clearly the God of creation. Those who have read this book from the beginning might be surprised to read Paul's words in Ephesians 4.6, as we have stressed that God is only 'The Father of His children' and not 'The Father of mankind.'

The 'golden rule' of Bible study is that words must be read in their context. The beginning of Ephesians indicates that Paul wrote only to believers. All had been born again. Hence, God was their Father and they were His children.

Experience teaches that many think God is everyone's Father. Many will read the word 'all' and assume that it includes them. Paul wrote more of The New Testament than any other writer and he never indicated that God was 'The Father of mankind.' He wrote the opposite in Galatians 3:26. Read his words to the Galatian believers.

> Galatians 3:26. NIV. '... in Christ Jesus you are all children of God through faith ...'

Note the words 'in Christ Jesus,' 'you are all,' and 'through faith.' These words only apply to believers. We also quote 2Corinthians 6:14-18 from the ERV.

> 2Corinthians 6:14-18. ERV. You are not the same as those who don't believe. So don't join yourselves to them. Good and evil don't belong together. Light and darkness cannot share the same room. How can there be any unity between Christ and the devil? What does a believer have in common with an unbeliever? God's temple cannot have anything to do with idols, and we are the temple of the living God. As God said, "I will live with them and walk with them; I will be their God, and they will be my people." "So come away from those people and separate yourselves from them, says the Lord. Don't touch anything that is not clean, and I will accept you." "I will be your father, and you will be my sons and daughters, says the Lord All-Powerful."

'God's people' once received teaching about not being involved with unbelievers and God's view of them. They were taught that without exceptions, God categorised unbelievers as 'those who don't believe,' 'evil,' 'darkness' and 'not clean.' God does not exaggerate. Titus 1:2 states that God does not lie. Believers can choose whether to:

- agree with God's view and obey Him.
- agree with God's view and disobey Him.
- disagree with God's view and disobey Him.

In Old Testament days, God made the promise to His earthly people that we read in 2Corinthians 6:16-18:

"'So come away from those people and separate

yourselves from them, says the Lord. Don't touch anything that is not clean, and I will accept you." "I will be your father, and you will be my sons and daughters, says the Lord All-Powerful."' 2Corinthians 6:16-18. ERV.

God's promise follows Paul's words in 2Corinthians 6:14-16. Paul also referred to 'the devil.' The significance of this is obvious. Paul stated in unequivocal words that there was a contrast between believers and unbelievers that required believers to be separate from unbelievers and he supported his instructions by reference to God's command and promise that He made to His earthly people. Those who were unaware of these verses may be surprised at:

- The contrast made between believer and unbeliever
- Paul's candidness in emphasising that contrast.

Put another way, neither believer nor unbeliever could read these five verses without realising:

- Why God was not the Father of all mankind.
- What God's view of unbelievers really is.

Ephesians 4:7-10

> Ephesians 4:7-10. NIV. 'But to each one of us grace has been given as Christ apportioned it. This is why it says: "When he ascended on high, he took many captives and gave gifts to his people." (What does "he ascended" mean except that he also descended to the lower, earthly regions? He who descended is the very one who ascended higher than all the heavens, in order to fill the whole universe.)' Ephesians 4:7-10. NIV.

The translators had difficulty translating these verses into understandable English. We quote three examples of Ephesians 4:7 from popular translations:

> GNB. 'Each one of us has received a special gift in proportion to what Christ has given.'
>
> GW. 'God's favor has been given to each of us. It was measured out to us by Christ who gave it.'
>
> NLT. 'He has given each one of us a special gift through the generosity of Christ.' Ephesians 4:7.

Each believer had received from Christ their own 'special gift.' The translators use words such as 'apportioned,' 'in proportion,' 'measured out' and 'given,' words associated with God's grace. We quote Ephesians 4:7-8 again before we comment further.

> 'But to each one of us grace has been given as Christ apportioned it. This is why it says: "'When he ascended on high, he took many captives and gave gifts to his people.'" Ephesians 4:7-8. NIV.

It seems that Paul wanted the believers to know that each and every believer received a 'special gift.'

- Believers received different individual 'special gifts.'
- The gifts were different but not indiscriminately given.

These gifts are additional to the divine blessings that all unbelievers receive when they become believers.

'This is Why it Says ...' Ephesians 4:8.

The 'it' in Ephesians 4:8, is The Old Testament. The quotation is from Psalm 68 that David the Psalmist wrote. This Psalm is well worth reading, but remember that David was one of God's earthly people, the Jews. Read David's words about the divine punishment of the Jew's enemies and those who sin and consider whether those who only preach about God's love mislead their hearers.

God detests sin. He is a loving God, but He is also righteous and must punish unrepentant sinners. In Psalm 68 we read totally contrasting words about God such as:

- Psalm 68:2, 'may the wicked perish before God.'
- Psalm 68:20, 'Our God is a God who saves ....'

In Ephesians 4:8, Paul quotes from Psalm 68:18.

> Psalm 68:18. 'When you ascended on high, you took many captives; you received gifts from people, even from the rebellious ...' Psalm 68:18. NIV.

We know why David used this analogy. Victorious armies plundered their enemies' possessions. These were given to those who assisted their commander to be successful.

The New Testament teaches us truths about Jesus' victories over His enemies.

Jesus has Defeated His Enemies

Jesus' birth, death, resurrection and ascension, when He sat down at His rightful place in Heaven, proved that He had defeated all His enemies. He will one day destroy them. We have limited space to comment further. We quote just three example of verses that you find on this very important matter in The New Testament.

> Hebrews 2:14. 'Since the children have flesh and blood, he too shared in their humanity so that by his death he might break the power of him who holds the power of death--that is, the devil ...'
>
> 1John 3:8. 'The one who does what is sinful is of the devil, because the devil has been sinning from the beginning. The reason the Son of God appeared was to destroy the devil's work.'

> Revelation 20:10. 'And the devil, who deceived them, was thrown into the lake of burning sulfur …. will be tormented day and night for ever and ever.'

Psalm 68:18. David was a Prophet

David was both a psalmist and a prophet. Prophets were not fully aware of God's plans but the analogy in Psalm 68:18 informed the Ephesian believers what victors did with the spoils of warfare in David's day.

Paul wrote that the victorious Christ was distributing gifts to His people on Earth from His elevated position at God's right hand. Read again Ephesians 4:7-13.

> 'But to each one of us grace has been given as Christ apportioned it. This is why it says: "When he ascended on high, he took many captives and gave gifts to his people." (What does "he ascended" mean except that he also descended to the lower, earthly regions? He who descended is the very one who ascended higher than all the heavens, in order to fill the whole universe.) So Christ himself gave the apostles, the prophets, the evangelists, the pastors and teachers, to equip his people for works of service, so that the body of Christ may be built up until we all reach unity in the faith and in the knowledge of the Son of God and become mature, attaining to the whole measure of the fullness of Christ.   Ephesians 4:7-13. NIV.

Paul added to David's analogy. Paul wanted the Ephesian believers to know that one who ascends must have been lower. This aptly referred to Jesus. He came from Heaven to this world. He completed the work that His Father gave Him to do. We now have the opportunity of being saved for eternity. After His death and resurrection, Jesus ascended to Heaven. It is important to note two matters:

1. Jesus is not only above all, He fills the whole universe.

2. Jesus has given gifts to every one of His people.

Jesus' Reason for Giving These Gifts

This is clearly stated. It is 'to equip his people for works of service, so that the body of Christ may be built up ...'

As some vital matters could be overlooked, we need to consider these gifts, and appreciate why they are given.

- Paul wrote, 'Christ himself gave ...' It is Jesus who decides what gifts He gives, and not believers.
- Note the emphasis in the two words 'Christ' and 'Himself.' The One giving is 'The Head of The Church.'
- Believers cannot ask for a gift, exchange their gift, or be trained to do what they have not been gifted to do.

If you accept that Jesus Christ is Lord, you must:

- only do what you are gifted to do.
- not do what you are not gifted to do.

The gifts are 'to equip his people for works of service.' 'Equip' is the word that most translators use, but some prefer 'prepare' or 'train.' Experience teaches the value of believers who use their divine gifts to better enable God's people to do God's work.

'Works of service'

Experience also teaches that not all believers are willing to work and to serve. The word 'works' means 'to toil' and 'to labour.' The word 'service' refers to a servant's work. You will look in vain in these verses for the gift of 'boss.' Neither will you find the gift of delegation.

'The body of Christ may be built up'

Not only when Paul wrote these words, but ever since

there has been a need for The Church to be 'built up.' Various similar words and expressions are used by the translators. The CEV so simply states:

> 'his people would learn to serve and his body would grow strong.' Ephesians 4:12. CEV.

Believers must use the gift they have been given to ensure that The Church continues to grow strong, but do you:

- expect God to ensure that The Church grows strong?
- pray that God will make The Church grow strong?

The verses in Ephesians 4:7-13 teach us that:

- the gifts that ensure The Church will grow strong have already been given by the victorious ascended Christ.
- problems will exist when believers fail to do 'works of service so that the body of Christ may be built up.'
- The Church will only be strong when believers serve using the gifts they have been given.

The truths might not be taught today. Those believers who think they know more than Paul knew about The Church should read his candid words. We quote from the CEV.

- Ephesians 4:14. 'stop acting like children.'
- Ephesians 4:17. 'stop living like stupid, godless people.'

Ephesians 4:11.

This verse has not been without its controversy.

> 'Christ himself gave the apostles, the prophets, the evangelists, the pastors and teachers ...'

It seems to be agreed that Christ is still giving The Church evangelists, pastors and teachers, but there seems to be three different views of the gifts Christ has given:

1. Christ still gives apostles and prophets.
2. There are five gifts because pastors and teachers are not one and the same gift.
3. A believer can only have one gift so that, for example, an evangelist cannot be a pastor or a teacher.

Paul encouraged the believers 'to keep the unity of the Spirit through the bond of peace.' But local churches, that should reflect what is true of The Church, are divided into groups that have dissimilar beliefs. It is worth being reminded of Ephesians 4:3.

> 'Make every effort to keep the unity of the Spirit through the bond of peace. ' Ephesians 4:3. NIV.

Apostles and Prophets

In Ephesians 2:20, Paul likened The Church to a building. He wrote that it was:

> '... built on the foundation of the apostles and prophets, with Christ Jesus himself as the chief cornerstone.'

The apostles and prophets were 'foundation gifts' to The Church. We read in Acts 1:21-22 that apostles needed an essential qualification that Peter stated unambiguously:

> Acts 1:21-22. NIV. "it is necessary to choose one of the men who have been with us the whole time the Lord Jesus was living among us, beginning from John's baptism to the time when Jesus was taken up from us. For one of these must become a witness with us of his resurrection."

Ephesians 2:20 refers to both the apostles and the

prophets as, 'the foundation,' and Acts 1:21-22 states that apostles must have seen Jesus after He rose again. So, we consider that there are no apostles or prophets today.

Evangelists

Some think that believers can be taught to be evangelists and that they have human skills that assist them to preach. We cannot in this book detail their work but we must emphasise that Christ gave evangelists to The Church. They are neither self-appointed nor appointed by men. Do not make the mistake of thinking that only evangelists can preach The Gospel. If you doubt this, read Acts. Note when Luke mentioned that believers preached The Gospel wherever they went to those they met. If you do decide to read Acts, as we suggest that you should, note also:

- How often believers took the opportunity of preaching The Gospel without thought of their own safety.
- What believers said to unbelievers about Jesus that resulted in the unbelievers being saved.

Paul wrote two letters to Timothy. 2Timothy 4:5 has been variously translated. We quote the NIV and the GNB. Read what believers, not just evangelists, should do:

> NIV: 'keep your head in all situations, endure hardship, do the work of an evangelist, discharge all the duties of your ministry.' 2Timothy 4:5. NIV.
>
> GNB: 'you must keep control of yourself in all circumstances; endure suffering, do the work of a preacher of the Good News, and perform your whole duty as a servant of God.' 2Timothy 4:5. GNB.

Pastors and Teachers

Some translators prefer 'shepherd' to 'pastor.' 'Shepherd' explains the spiritual function of the gift. Sheep cannot survive on their own. They need shepherds to care for them. Believers need spiritual shepherds to guide them, protect them from danger, and ensure they always have food to eat.

Hence, we disagree with those who consider that pastors and teachers are two separate gifts. Believers need a shepherd who can teach God's Word to guide and care for them. Spiritual shepherds:

- will know the dangers that confront the sheep and what is best for them.
- will have the ability to feed the sheep with God's Word. The risen victorious Christ would not entrust His 'sheep' to shepherds who could not feed them.

Some translations of Ephesians 4:11 state that pastors and teachers are one and the same. For example:

> Ephesians 4:11. ERV: 'and some to care for and teach God's people.'
>
> Ephesians 4:11. Wuest: 'some as pastors who are also teachers.'

Ephesians 4:12-14.

> Ephesians 4:11-14. NIV. 'So Christ himself gave the apostles, the prophets, the evangelists, the pastors and teachers, to equip his people for works of service, so that the body of Christ may be built up until we all reach unity in the faith and in the knowledge of the Son of God and become mature, attaining to the whole measure of the fullness of Christ. Then we will no longer be infants, tossed back and forth by the waves, and blown here and there by every wind of teaching and by the cunning and craftiness of people in their deceitful scheming.

'So that The Body of Christ may be Built Up'
Part 1:
Infants

Paul stated so simply and candidly the reason why Christ gave gifts to believers, and why they need equipping for acts of service. We ask two questions:

1: What happens if believers do not use their gifts?

Answer: They will all remain spiritual infants.

2: Could all believers reach spiritual maturity?

Answer: "Yes." Ephesians 4:13 states, 'until we all reach unity in the faith and in the knowledge of the Son of God and become mature, attaining to the whole measure of the fullness of Christ.'

You might have a low opinion of your spiritual ability or consider yourself ungifted. You might even be lazy and let other believers build up the Body of Christ. Experience teaches that few believers use their gifts. Those who do not need to be taught that there are no ungifted believers and all Christ's people are included in these words:

> 'to equip his people for works of service, so that the body of Christ may be built up.'   Ephesians 4:12. NIV.

It is vital that believers ascertain the gift that the ascended Christ has given to them. Every gift is needed for the works of service that build up the body of Christ.

'Then we will no longer be infants'

All believers begin their spiritual life as infants because they are born again of The Holy Spirit. Christ has given gifts so that His people can mature. Paul stated what 'maturity' is. We do not need to guess. We ask two questions as we consider first what spiritual maturity is not:

1: Have believers reached spiritual maturity when they know every verse in The Bible?

Answer: "No."

2: Have believers reached spiritual maturity when they can win every argument about Christianity?

Answer: "No."

'So that The Body of Christ may be Built Up'
Part 2:

Maturity

Keep in mind that Paul wanted the Ephesian believers to know that they were obliged 'to keep the unity of the Spirit through the bond of peace.'

Maturity follows Unity

We read Paul's teaching about unity prior to his teaching about maturity. We have little doubt that some believers think that they are spiritually mature, but this is based on one or more of three incorrect opinions:

1: Their own opinion.

2: Their family's opinion.

3: Their church's opinion.

Only God's Word, The Bible, is the guide of spiritual maturity. It is the only guide that counts with God. How many using God's Word might discover how spiritually immature they really are? So, before studying the dangers and the consequences of staying spiritual infants, we summarise the truths in Ephesians 4:1-12, and make the verses personal to you:

1. You have been invited by God to be one of His people.

Live as His people should live. Be humble, gentle and patient. Accept others with love.

2. You and all believers are united and joined together with peace through The Holy Spirit. Do all you can to continue letting unity and peace hold you together.
3. The ascended Christ gave you a gift. He chose that particular gift for you.
4. Christ's gift was not given to you for your own benefit. He gave it to you to prepare you for works of service that will make His Church, His body, stronger.
5. You have the option of using or not using your gift.

It is so important you appreciate that:

- Christ's gifts were given for the benefit of The Church.
- believers who do not use their gifts do not make The Church stronger.

'The Christian life is like a bed of roses' teaching is not true. Hebrews 11:35-40 should be read by those who disagree. God expects every believer to use their gift and that involves 'work.' Paul referred to 'works of service.'

We unhesitatingly say to believers that if your view of the Christian life is that it is acceptable for you to 'take it easy' and not use the gift that Christ gave you, your view is contrary to God's Word.

Many years ago, believers were taught that they had been 'saved to serve.' Although it is not scriptural, we can appreciate why preachers used this expression. It is most unlikely that after listening to such teaching, the majority of believers only attended church services and did nothing else. That seems to be what happens today.

A believer's obligation to God includes so much more than 'service,' but must include it.

Ephesians 4:13-16.

To study these verses in context we begin at verse 12:

> Ephesians 4:12-16. 'Christ gave these gifts to prepare God's holy people for the work of serving, to make the body of Christ stronger. This work must continue until we are all joined together in what we believe and in what we know about the Son of God. Our goal is to become like a full-grown man--to look just like Christ and have all his perfection. Then we will no longer be like babies. We will not be people who are always changing like a ship that the waves carry one way and then another. We will not be influenced by every new teaching we hear from people who are trying to deceive us--those who make clever plans and use every kind of trick to fool others into following the wrong way. No, we will speak the truth with love. We will grow to be like Christ in every way. He is the head, and the whole body depends on him. All the parts of the body are joined and held together, with each part doing its own work. This causes the whole body to grow and to be stronger in love.' Ephesians 4:12-16. ERV.

Muse on these verses before reading our commentary because they illustrate:

- how The Church is made stronger.
- the dangers that exist for immature believers.

You will hear sermons that give the impression that the local church attended by the preacher has discovered the secret of successful evangelism. As you read Ephesians, you will note that Paul did not mention evangelical activities and we think we know why. There was something far more important that he required them to do. We again quote Ephesians 4:1 and ask you to reflect upon it.

> I beg you to live the way God's people should live, because he chose you to be his. Ephesians 4:1. ERV.

The fact that Paul pleaded with the Ephesian believers to do what he required, suggests to us it is something that:

- is not usually done by believers.
- does not come naturally to believers.

The absence of any mention of spiritual activities and the wording of Ephesians 4:1 would also suggest to us that a believer's spiritual condition is more important than their gift. You might be an evangelist, but:

- are you humble, gentle, and patient? Ephesians 4:2.
- do you love other believers? Ephesians 4:2.
- do you seek peace and unity? Ephesians 4:3.

Other matters relating to how believers live need to be considered. We ask you questions:

1: Does the gift that you have been given make you proud and arrogant, even unfriendly and unapproachable?

2: If you have a 'public gift,' such as the gift of an evangelist, do you consider that you are superior to other believers, and your gift superior to their gifts?

Questions: Your Gift and The Local Church

1: If you do not use the gift given you by Christ, how does The Church become stronger?

2: If you have the gift of pastor and teacher, but your priorities in life are your worldly activities, how do those you should be caring for mature spiritually?

Ephesians 4:13. 'This work must continue …'

'This work' refers to the preparing of God's people for the

work of serving so that The Church will become stronger. 'This work must continue until ...' is how the easier-to-read translations begin Ephesians 4:13. Paul urged the Ephesian believers to continue to serve. It was the only way The Church would become stronger.

Ephesians 4:13. 'until we all attain'

This verse is variously translated. Some translators, like Wuest, have accurately translated Ephesians 4:13 from the original language. Others have made the original language more understandable in English.

> Wuest: 'until we all attain to the unity of the Faith and of the experiential, full, and precise knowledge of the Son of God, to a spiritually mature man, to the measure of the stature of the fulness of the Christ ...'
>
> CEV: 'This will continue until we are united by our faith and by our understanding of the Son of God. Then we will be mature, just as Christ is, and we will be completely like him.'
>
> GW: 'This is to continue until all of us are united in our faith and in our knowledge about God's Son, until we become mature, until we measure up to Christ, who is the standard.'   Ephesians 4:13, Wuest, CEV, and GW.

Jesus - The Standard for Unbelievers

God's required standard for mankind is sinlessness. Believers correctly preach the pointlessness of anyone comparing themselves with others to see if they are above or below human standards.

Only Jesus was sinless. Jesus is God's standard for unbelievers. So, believers preach that unless unbelievers repent and accept Jesus as their Saviour, God will punish them for their sin.

Jesus - The Standard for Believers

Ephesians 4:13 states that Jesus is the standard for believers. If they want to know if they are mature, they must not compare themselves with other believers. Jesus is the only standard. Paul did not pretend that he had reached the required standard. He was seeking to attain it. We do not have the space to refer to the admissions that Paul made in his letters about the constant battle he had between right and wrong.

Ephesians 4:13 – Becoming Mature

We do not know your view of how The Church has progressed in the last 2000 years, or how it is progressing today. At the time you read this book you might be seeing a time of God's blessing. On the other hand, you might be 'ploughing a lone furrow,' in a godless area waiting for the time of blessing that you have so often prayed for.

Studying Ephesians 4:13 will teach you that God's eternal plan will succeed and Jesus will be the head of everything in Heaven and on Earth.

So that we do not mislead you, we state that if you are not yet a believer, and you remain an unbeliever, God's wonderful blessings will never be yours.

If you are a believer, you are part of God's eternal plan. Your eternal future could not be better. It is better than words can adequately express or believers can presently understand. Keep this in mind as we continue to study Ephesians 4:13.

Ephesians 4:13. NIV. 'until we all reach unity in the faith and in the knowledge of the Son of God and become mature, attaining to the whole measure of the fullness of Christ.'   Ephesians 4:13. NIV.

We underline the four aspects of spiritual maturity referred to in Ephesians 4:13 for your personal consideration:

1. 'until <u>we all</u> …'
2. 'until we all reach <u>unity in the faith</u> …'
3. 'until we all reach unity in the faith <u>and in the knowledge of the Son of God</u> …'
4. 'until we all reach unity in the faith and in the knowledge of the Son of God <u>and become mature, attaining to the whole measure of the fullness of Christ</u>.'

Ephesians 4:13 – 'We all …. become mature'

There will come a time when The Church is mature. Paul emphasised in Ephesians that believers must remain united because unity is the end result of God's eternal plan. God has not disclosed every aspect of His eternal plan, but we do know from the verses we have read that believers can say:

"we are united with Christ. Even before He made the world, God loved us, chose us in Christ to be holy and without fault in His eyes, and adopted us into His own family by bringing us to Himself through Jesus Christ. This is what He wanted to do, and it gave Him great pleasure. God has now revealed to us His mysterious plan regarding Christ, a plan to fulfill His own good pleasure. And this is God's plan: At the right time He will bring everything together under the authority of Christ—everything in heaven and on earth. Furthermore, because we are united with Christ, we have received an inheritance from God who makes everything work out according to His plan." Ephesians 1: 3-5; 9-11. NLT.

Ephesians 4:14-16.

Ephesians 4:14-16. NIV. 'Then we will no longer be

> infants, tossed back and forth by the waves, and blown here and there by every wind of teaching and by the cunning and craftiness of people in their deceitful scheming. Instead, speaking the truth in love, we will grow to become in every respect the mature body of him who is the head, that is, Christ. From him the whole body, joined and held together by every supporting ligament, grows and builds itself up in love, as each part does its work.' Ephesians 4:14-16. NIV.

We have learnt two important truths about all believers:

1. Irrespective of their actual age, they begin their new lives in Christ as spiritual infants.

2. They will one day be spiritually mature because they will have reached 'unity in the faith and in the knowledge of the Son of God.'

We are going to learn that there is no automatic progression from spiritual infancy to spiritual maturity. Believers can choose to remain spiritual infants. Consider your own spiritual progress and the choice you have made as we study Ephesians 4:14-16. We are sure that no believer would want to be in the spiritual situation so aptly described by Paul as he uses the illustration of a sailing ship during a storm.

Note 1: Even in the days of the early church there were those teaching false doctrine. Paul referred to them as 'deceitful schemers,' 'cunning and crafty.'

Note 2: Paul did not take the view that everyone was entitled to their own beliefs or to be heard.

Only a foolish believer would choose to be in a small sailing ship that was out of the shipmaster's control during a storm. But how many believers never bother to check whether what they are taught is true or false?

We understand the reason for Paul's uncomplimentary words about false teachers. He, like us, must have witnessed the problems they bring to immature believers.

Common sense tells us that it will be some time before new believers have the spiritual knowledge necessary to recognise false teachers and their teaching. But how many believers simply never mature:

- If you had been saved for one year and the 'spiritual' part of your week consisted only of the time you attended church on a Sunday, would you be offended if someone said that you were a spiritual infant?
- If, some 20 years later, they still only assessed you as a spiritual infant, would you be offended? Would you retort that you must have grown spiritually because you had spent some 1000 hours attending church?

Ephesians 4:15-16. The Wrong Answer

The Question: How do believers spiritually mature?

We judge that few would have given Paul's answer. Experience teaches that many would have referred to a believer's knowledge of The Bible. Consider carefully Paul's answer and his positive assertion 'we will grow:'

- The word 'instead' tells us that believers can choose.
- As there is no third option, believers can choose either:
  - to be spiritual infants and the easy target of those who teach error.
  - to speak the truth in love and 'grow to become in every respect the mature body of him who is the head, that is, Christ.'

'Love,' is referred to twice in Ephesians 4:15-16. There is a simplicity in Paul's teaching. If believers speak the truth in love, The Church will build itself up in love. Hence:

- Only 'the truth' will build up The Church.
- Truth without love will not build up The Church.

Paul stated how the human body is held together and grows. Truth and love need work. 'As each part does its work,' is variously translated, for instance:

BBE: 'the full working of every part.'

NLT: 'as each part does its own special work.'

Paul did not envisage the existence of lazy believers. Believers must be active. Re-read Ephesians 4:12. Paul stated what is expected of those who have received 'gifts' and the reason. Reconsider the words 'for works of service.' No believer is exempt and no believer excused.

Ephesians 4:17-32.

> Ephesians 4: 17-32. NIV. 'So I tell you this, and insist on it in the Lord, that you must no longer live as the Gentiles do, in the futility of their thinking. They are darkened in their understanding and separated from the life of God because of the ignorance that is in them due to the hardening of their hearts. Having lost all sensitivity, they have given themselves over to sensuality so as to indulge in every kind of impurity, and they are full of greed. That, however, is not the way of life you learned when you heard about Christ and were taught in him in accordance with the truth that is in Jesus. You were taught, with regard to your former way of life, to put off your old self, which is being corrupted by its deceitful desires; to be made new in the attitude of your minds; and to put on the new self, created to be like God in true righteousness and holiness. Therefore each of you must put off falsehood and speak truthfully to your neighbor, for we are all members of one body. "In your anger do not sin": Do not let the sun go down

> while you are still angry, and do not give the devil a foothold. Anyone who has been stealing must steal no longer, but must work, doing something useful with their own hands, that they may have something to share with those in need. Do not let any unwholesome talk come out of your mouths, but only what is helpful for building others up according to their needs, that it may benefit those who listen. And do not grieve the Holy Spirit of God, with whom you were sealed for the day of redemption. Get rid of all bitterness, rage and anger, brawling and slander, along with every form of malice. Be kind and compassionate to one another, forgiving each other, just as in Christ God forgave you.

Paul set out in clear and positive language:

- The difference between believers and unbelievers.
- The way believers should behave in this wicked world where the majority are unbelievers.

We explain the various terms used by Paul and note the way he described those who are not saved. We divide these verses into sections for ease of commentary and quote the NLT so that you will have an alternative translation of Paul's words:

Ephesians 4: 17-20. NLT.

> With the Lord's authority I say this: Live no longer as the Gentiles do, for they are hopelessly confused. Their minds are full of darkness; they wander far from the life God gives because they have closed their minds and hardened their hearts against Him. They have no sense of shame. They live for lustful pleasure and eagerly practice every kind of impurity. But that isn't what you learned about Christ.   Ephesians 4:17-20. NLT.

Do not be misled by those who tell you that Paul wrote his own opinions. They seem unaware that whenever Paul wrote his own opinion, he indicated in the text that it was his opinion. This 'Paul's Opinions Notion' is used by those who want to introduce their own ideas into the local church. Even if what they said was true, for a reason unknown to us, they foolishly consider that their opinions are superior to Paul's opinions. They are like those referred to in Ephesians 4:17 - 'hopelessly confused.'

It is obvious from Ephesians 4:17 that Paul wanted to leave the Ephesian believers in no doubt that what he wrote was not optional. It was 'a command.' Not only did he state his reason for writing it, he stated his authority. When you read Paul's 'command' you wonder why, having stated his authority, he also added why he wrote it. Why did he not simply write, 'With the Lord's authority I say this?' First, we must consider who 'the Gentiles' were.

'The Gentiles'

This is Paul's last reference in Ephesians to 'the Gentiles.' Those who have read Ephesians from the beginning will know that Paul was a Jew before he was saved whereas the Ephesian believers were Gentiles. There are five references to Gentiles in Ephesians. We cannot now study all of them but quote them from the NLT so that you will appreciate Paul's condemnation of their sinful behaviour in Ephesians 4:17-20.

> Ephesians 2:11-12: Don't forget that you Gentiles used to be outsiders. You were called "uncircumcised heathens" by the Jews, who were proud of their circumcision, even though it affected only their bodies and not their hearts. In those days you were living apart from Christ. You were excluded from citizenship among the people of Israel, and you did not know the covenant

promises God had made to them. You lived in this world without God and without hope.

Ephesians 3:1-2: I, Paul, a prisoner of Christ Jesus for the benefit of you Gentiles .... assuming, by the way, that you know God gave me the special responsibility of extending His grace to you Gentiles.

Ephesians 3:6-8: And this is God's plan: Both Gentiles and Jews who believe the Good News share equally in the riches inherited by God's children. Both are part of the same body, and both enjoy the promise of blessings because they belong to Christ Jesus. By God's grace and mighty power, I have been given the privilege of serving Him by spreading this Good News. Though I am the least deserving of all God's people, He graciously gave me the privilege of telling the Gentiles about the endless treasures available to them in Christ.

Ephesians 4:17-20: With the Lord's authority I say this: Live no longer as the Gentiles do, for they are hopelessly confused. Their minds are full of darkness; they wander far from the life God gives because they have closed their minds and hardened their hearts against Him. They have no sense of shame. They live for lustful pleasure and eagerly practice every kind of impurity. But that isn't what you learned about Christ.

The Gentiles were idolaters. Paul had preached The Gospel in Ephesus. He knew the reaction of the Ephesians. The majority rejected The Gospel. He knew first-hand that few were prepared to repent and accept Jesus as their Saviour. He was well aware that the majority wanted to continue being idolatrous and sinning, a lifestyle they would have to turn their backs on if they repented and believed The Gospel. Hence, what we read in Ephesians 4:17-20 is Paul's accurate first-hand account of the lifestyles and thoughts of Gentile unbelievers.

As Paul was writing about the behaviour of the idolatrous Gentiles 2000 years ago, some readers might assume that because society has progressed, what we have read in Ephesians 4:17-20 is historical.

Maybe respectability has hidden behind closed doors the immorality that Paul referred to, but it did not only apply to his own day. Sadly, some believers seem to consider that respectable sinners deserve special treatment so that only 'one-half' of The Gospel is presented to them.

We need to state clearly that Paul did not only emphasise repentance when he preached The Gospel in Ephesus because the idolatrous Gentiles had 'no sense of shame' and lived 'for lustful pleasure and eagerly practice every kind of impurity.' Re-read and consider what he said as he said farewell to the Ephesian local church elders.

> Acts 20:20-21. NLT. "'I never shrank back from telling you what you needed to hear, either publicly or in your homes. I have had one message for Jews and Greeks alike—the necessity of repenting from sin and turning to God, and of having faith in our Lord Jesus.'"

We must analyse Paul's words to understand what the man who was specifically chosen by Jesus to be personally responsible for spreading The Gospel to both Jews and Gentiles said when he preached it to the many diverse inhabitants who lived in the countries between Damascus in Syria, and Ephesus, which is in Turkey today, but was in Greece in Paul's day.

As we read Acts 20:20-21, three statements that Paul made are pertinent to our analysis:

1. 'I never shrank back.' This tells us that Paul did not find it easy to preach what unbelievers 'needed to hear.' We refer to this meaningful word 'needed' in Paragraph 3.

2. 'I have had one message for Jews and Greeks alike,' tells us that Paul preached the one and only message that unbelievers need irrespective of their differences.

3. The expression 'what you needed to hear' in Acts 20:20, and the words 'the necessity' in Acts 20:21, indicates to us that every unbeliever must be told of this 'necessity' when they are presented with The Gospel.

4. The 'necessity' has two parts:

   1) 'repenting from sin and turning to God.'

   2) 'having faith in our Lord Jesus.'

We consider that we can tell every believer that whether or not they find it difficult to do, and irrespective of who they are communicating to, they are not faithfully telling unbelievers The Gospel unless they emphasise its two essential parts, that we abridge to 'repenting from sin and having faith in Jesus.'

We know that this will require believers to stop being naïve and accept what The Bible teaches about sin, sinning and sinners. The Bible teaches that these have not changed since the first sin was committed. Consider Paul's words in Ephesians 4:18 carefully.

> Ephesians 4:18. 'Their minds are full of darkness; they wander far from the life God gives because they have closed their minds and hardened their hearts against him.' Ephesians 4:18. NLT.

If you want confirmation that Paul's words in Ephesians 4:18 are supported by one of Jesus' disciples, who would not have contradicted what Jesus taught, you must read John 3:16-21. What The Bible teaches about sin and sinners is unambiguous. The majority of the human race, and that includes every believer's unbelieving family, friends and work colleagues, prefer their sin to God's

Salvation. In Ephesians 4:17-20 we read why:

- The Gospel is rejected.
- it is so difficult to get people to listen to The Gospel.
- the greater part of the few who listen to The Gospel reject it.

Ephesians 4:20.

> 'But that isn't what you learned about Christ.' Ephesians 4:20. NLT.

Ephesians 4:20 commences with that so important word 'but.' The contrast it introduces is so important to a correct understanding of The Gospel and God's Salvation. We now quote Ephesians 4:17-20 emphasising the pronouns.

> Ephesians 4:17-20. NLT.
>
> 17. '... Live no longer as the Gentiles do, for <u>they</u> are hopelessly confused. 18 <u>Their</u> minds are full of darkness; <u>they</u> wander far from the life God gives because <u>they</u> have closed <u>their</u> minds and hardened <u>their</u> hearts against him. 19 <u>They</u> have no sense of shame. <u>They</u> live for lustful pleasure and eagerly practice every kind of impurity.'
>
> 20. But that isn't what <u>you</u> learned about Christ.

'They' and 'their' are the pronouns in Ephesians 4:17-19, but 'you' is the pronoun in Ephesians 4:20.

An Important Note to Every Reader

Without exception, Ephesians 4:17-20 states the spiritual status of everyone. So if you are not one of the 'you' referred to in Ephesians 4:20, you are one of the 'they' referred to in Ephesians 4:17-19.

Many, and you might be one of them, think that they are one of the 'you' even though in reality, they have never:

- repented of their sins.
- received Jesus as their Saviour.

If you are not yet a believer, those responsible for this book want you to be saved. So, we make being saved personal to you. So that it will have the greatest impact upon you, we quote Ephesians 4:18 and ask a question that we trust will make the verse personal to you.

> Ephesians 4:18 NLT. 'Their minds are full of darkness; they wander far from the life God gives because they have closed their minds and hardened their hearts against him.'

Question: Have you closed your mind and hardened your heart against the life God gives?

Note the two distinct acts, and the order that Paul wrote them, as you consider your answer:

- Closing your mind.
- Hardening your heart.

Our Experience

- We have been present when people have forcibly tried to prevent The Gospel from being preached.
- We have seen husbands drive their wives to church services, drive away and return to drive them home.
- We have known families where an unsaved husband will not set foot inside a church, but willingly assists their saved wife to do various tasks for the church.
- We knew one husband who read a portion of The Bible daily to his saved wife who was blind. He would not enter a church, even to attend the wedding services of

his close relatives.

We have witnessed The Gospel preached many times. We have seen a few respond to it when they first heard it. Some needed to hear it many times before responding to it. The vast majority who heard it never responded to it and did not want to hear it again. A few heard it weekly for many years. They knew exactly what The Gospel required, but never responded to it.

Closing the Mind and Hardening the Heart.

Paul referred to those who have closed their minds and hardened their hearts against the life that God gives. How does this happen? Has it happened to you? These are questions that need to be seriously considered.

Unless you are saved, your eternal destiny is Hell. You could have eternal life. It begins immediately you repent and accept Jesus as your Saviour. It never ends. When your earthly life ends, you will live with God forevermore.

Would this scenario be true of you? You heard The Gospel for the first time but, for one reason or another, you closed your mind and rejected God's invitation to repent, accept Jesus as your Saviour, and receive God's eternal life. We read in Ephesians 4:18 that you not only closed your mind to God's eternal life, you hardened your heart to it.

We know what happens when our hearts and minds differ. In the conflict that ensues within us. it is often the heart that succeeds. But, if heart and mind agree, there is no conflict and this results is a decision that is hard to change.

Experience proves that what Paul wrote is correct. Many years ago, those who heard The Gospel regularly but who did nothing about it were called 'Gospel hardened.' We have witnessed unbelievers who heard The Gospel regularly. They ignored it. They also ignored the change in the lifestyle of those who believed The Gospel. The change proved to them over many years that The Gospel was true, but they never believed it. They closed their minds and hardened their hearts to The Gospel and to the eternal life that God gives. Ephesians 4:18 is true.

Believers can tell you about a time and a place that they heard The Gospel and they:

- believed it.
- still believe it.

We can tell you that you need not stay an unbeliever. What Paul wrote in Ephesians 4:17-19 once described the Ephesian believers. They are now described in Ephesians 4:20 because they:

- repented of their sin.
- believed The Gospel.

Question: What was now expected of them?

We read the Answer in the next four verses.

> Ephesians 4:21. 'Since you have heard about Jesus and have learned the truth that comes from Him, throw off your old sinful nature and your former way of life, which is corrupted by lust and deception. Instead, let the Spirit renew your thoughts and attitudes. Put on your new nature, created to be like God—truly righteous and holy.'   Ephesians 4:21-24. NLT.

The Ephesian believers could change because they had:

- 'heard about Jesus.'
- 'learned the truth that comes from him.'

Once again we read the expression 'the truth.' It is always associated with Jesus. It is used some 54 times by Paul.

'The truth,' is clearly of vital importance. But once believers have accepted it, they have obligations and Paul does not hold back in stating what God requires but note that:

- only when believers have decided how they are going to live will The Holy Spirit do His work of renewing their thoughts and attitudes.
- believers cannot put on their new nature until they have thrown off their old sinful nature and former way of life.

If you are not yet a believer, unlike a believer, you cannot put on a new nature. You do not have one. You only have the sinful nature referred to in Ephesians 4:22 as:

'your …. way of life, which is corrupted by lust and deception.'

Unbelievers might disagree that these words represent an accurate way of describing how they live. That is probably why Paul referred to 'deception.'

Deception

The word, 'deception,' appears six times in The New Testament. Sin is misleading. Do not be deceived by it.

A New Nature

'like God—truly righteous and holy.'

If you do not want to be deceived by sin and you want a new nature, you need Jesus to save you from your sin.

Ephesians 4:25-29.

These five verses are self-explanatory.

> 'So stop telling lies. Let us tell our neighbors the truth, for we are all parts of the same body. And "don't sin by letting anger control you." Don't let the sun go down

> while you are still angry, for anger gives a foothold to the devil. If you are a thief, quit stealing. Instead, use your hands for good hard work, and then give generously to others in need. Don't use foul or abusive language. Let everything you say be good and helpful, so that your words will be an encouragement to those who hear them. Ephesians 4:25-29. NLT.

Paul did not hold back in telling believers to stop sinning. The Gospel begins with sin and repentance. In every place on Earth, anyone and everyone who will repent and believe The Gospel can be saved.

Repentance cannot be excluded from The Gospel because those who want to be saved must turn their backs on their past way of life. Put another way, unbelievers please themselves how they live whereas believers live to please a holy God. Those who are not willing to repent of their past sins, change their lifestyle and stop sinning, cannot be saved.

Ephesians 4:30-32.

> And do not bring sorrow to God's Holy Spirit by the way you live. Remember, He has identified you as His own, guaranteeing that you will be saved on the day of redemption. Get rid of all bitterness, rage, anger, harsh words, and slander, as well as all types of evil behavior. Instead, be kind to each other, tenderhearted, forgiving one another, just as God through Christ has forgiven you. Ephesians 4:30-32. NIV.

We are unable now to write in detail about 'The Trinity,' but The Bible teaches that God the Father, God the Son and God The Holy Spirit participate in the Salvation of every believer. God The Holy Spirit indwells every believer from the moment they are saved. The Holy Spirit is always referred to in The Bible as 'He' as 'He' is a divine Person. It is wrong to refer to The Holy Spirit as 'it.' The words 'And do not bring sorrow to God's Holy Spirit by the way you live' indicates His personal involvement with all believers. His holiness is clearly indicated by His Name.

Experience teaches that many believers only have vague ideas about The Holy Spirit and the work He does today. Before we consider Ephesians 4:30, we quote, without comment, each verse in Ephesians that mentions Him.

The Holy Spirit

> Ephesians 1:13. And now you Gentiles have also heard the truth, the Good News that God saves you. And when you believed in Christ, He identified you as His own by giving you The Holy Spirit, whom He promised long ago.
>
> Ephesians 2:18. Now all of us can come to the Father through the same Holy Spirit because of what Christ has done for us.
>
> Ephesians 4:30. And do not bring sorrow to God's Holy Spirit by the way you live. Remember, He has identified you as His own, guaranteeing that you will be saved on the day of redemption.

Ephesians 4:30 is a solemn caution, but it does contain a wonderful fact about every believer's eternal salvation. God The Holy Spirit indwells all believers and He can be grieved by their conduct. Sinful believers do not lose their Salvation. The above three verses contradict the teaching that believers:

- do not receive The Holy Spirit when they are saved.
- can lose their Salvation by the way they live.

Ephesians 4:30 tells us in the plainest terms that although a believer's sinful life will grieve The Holy Spirit, God has guaranteed their Salvation. The words, 'you will be saved,' could not be more simply written. Consider these words in their context because Ephesians 4:31 clearly indicates that Paul was not writing to sinless believers. Paul wrote

> Ephesians 4:31. NIV. 'Get rid of all bitterness, rage, anger, harsh words, and slander, as well as all types of evil behavior.' Ephesians 4:31. NIV.

Ephesians 4:32 provides a contrast to Ephesians 4:31.

> Ephesians 4:32. NTL. 'Instead, be kind to each other, tenderhearted, forgiving one another, just as God through Christ has forgiven you. Ephesians 4:32. NTL.

Translators have provided us with a variety of opening words that amplify the word 'instead:'

- Lexham: 'Become kind to …'
- Weymouth: 'On the contrary learn to be kind …'
- Wuest: 'And be becoming kind …'
- Young: 'and become one to another kind …'

Would we be wrong in thinking that the sins of Ephesians 4:31 come naturally and easily to us and that being kind, tenderhearted, and forgiving is really difficult especially when we have been wronged? Paul knew how difficult the change would be hence, they would have to:

- learn to be kind, tenderhearted, and forgiving.
- remember that God had forgiven them.

Muse upon 'Paul's incredible statement' that concludes Ephesians 4. It is so important that we are quoting it in three translations so that you can check the tenses. Ask yourself this question about Paul's statement. When Paul wrote it, had the Ephesians already been forgiven?

- BBE: 'having forgiveness for one another, even as God in Christ had forgiveness for you.'
- ERV: 'Forgive each other the same as God forgave you through Christ.'
- GNB: 'forgive one another, as God has forgiven you through Christ.'

The believers had already been forgiven because of what Christ had done for them. Christ's death and resurrection on their behalf was in the past, but it enabled God to forgive sins that would be committed in the future. When they accepted what Christ had already done on their behalf, God forgave them and gave them His Salvation.

The Ephesian believers were not forgiven because of what they had done. They were forgiven because of what Christ had done for them. It really is foolish to believe that Christ's death and resurrection can only result in God's temporary forgiveness. Put another way, we never at any time deserved God's forgiveness. Salvation is not, never has been, and never will, be based on what we do. To suggest either that sinners can earn God's Salvation, or that believers can lose it, demeans The Work of Christ.

A Time to be Candid

If you are not yet a believer, 'Paul's incredible statement,' that we have referred to above does not apply to you. But if you are a believer, we challenge you to think of anything more amazing. As you know from reading Ephesians 4, Paul has not kept secret the sins that believers commit. And yet every single one of them is included in his incredible statement.

EPHESIANS 5. NIV.

Follow God's example, therefore, as dearly loved children and walk in the way of love, just as Christ loved us and gave himself up for us as a fragrant offering and sacrifice to God. But among you there must not be even a hint of sexual immorality, or of any kind of impurity, or of greed, because these are improper for God's holy people. Nor should there be obscenity, foolish talk or coarse joking, which are out of place, but rather thanksgiving. For of this you can be sure: No immoral, impure or greedy person--such a person is an idolater--has any inheritance in the kingdom of Christ and of God. Let no one deceive you with empty words, for because of such things God's wrath comes on those who are disobedient. Therefore do not be partners with them. For you were once darkness, but now you are light in the Lord. Live as children of light (for the fruit of the light consists in all goodness, righteousness and truth) and find out what pleases the Lord. Have nothing to do with the fruitless deeds of darkness, but rather expose them. It is shameful even to mention what the disobedient do in secret. But everything exposed by the light becomes visible--and everything that is illuminated becomes a light. This is why it is said: "Wake up, sleeper, rise from the dead, and Christ will shine on you." Be very careful, then, how you live--not as unwise but as wise, making the most of every opportunity, because the days are evil. Therefore do not be foolish, but understand what the Lord's will is. Do not get drunk on wine, which leads to debauchery. Instead, be filled with the Spirit, speaking to one another with psalms, hymns, and songs from the Spirit. Sing and make music from your heart to the Lord, always giving thanks to God the Father for everything, in the name of our Lord

Jesus Christ. Submit to one another out of reverence for Christ. Wives, submit yourselves to your own husbands as you do to the Lord. For the husband is the head of the wife as Christ is the head of the church, his body, of which he is the Savior. Now as the church submits to Christ, so also wives should submit to their husbands in everything. Husbands, love your wives, just as Christ loved the church and gave himself up for her to make her holy, cleansing her by the washing with water through the word, and to present her to himself as a radiant church, without stain or wrinkle or any other blemish, but holy and blameless. In this same way, husbands ought to love their wives as their own bodies. He who loves his wife loves himself. After all, no one ever hated their own body, but they feed and care for their body, just as Christ does the church-- for we are members of his body. "For this reason a man will leave his father and mother and be united to his wife, and the two will become one flesh." This is a profound mystery--but I am talking about Christ and the church. However, each one of you also must love his wife as he loves himself, and the wife must respect her husband.

                                              Ephesians 5. NIV.

EPHESIANS 5. COMMENTARY.

Ephesians 5 continues the teaching of Ephesians 4. If you are reading this book chapter by chapter, re-read Ephesians 4 from Ephesians 4:11.

We know that the risen Lord Jesus Christ gave gifts to His Church so that believers, God's people, would be equipped to do His work and The Church, 'the body of Christ,' would be built up. This maturing activity was essential because the Ephesian believers needed to be able to detect false teachers and their clever lies.

Note as you read Ephesians 5 that Paul continued to instruct the believers as to how they should live without mentioning excuses or exceptions. The opening two verses state the standard of behaviour required and the reasons why believers can choose to attain it.

Ephesians 5:1-2.

> 'Follow God's example, therefore, as dearly loved children and walk in the way of love, just as Christ loved us and gave himself up for us as a fragrant offering and sacrifice to God.'   Ephesians 5:1-2. NIV.

In Ephesians 5:1 we read that believers must 'Follow God's example.' They are not asked to do their best to this and we are told the reason. Believers are the children that God loves. Note that no distinction is made between 'mature' and 'immature' believers, for instance, elders and those who have only recently been saved.

In Ephesians 5:2 we read that believers must 'walk in the way of love.' The ERV translates these words so simply:

'Live a life of love.' Ephesians 5:2. ERV.

As in Ephesians 5:1, it is not 'try to' or 'do your best to' and once again the reason is stated. Christ loved believers and offered Himself as a sacrifice for them. It was when they were unlovable sinners that Christ died for them. He paid the penalty that their sin deserved. No one can understand why the sacrifice of 'The Holy One' who could not, and did not sin, was part of God's Plan of Salvation but believers can truthfully sing 'we believe it was for us He hung and suffered there.'

How grateful believers are that God does not require us humans to understand divine truth. God's requirement is only that we believe it. We are all capable of believing.

God's Approval

We cannot now comment on The Old Testament verses dealing with the fragrances, offerings and sacrifices that God approved of as they foreshadowed Jesus' death. Because He loved those who would believe in Him, Jesus was willing to give Himself up as a fragrant offering and sacrifice to God.'

God's Disapproval

We must contrast the fragrances, offerings and sacrifices mentioned above that God approved of with God's disapproval of those who ignore or belittle Jesus who made it possible for God to offer His Salvation to every sinner, and to give His Salvation to sinners who are willing to repent and accept Jesus as their Saviour.

Whether you are a believer or are not yet a believer, time spent reading and reflecting on these verses will be time well spent. We quote without comment Ephesians 5:2, and extracts from Isaiah 53:10-12, and Hebrews 10:29-31.

> Ephesians 5:2. 'and walk in the way of love, just as Christ loved us and gave himself up for us as a fragrant offering and sacrifice to God.'

> Isaiah 53:10-12. (Extract) NirV. 'The LORD says, "It was my plan to crush him and cause him to suffer .... I made his life a guilt offering to pay for sin .... My plan will be brought about through him .... After he suffers .... he .... will make many people godly because of what he will accomplish. He will be punished for their sins .... he was willing to give his life as a sacrifice ....He took the sins of many people on himself. And he gave his life for those who had done what is wrong."
>
> Hebrews 10:29-31. (Extract) NirV. 'What should be done to anyone who has hated the Son of God or has said no to him? Don't you think people like that should be punished more than anyone else? ... We know the One who said, "I am the One who judges people. I will pay them back." .... It is a terrible thing to fall into the hands of the living God.'

Ephesians 5:3-4.

> 'But among you there must not be even a hint of sexual immorality, or of any kind of impurity, or of greed, because these are improper for God's holy people. Nor should there be obscenity, foolish talk or coarse joking, which are out of place, but rather thanksgiving. Ephesians 5:3-4. NIV.

In these two verses, Paul continues to state the sinful things that believers must not do.

Ephesians 5:1 begins with this instruction: 'Follow God's example.' Believers must 'follow God's example' and 'walk in the way of love' as they are God's 'dearly loved children.'

In Ephesians 5:2 it is Christ who is the believers' example. They are expected to 'walk in the way of love' as 'Christ loved us and gave himself up for us as a fragrant offering and sacrifice to God.'

In Ephesians 5:3-4 Paul stated that the believers are 'God's holy people.' Hence, not only must there be no improper behaviour, there must be no inappropriate talk. Note that greed is mentioned alongside immorality and impurity. Many believers would have considered greed less sinful than immorality and impurity, but they are 'God's holy people' and they must think like God.

Isaiah 55 is a chapter that we would recommend all who would live wisely and well. In this chapter we read God's words to His earthly people, the Jews. He wanted them to think about how they were living, how they could and should live, and be fulfilled.

We read two verses in Isaiah 55 that so clearly state what God required the Jews to do, and a verse declaring what God wanted them to know. We suggest that then as now, people would consider:

- how they lived was good enough for God.
- God would accept their best efforts to comply with a standard considered acceptable by 'conventionally correct society' and described by words such as 'respectable' 'decent' and 'well thought of.'

As we seem to be living in a period when preachers try to ensure that unbelievers are not offended, these two verses and the declaration that follows them are probably not well-known. Those who desire to faithfully proclaim The Gospel should reflect on them and memorise them. They state in a few simple words the gulf that exists between God and His sinful creatures. Only repentance, and faith in Jesus will bridge this gulf.

Isaiah 55:6-7. AV. 'Seek the LORD while he may be found; call on him while he is near. Let the wicked forsake their ways and the unrighteous their thoughts. Let them turn to the LORD, and he will have mercy on them, and to our God, for he will freely pardon.'

Isaiah 55:8. AV. '"For my thoughts are not your thoughts, neither are your ways my ways," declares the LORD.'

We revert to Ephesians 5.

We like the ERV translation of Ephesians 5:3-4. These two verses state in simple, unequivocal words what believers must not do, and should do.

Ephesians 5:3-4. 'But there must be no sexual sin among you. There must not be any kind of evil or selfishly wanting more and more, because such things are not right for God's holy people. Also, there must be no evil talk among you. Don't say things that are foolish or filthy. These are not for you. But you should be giving thanks to God.'

Ephesians 5:5-8.

> 5. 'You can be sure that no immoral, impure, or greedy person will inherit the Kingdom of Christ and of God. For a greedy person is an idolater, worshiping the things of this world. 6. Let no one deceive you with empty words, for because of such things God's wrath comes on those who are disobedient. 7. Therefore do not be partners with them. 8. For you were once darkness, but now you are light in the Lord. Live as children of light …' Ephesians 5:5-8. NIV.

Paul mentioned The Kingdom of Christ and of God in these four verses, and stated in unequivocal words that not everyone will inherit this Kingdom.

Experience teaches that what the clergy say, especially at funeral services, about entry to this Kingdom, contradicts the simple and clear words written by Paul. However, Jesus spoke about this matter and unsurprisingly, what He said also contradicts what the clergy say. So, we need to learn more about this Kingdom and what determines who will, and who will not inherit it.

We quote Jesus' words. He was speaking to Nicodemus about The Kingdom of God and The New Birth. It was a second birth involving The Holy Spirit. John 3:3-7. ERV:

> John 3:3-7. 'Jesus answered, "I assure you, everyone must be born again. Anyone who is not born again cannot be in God's kingdom." 4 Nicodemus said, "How can a man who is already old be born again? Can he go back into his mother's womb and be born a second time?" 5 Jesus answered, "Believe me when I say that everyone must be born from water and the Spirit. Anyone who is not born from water and the Spirit cannot enter God's kingdom. 6 The only life people get from their human parents is physical. But the new life that the Spirit gives a person is spiritual. 7 Don't be surprised that I told you, 'You must be born again.'

We could not have a more positive readily understandable, statement than Jesus' first statement in John 3:3. "'I assure you, everyone must be born again. Anyone who is not born again cannot be in God's kingdom.'"

Jesus' second statement in John 3:5, "'Believe me when I say that everyone must be born from water and the Spirit. Anyone who is not born from water and the Spirit cannot enter God's kingdom' is as positive, but not as readily understandable to us, as His first statement. However, we read in John 3:10 that Jesus said to Nicodemus:

"'You are an important teacher of Israel ...'"

So, we know that Nicodemus was very well acquainted with The Old Testament, and he would know that Jesus was referring to The Holy Spirit when He mentioned 'water.' The AMPC+ translation informs its readers when a literal translation of the text does not provide the real or implied meaning of the text. It prints a word that is understandable in English that assists to convey the real meaning of the text. The additional words are printed between open brackets '[' and closed brackets ']' to ensure that readers know that the word is not in the original text. We quote John 3:5 from the AMPC+:

"'Jesus answered, I assure you, most solemnly I tell you, unless a man is born of water and [even] the Spirit, he cannot [ever] enter the kingdom of God.'"

Nicodemus knew, or should have known, that The Old Testament word 'water' did not always refer to real water. It might refer to God's divine cleansing power as in Ezekiel 36:25. We like the CEV translation of this verse:

"'I will sprinkle you with clean water, and you will be clean and acceptable to me. I will wash away everything that makes you unclean, and I will remove your disgusting idols.'" Ezekiel 36:25.

We quote Ezekiel 36:25 in its context, Ezekiel 36:21-27, so that you will know what God said to His idol-worshipping sinful people, the Jews. They had been taken captive to foreign lands when various armies successfully attacked Israel. Note that God referred to:

- 'clean water' in Ezekiel 36:25.
- 'My Spirit' in Ezekiel 36:27.

Ezekiel 36:21-27. CEV. "'I care what those foreigners think of me, 22 so tell the Israelites that I am saying: You have disgraced my holy name among the nations where you now live. So you don't deserve what I'm going to do for you. I will lead you home to bring honor to my name 23. and to show foreign nations that I am holy. Then they will know that I am the LORD God. I have spoken. 24 I will gather you from the foreign nations and bring you home. 25 I will sprinkle you with clean water, and you will be clean and acceptable to me. I will wash away everything that makes you unclean, and I will remove your disgusting idols. 26 I will take away your stubborn heart and give you a new heart and a desire to be faithful. You will have only pure thoughts, 27 because I will put my Spirit in you and make you eager to obey my laws and teachings.'" Ezekiel 36:21-27. CEV.

You will now know why Jesus mentioned water when He discussed the necessity of 'being born again' with Nicodemus. Note John 3:6:

John 3:6. CEV. 'The only life people get from their human parents is physical. But the new life that the Spirit gives a person is spiritual. 7 Don't be surprised that I told you, 'You must be born again.'

Nicodemus also learnt about the divine work of The Holy Spirit, in the new spiritual life that 'the Spirit gives.'

A Time to Reflect

We cannot provide the details now, but it appears from the little that we read about Nicodemus in The Gospels that his personal discussion with Jesus resulted in his 'new life.'

We have already mentioned that we publish this book to:

- encourage believers to study The Bible. We know that God speaks to those who read His Word. Believers who read The Bible just to fill their head with information will not be as blessed as those who want to learn the spiritual truths that The Holy Spirit will reveal to those who put into practice what they learn.

- inform those not yet believers what The Bible teaches is a 'must' before they can possess God's Salvation, become one of God's dearly loved children, and know that Heaven is their eternal home.

What we have already studied in Ephesians, coupled with

Jesus' words in John 3 confirms six truths:

1. Born again believers are God's dearly loved children.
2. We are neither God's dearly loved children when we are born into this world, nor do we enter the Kingdom of God. We are born sinners who must be born again.
3. We enter the Kingdom of God when we are born again.
4. We cannot be born again unless The Holy Spirit is involved in our new birth.
5. Receipt of The Holy Spirit when we are born again is God's guarantee that He has identified us as His own.
6. The Holy Spirit will be our security until that future day in Heaven when our Salvation will be complete.

Now we have studied what Jesus said about The Kingdom of God we revert to Ephesians 5 and quote again Ephesians 5:5-8.

Ephesians 5:5-8.

> 5. 'You can be sure that no immoral, impure, or greedy person will inherit the Kingdom of Christ and of God. For a greedy person is an idolater, worshiping the things of this world. 6. Let no one deceive you with empty words, for because of such things God's wrath comes on those who are disobedient. 7. Therefore do not be partners with them. 8. For you were once darkness, but now you are light in the Lord. Live as children of light ...'   Ephesians 5:5-8. NIV.

Paul mentioned The Kingdom of Christ and of God in these four verses, and stated in unequivocal words that not everyone will inherit this Kingdom.

Both Ephesians 5:5 and Ephesians 5:6 begin with words emphasising that what is written is 'nothing but the truth:'

- 'You can be sure that …' Ephesians 5:5.
- 'Let no one deceive you …' Ephesians 5:6.

Note that in both verses we read the opposite to what we know about The Kingdom of Christ and of God. We have no difficulty associating how believers live with their relationship to this divine Kingdom. We would also expect that those who do not belong to this Kingdom:

- are associated with 'the things of this world' and we can understand Paul's emphasis on the words 'this world' in Ephesians 5:5.
- have not repented of their sin and been born again and in consequence Paul wrote that they were 'those who are disobedient.' Ephesians 5:6.

We are not surprised that no immoral or impure person will inherit this divine Kingdom, but what might surprise us is Paul's inclusion of the 'greedy' with the immoral or impure. Was he referring to Proverbs 23:2? Few today have a good knowledge of The Old Testament. Hence, most of us will be taken aback by what Solomon wrote about gluttony. We quote Proverbs 23:2 in its context:

Proverbs 23:1. 'When you sit to dine with a ruler, note well what is before you, 2 and put a knife to your throat if you are given to gluttony. 3 Do not crave his delicacies, for that food is deceptive. 4 Do not wear yourself out to get rich; do not trust your own cleverness. 5 Cast but a glance at riches, and they are gone, for they will surely sprout wings and fly off to the sky like an eagle.' Proverbs 23:1-5. NIV.

We do not consider that Paul was referring to a 'big eater' but to a 'covetous' person. The AMPC adds these words to express the true meaning of the original language, 'who has lustful desire for the property of others and is greedy for gain.' Hence, they 'worship' material things.

Jesus taught His disciples to pray. In that prayer we read

these now famous words:

'your kingdom come ...' Matthew 6:10. NIV.

After teaching His disciples how to pray, Jesus taught them what their spiritual aspirations should be as they waited for the coming Kingdom. He mentioned Earth and Heaven. The contrast between them is beyond human understanding but Jesus used the simplest of words to illustrate why His disciples should concentrate on the things that will last for eternity. He said:

"Do not store up for yourselves treasures on earth, where moths and vermin destroy, and where thieves break in and steal. But store up for yourselves treasures in heaven, where moths and vermin do not destroy, and where thieves do not break in and steal. For where your treasure is, there your heart will be also." Matthew 6:19-21. NIV.

We revert to Ephesians 5:7-8. We have read in Ephesians 5 about the sins that believers should not do, along with other behaviour like immorality, impurity and idolatry. We have also read that those who commit these sins have no inheritance in the kingdom of Christ and of God, and that God's wrath in on those who disobey Him. We cannot be therefore be surprised by Paul's unambiguous instruction:

'Therefore do not be partners with them.' Ephesians 5:7.

Although Paul does not state so, what we have read in Ephesians 5:5-6 describes the sins of unbelievers. This is obvious when we read Ephesians 5:8.

'For you were once darkness, but now you are light in the Lord. Live as children of light ...' Ephesians 5:5-8. NIV.

In all Paul's letters, apart from Philippians, he stated how believers must behave.

The Ephesian Believers' Background

The Ephesians were Gentiles. They had no knowledge of

God until they heard The Gospel. Unlike the Jews, who knew The Ten Commandments and The Old Testament prior to hearing The Gospel, the Ephesians were idolaters. Their lives reflected the moral standards of the day. We can judge from Ephesians 5 that those standards were low. As this book might be read by young people we do not refer further to this matter but we must mention Paul's assessment of the sins:

- Ephesians 5:3. '… improper for God's holy people.'
- Ephesians 5:4-5. '… out of place …'

Ephesians 5:5-20.

'You can be sure that no immoral, impure, or greedy person will inherit the Kingdom of Christ and of God. For a greedy person is an idolater, worshiping the things of this world. Let no one deceive you with empty words, for because of such things God's wrath comes on those who are disobedient. Therefore do not be partners with them. For you were once darkness, but now you are light in the Lord. Live as children of light (for the fruit of the light consists in all goodness, righteousness and truth) and find out what pleases the Lord. Have nothing to do with the fruitless deeds of darkness, but rather expose them. It is shameful even to mention what the disobedient do in secret. But everything exposed by the light becomes visible—and everything that is illuminated becomes a light. This is why it is said: "Wake up, sleeper, rise from the dead, and Christ will shine on you." Be very careful, then, how you live—not as unwise but as wise, making the most of every opportunity, because the days are evil. Therefore do not be foolish, but understand what the Lord's will is. Do not get drunk on wine, which leads to debauchery. Instead, be filled with the Spirit,

> speaking to one another with psalms, hymns, and songs from the Spirit. Sing and make music from your heart to the Lord, always giving thanks to God the Father for everything, in the name of our Lord Jesus Christ.　　　　　　　　　Ephesians 5:5-20. NIV.

The 'Do' and 'Must Not Do' of Christianity

There are unbelievers and believers who associate God's Salvation with a list of things you must not do, or to express it another way, unbelievers think that if they were saved, they would have to stop doing almost everything they enjoy doing. Some believers try to assist unbelievers to overcome this problem by telling them that believers stop wanting to do the things they once enjoyed doing.

You will not read this notion in The New Testament. Paul would have disagreed with it. Six times in Paul's letters, although not in Ephesians, he refers to The Gospel he preached as The Gospel of God. Hence, The Gospel:

- did not belong to Paul. He could not change it.
- does not belong to us. We cannot change it.

We read in Acts 20:21 what Paul said about The Gospel he preached for three years when he lived, preached The Gospel, and taught believers in Ephesus. Note in Acts 20:21 that The Gospel Paul preached to both the Jews and the Gentiles had two parts, and both were necessary. The word 'must' is in the first part, and the word 'have' is in the second part and implies 'must have.' Paul said,

"'I have declared to both Jews and Greeks that they must turn to God in repentance and have faith in our Lord Jesus. Acts 20:21. NIV.'"

We like the GNB translation of this verse:

'To Jews and Gentiles alike I gave solemn warning that

they should turn from their sins to God and believe in our Lord Jesus.' Acts 20:21. GNB.

Hence, unbelievers must:

- 'turn to God in repentance.'
- 'have faith in our Lord Jesus.'

You can check that what we write is correct by reading Acts 20:21. If unbelievers will not repent of their sins, they cannot be saved. Repentance means 'turning your back on your way of life and beginning a life that pleases God.'

There are believers who foolishly believe that God's love will ensure that on the Day of Judgment, everyone will be forgiven. That belief is the opposite of what Paul wrote in Ephesians 5. So, as we consider both the teaching relating to believers in Ephesians 5, and the things that believers must not do, keep the thought of 'must turn to God in repentance' in mind.

God's Dear Children and God's Holy People

> Ephesians 5:1. Follow God's example, therefore, as dearly loved children 2. and walk in the way of love, just as Christ loved us and gave himself up for us as a fragrant offering and sacrifice to God. 3 But among you there must not be even a hint of sexual immorality, or of any kind of impurity, or of greed, because these are improper for God's holy people. Ephesians 5:1-3. NIV.

God's Dear Children

Both God's love and Christ's love are mentioned by Paul in Ephesians 5:1-2 and both refer to a specific group. The pronoun he used is 'us.' It refers to 'God's dear children.'

God's Holy People

In Ephesians 5:3 we read that the sins Paul mentioned are

improper for 'God's holy people.' Paul referred only to a specific group. The pronoun he used is 'you.'

Everybody

It is our sincere prayer that unbelievers who read this book will become believers, and so we clarify from time to time what we write to ensure that it is crystal clear. Hence, we state that everybody can be saved. However, only those who repent and believe in Jesus are saved.

If Paul had meant 'everybody' in Ephesians 5, he would have used the word 'everybody.' But, he would have wasted his time writing to those who were not saved about their way of life as they were not 'God's Holy People.'

Only those Paul identified as 'God's dear children and Gods holy people' could change their ways. In Ephesians 5:16 we read that 'the days are evil.' Let us be clear about this. Paul was referring to the unbelievers in Ephesus being evil. Hence, the Ephesian believers, 'Gods holy people' lived in evil days surrounded by evil unbelievers.

Holy and Evil

The distinction in Ephesians 5:5 is between believers who are holy and unbelievers who are evil. 'Evil' means evil. Believers must not attempt to make the words 'holy' and 'evil' mean other than 'holy' and 'evil.'

God's Wrath: Some Important Questions

In Ephesians 5:6 we are told that, 'God's wrath comes on those who are disobedient.' The meaning of these words is crystal clear. We need to ask four important questions about those who occupy pulpits or preach elsewhere:

1. Why do they mention God's love and ignore His wrath?
2. Would mentioning 'God's wrath' embarrass them?
3. Does 'God's wrath' not fit in with their one-sided and

misguided view of God?

4. Do they ignore 'God's wrath' because it might make them less popular?

We quote Acts 20:26-27 from the NIV and the NLT:

Acts 20:26-27. NIV. "'I declare to you today that I am innocent of the blood of any of you. For I have not hesitated to proclaim to you the whole will of God.'"

The NLT translates Acts 20:26-27 even more dramatically:

Acts 20:26-27 "'I declare today that I have been faithful. If anyone suffers eternal death, it's not my fault, for I didn't shrink from declaring all that God wants you to know.'"

We know from The New Testament that Paul was a man of both moral and spiritual integrity. How should we describe preachers who deliberately avoid preaching about God's wrath? We remind you again of Paul's words in Ephesians 5:6.

'God's wrath comes on those who are disobedient.'

Whether you are a believer or an unbeliever, God demands your obedience.

False Believers: 'Let No One Deceive You ...'

If you think you are believer, but are blasé as to whether or not you are obedient to God, may we suggest that you ask yourself if you have ever repented of your sins and turned your back on your old way of life. A simple test is to consider if it is obvious from how you now live that there has been a visible change in your lifestyle.

Experience teaches that many have been deceived into thinking that they are saved. Yet there was never a moment in their lives when they repented of their sin and turned their back on their old way of life. Could that be the reason why Ephesians 5:6, that refers to God's wrath, begins with the words:

- 'let no one deceive you ...' NIV.
- 'don't be fooled ...' NLT.

Ephesians 5:5-8

As it is vital to your eternal welfare, before we mention the contrasts between believers and unbelievers, we quote Paul's blunt statement in Ephesians 5:5-8 from the NLT:

> Ephesians 5:5-8. NLT. 'You can be sure that no immoral, impure, or greedy person will inherit the Kingdom of Christ and of God. For a greedy person is an idolater, worshiping the things of this world. Don't be fooled by those who try to excuse these sins, for the anger of God will fall on all who disobey Him. Don't participate in the things these people do. For once you were full of darkness, but now you have light from the Lord. So live as people of light!' Ephesians 5:5-8. NLT.

Darkness and Light

Paul's bluntness continued. He stated the believers were 'once darkness.' Paul was correct. The longer you live as a believer the more you will realise that darkness 'saturates' unbelievers.' Hence, an old children's spiritual song (you can download the words and the music from the Internet) states unambiguously where unbelievers, who want to be believers, must begin:

'There's a way back to God from the dark path of sin,
There's a door that is open and all may go in,
At Calvary's Cross is where you begin,
When you come as a sinner to Jesus.'

If, at this present time, you are earnestly seeking to

teach unbelievers Christian truths, believing that this will bring them to a knowledge of Salvation, we need to tell you that you will not succeed. You might find it difficult, or even embarrassing, but The Gospel, God's Good News, begins with the subject of sin and repentance. Sinner must realise that they need saving from their sins. Otherwise, they will never repent and have faith in The Lord Jesus.

Ephesians 5:8-14.

These verses contrast God's children, who are no longer 'darkness,' from unbelievers who are. The light that God's children possess can produce fruit that will be well-pleasing to The Lord. We are told exactly what the fruit is. Before we consider this further, we need to look at Paul's very positive statement in Ephesians 5:11.

> Ephesians 5:11. NIV. 'Have nothing to do with the fruitless deeds of darkness, but rather expose them.'

Some believers have spent many years living for God, seeking to please Him in everything they do. They toil day by day to make The Gospel known to unbelievers.

Some readers might consider that 'fruit' is equivalent to 'success,' that is, the number of unbelievers saved. But that is not so. The fruit of the light in Ephesians 5:9 cannot be counted or weighed. It is contrasted in Ephesians 5:11 with 'the fruitless deed of darkness.' The importance of this contrast leads us to ask three questions that readers will answer for themselves:

1. Are you involved with 'the fruitless deeds of darkness?'
2. Do you expose 'the fruitless deeds of darkness?'
3. Are unbelievers who live in darkness mystified that you have nothing to do with their darkness because you have never told them that or why you live in light?

Another Contrast: The Secret and The Visible
Ephesians 5:12-14.

> Ephesians 5:12-14. NIV. 'It is shameful even to mention what the disobedient do in secret. But everything exposed by the light becomes visible--and everything that is illuminated becomes a light. This is why it is said: "Wake up, sleeper, rise from the dead, and Christ will shine on you." Ephesians 5:12-14. NIV.

Read John 3:1-15. John records the dialogue between Jesus and a religious man. Jesus told him two truths:

1. He must be born again.
2. The consequences of not being born again.

Jesus stated why He had come into the world to die.

Read John 3:16-36. Read what John wrote about God's universal offer of Salvation and why unbelievers hate the light and would prefer to live in the darkness. John wrote that they love sinning and the light would expose their sins.

John clearly indicates the difference between a believer's and an unbeliever's present life and their futures. Believers presently possess God's everlasting life, but God's everlasting wrath is now abiding on unbelievers.

We quote John 3:19-21 below. Read about unbelievers, and light and darkness. This vital truth is rarely, if ever, mentioned from the pulpit and might explain why so few know about it. Note in particular that:

- unbelievers willingly live in the darkness and love it.
- what unbelievers do is referred to as 'evil.'

The Bible teaches that God detests sin, so never ignore or diminish God's view of sin. Believers who do this deceive unbelievers. This must please Satan. Experience teaches that many believers do not understand why unbelievers resist hearing or believing The Gospel. Jesus taught that only a few choose to travel the narrow road to Heaven, the majority choosing to travel the broad road to Hell. Are you surprised that believers, who are aware of the awful eternal punishment for sin that unbelievers will suffer in Hell, never make their unbelieving loved ones aware of it?

This is the Verdict: John 3:19-21.

> 'This is the verdict: Light has come into the world, but people loved darkness instead of light because their deeds were evil. Everyone who does evil hates the light, and will not come into the light for fear that their deeds will be exposed. But whoever lives by the truth comes into the light, so that it may be seen plainly that what they have done has been done in the sight of God.'　　　　　　　　　　　　John 3:19-21. NIV.

Ephesians 5:14: 'Wake Up'

> 'This is why it is said: '"Wake up, sleeper, rise from the dead, and Christ will shine on you."'　　Ephesians 5:14.

We have considered things done secretly or openly in Ephesians 5:12-14, and in darkness or light in John 3:19-21. These three question make the verses personal to you:

1: Are you doing something secretly because you would be ashamed if others knew about it?

2: Are you doing something that you would prefer that Christ did not know about?

3: Do you need a 'wake-up call' to stop you doing evil to enable you to come into the light?

We read in Ephesians 5:12-14, "'Wake up, sleeper, rise from the dead, and Christ will shine on you.'" This saying combines the truth in some Old Testament verses in Isaiah about a resurrection that related to the Jews. Paul used it as a 'wake-up call.' He had written that what the disobedient do in secret will become visible when exposed by the light. Paul tells the Gentile Ephesians that it is possible to 'wake-up' and stop being disobedient, to come into the light and receive the blessing of the light that only Christ can give. Light makes things visible, but divine light exposes the true character of everything.

Believers should live in light as children of light and expose the hidden things of darkness. Although believers' lives should expose the things that the ungodly do, believers do not talk about it because 'it is shameful even to talk about the things that ungodly people do in secret.'

Candid Instructions for Christian Living

Ephesians 5:14-20.

Some object to those who speak candidly. Some have the idea that 'the Christian approach,' should always be a 'soft and gentle approach.' Presumably, they would have criticised Paul for his bluntness because, in relatively few words, he instructed the Ephesian believers:

- to be careful how they lived and not to live unwisely.
- to make the most of every opportunity.
- not to be foolish, and not to get drunk.

It would be difficult think of more candid instructions than these, but we know why they must be obeyed. Four words needed to be at the forefront of believers' minds:

'The days are evil.'

The days are still evil.

'The Days are Evil'

Question: Does God expect believers to fight evil using their own resources?

The Answer is: "No." These five truths in Ephesians 5:17-19 should amaze believers. It is possible for believers to:

1. 'understand what the Lord's will is.'
2. 'be filled with the Spirit.'
3. speak to other believers, 'with psalms, hymns, and songs from the Spirit.'
4. 'sing and make music from your heart to the Lord.'
5. live 'continually giving thanks to God the Father for everything, in the name of our Lord Jesus Christ.'

As mentioned above, these five truths apply to believers, but they are optional. However, we cannot imagine that any believer would be so foolish as to choose to ignore them as they involve living in harmony with God the Father, God the Son and God The Holy Spirit.

Re-read the verses considering the involvement of 'The Godhead.' It must be foolish to seek to 'go it alone' in days that are characterised by evil. It cannot be other than wise but to be obedient to the instructions that are written prior to Ephesians 5:17, and those that follow Ephesians 5:20.

Experience teaches that what we will shortly study has been classed by some believers as 'old-fashioned.' It is probably because Paul used the relationship between a husband and a wife to illustrate this divine eternal truth that had never previously been revealed.

Ephesians 5:21-33.

We comment on Ephesians 5:21 and Ephesians 5:32 before considering this final section of Ephesians 5.

> Ephesians 5:21-33. NIV. 'Submit to one another out of reverence for Christ. Wives, submit yourselves to your own husbands as you do to the Lord. For the husband is the head of the wife as Christ is the head of the church, his body, of which he is the Savior. Now as the church submits to Christ, so also wives should submit to their husbands in everything. Husbands, love your wives, just as Christ loved the church and gave himself up for her to make her holy, cleansing her by the washing with water through the word, and to present her to himself as a radiant church, without stain or wrinkle or any other blemish, but holy and blameless. In this same way, husbands ought to love their wives as their own bodies. He who loves his wife loves himself. After all, no one ever hated their own body, but they feed and care for their body, just as Christ does the church-- for we are members of his body. "For this reason a man will leave his father and mother and be united to his wife, and the two will become one flesh." This is a profound mystery--but I am talking about Christ and the church. However, each one of you also must love his wife as he loves himself, and the wife must respect her husband.'   Ephesians 5:21-33. NIV.

Ephesians 5:21 continues Paul's practice of stating:

- the instruction.

- the reason for the instruction.

Ephesians 5:21 will test our spirituality. We will only do what we are instructed to do if we want to revere Christ.

Read and reread these nine words:

> 'Submit to one another out of reverence for Christ.' Ephesians 5:21. NIV.

'Be willing to serve each other out of respect for Christ,' is how the ERV translates this verse and makes it easy to understand for English readers. No two translations of this verse are the same but Wuest's translation is 'putting yourselves in subjection to one another …' This translation accurately expresses what believers must do.

- 'Putting yourselves' emphasises pro-activeness.
- 'In subjection' indicates selflessness and humility.
- 'To one another' eliminates choosing only some.

Our comments on Ephesians 5:8-10 could be condensed to 'live as children of light and find out what pleases the Lord.' If believers want to please the Lord, it will show their reverence for Him. Believers have a choice to:

- please the Lord.
- please themselves.

Believers can do one or the other, but not both simultaneously. Ephesians 5:21 states what pleases the Lord. How many believers are willing to obey other believers? It might be somewhat easier to obey those that we respect. Believers cannot pick and choose.

Equality is now part of the political agenda but Paul did not write to 'all and sundry.' He wrote to believers, those who:

- 'are light in the Lord, children of light.'
- 'understand what the Lord's will is.'
- can 'be filled with the Spirit.'

What unbelievers cannot do because they are not God's children, believers can do because they are, and they do it 'out of reverence for Christ.'

> 'This is a profound mystery--but I am talking about Christ and the church.'   Ephesians 5:32. NIV.

Ephesians 5:32. A Profound Mystery; A Secret.

Christ and the Church

Paul used the word 'mystery' many times in his letters, and several times in Ephesians. Those who have read Ephesians from the beginning will recall that it refers to truth previously unknown. So, you will not read these truths in The Old Testament, as the prophets were unaware of them. Jesus never referred to them, so His apostles and disciples were unaware of them until they learnt them from Paul. We too must learn each truth. We quote these truths using the ERV translation. This translation uses the word, 'secret,' to avoid readers assuming that the truths are mysterious or shadowy. We quote Ephesians 1:9-10, and Ephesians 3:3-12.

Ephesians 1:9-10. ERV. 'he let us know his secret plan. This was what God wanted, and he planned to do it through Christ.' God's goal was to finish His plan when the right time came. He planned that all things in heaven and on earth be joined together with Christ as the head.

Ephesians 3:3-12. ERV. 'God let me know his secret plan by showing it to me. I have already written a little about this. And if you read what I wrote, you can see that I understand the secret truth about Christ. People who lived in other times were not told that secret truth. But now, through the Spirit, God has made it known to his holy apostles and prophets. And this is the secret truth: that by hearing the Good News, those who are not Jews will share with the Jews in the blessings God has for his people. They are part of the same body, and they share in the promise God made through Christ Jesus. By God's special gift of grace, I became a servant to tell that Good News. He gave me that grace by using his power. I am the least important of all God's people. But he gave me this gift--to tell the non-Jewish people the Good News about the riches Christ has. These riches are too great to understand fully. And God gave me the work of telling all people about the plan for his secret truth. That secret truth has been hidden in him since the beginning of time. He is the one who created everything. His purpose was that all the rulers and powers in the heavenly places will now know the many different ways he shows his wisdom. They will know this because of the church. This agrees with the plan God had since the beginning of time. He did what he planned, and he did it through Christ Jesus our Lord. In Christ we come before God with freedom and without fear. We can do this because of our faith in Christ.'

Believers are very privileged. If you are not yet a believer, note that the above verses only become real to those who:

- have 'faith in Christ.'
- can honestly refer to Christ Jesus as "our Lord."

Only believers have the privilege of coming before God with freedom and without fear. They have not earned this privilege or the right to come before God with boldness:

- A believer's boldness or confidence is based on what Jesus did for them when He was crucified. He was punished by God for their sins. Because they have repented and accepted Jesus as their Saviour, God can forgive them and bestow His Salvation on them.
- God regards believers as 'in Christ.' God wants them to come before Him do so fearlessly. God initiated 'The Plan of Salvation,' and Jesus came into the world to fulfill this plan to save sinners who repent and accept Jesus as their Saviour.

If you are not yet a believer, you too could have this confidence to come before God. It is available to anyone and everyone, everywhere who will repent of their sin and put their faith in The Lord Jesus Christ. Those who do will be God's children, children of light. They will also become members of a very special body called 'The Church.'

Ephesians 5:32. The Secret Truth

Paul wrote 'that secret truth is very important--I am talking about Christ and the church.' We abridge what we read about this secret truth in Ephesians 3:6-12. ERV.

> 'by hearing the Good News, those who are not Jews will share with the Jews in the blessings God has for his people. They are part of the same body, and they share in the promise God made through Christ Jesus .... His purpose was that all the rulers and powers in the heavenly places will now know the many different ways He shows His wisdom. They will know this because of the church .... In Christ we come before God with freedom and without fear. We can do this because of our faith in Christ.' Ephesians 3:6-12. ERV. (Abridged)

Our Commentary

The Church was originally composed of Jewish believers. They sincerely, but incorrectly, believed that The Gospel could only be preached to Jews, although Peter preached it on one occasion to a Roman household. After Paul was saved, he travelled to many countries preaching The Gospel to both Jews and Gentiles.

An Important Note

The Jews were born sinners. They had some knowledge of God and The Old Testament. The Gentiles were also born sinners. They were idolaters who had no knowledge of God or The Old Testament. To receive the forgiveness of their sin and God's Salvation, both Jews and Gentiles needed to hear The Gospel, repent, and believe in Jesus.

Ephesians 5:23-32. The Church of God and Marriage.

We cannot read about the secret truth revealed to Paul without realising how important The Church is to God. In note form, Ephesians 5:23-32. ERV, teaches:

Ephesians 5:23.

- Christ is the head of The Church.
- The Church is Christ's body.
- Christ is the Saviour of The Church.

Ephesians 5:24.

- The Church submits to Christ.

Ephesians 5:25-27.

- Christ loved The Church.
- Christ gave Himself up to make The Church holy.
- Christ cleans and edifies The Church.
- Christ will present The Church to Himself. It will be:
  - glorious.
  - without blemish.
  - holy and blameless.

Ephesians 5:29-30.

- Christ feeds and cares for The Church.
- Believers are members of His body.

Ephesians 5:31-32.

- Paul wrote '… two will become one …. I am talking about Christ and The Church.'

Interwoven in what we learn about The Church are

instructions as to how husbands and wives should behave towards each other.

The Behaviour of Husbands and Wives.

We cannot separate Paul's instructions to husbands and wives from the secret truths we read about Christ and The Church. Ephesians 5:27-28 is a good example of this:

> Ephesians 5:27-28. ERV. 'Christ died so that he could give the church to himself like a bride in all her beauty. He died so that the church could be holy and without fault, with no evil or sin or any thing wrong in it. And husbands should love their wives like that. They should love their wives as they love their own bodies. The man who loves his wife loves himself ...'

Ephesians 5:31 is a quotation from Genesis 2:

> Genesis 2:22-24. NIV. 'Then the LORD God made a woman from the rib he had taken out of the man, and he brought her to the man. The man said, "This is now bone of my bones and flesh of my flesh; she shall be called 'woman,' for she was taken out of man." That is why a man leaves his father and mother and is united to his wife, and they become one flesh.'

The Head and The Body

- Christ is the head of The Church and The Church is Christ's body.
- The Church submits to Christ.
- Believers are members of Christ's body.
- Christ feeds and cares for His body.

Before we comment further on the important interrelation

of The Church, marriage, and Adam and Eve, we need to bring to your attention to Paul's farewell message to the Ephesian church elders in Acts 20. Previously in this book, for the sake of simplicity, we have referred to believers and unbelievers. We could have used other names such as:

- The people of God and unbelievers.
- The Church of God and unbelievers.

Our objective has always been to inform readers that they belong to only one of two groups, and to inform those not yet believers of the opportunity they have to repent, believe The Gospel and be eternally saved. We trust we have made it clear that no one need remain an unbeliever and receive God's eternal punishment for their sins. It is obvious that many choose to do so, but we trust we have made it clear that this is a matter of choice. Every believer has made a positive choice to be saved. They are powerless to ensure that others do the same.

False Doctrine; False Teachers; The Truth

Believers are not protected from false teachers who teach false doctrines. It is not only unbelievers that are misled. There is no lack of those who falsely claim to be part of The Church. Be cautious when making assumptions.

Two False Assumptions

1. Some think that false teachers and false teaching are relatively new. They are not. Read Acts 20. When Paul spoke about them, he regarded them as imminent.
2. Some think that 'The Truth' is unascertainable. That is also wrong. Read Acts 20. 'The Truth' is ascertainable. Paul referred to 'The Truth' as 'the whole will of God.'

What we believe is either:

1. right or wrong.
2. true or false.

'The Whole Will of God'

How do we ascertain 'the whole will of God?' We read God's Word, The Bible. There is a very simple test.

- If it is not in God's Word, it must be foolish to believe it.
- If it is in God's Word, it must be foolish to disbelieve it.

We mention three truths in Acts 20. Paul referred to:

1. The Gospel.
2. A believer's responsibility to be faithful.
3. The Price God paid for The Church.

The Gospel

Acts 20:20-21. GNB. 'You know that I did not hold back anything that would be of help to you as I preached and taught in public and in your homes. To Jews and Gentiles alike I gave solemn warning that they should turn from their sins to God and believe in our Lord Jesus.'

A Believer's Responsibility to be Faithful

Acts 20:26-27. NLT. 'I declare today that I have been faithful. If anyone suffers eternal death, it's not my fault, for I didn't shrink from declaring all that God wants you to know.'

The Price God Paid for The Church

'So guard yourselves and God's people. Feed and shepherd God's flock—His church, purchased with His own blood—over which the Holy Spirit has appointed you as elders. I know that false teachers, like vicious wolves, will come in among you after I leave, not sparing the flock.' Acts 20:28-29. NLT.

We ask four questions about Paul's statements. Readers

will supply their own answers to the first three questions:

1. Do you think of The Gospel as a solemn warning to unbelievers to 'repent, and turn to God, and believe in our Lord Jesus?'
2. Are you unfaithful to God as you shrink from declaring all that God wants unbelievers to know?
3. Do you refer to The Church as "my church," not realising that it belongs to God and that He purchased it with the blood shed by The Lord Jesus Christ on the Cross?
4. Do you regard the local church as belonging to its members? Note that a golf or tennis club or other organisation belonging to its members will be governed by its Rule Book. It will not be governed by God's Word. Voting and majority decisions might be appropriate to clubs and the like, but not to God's Church.

The Church and Genesis 2:22-24.

- The Head, Christ, and the body, the members, are one.
- Husband and wives become one.

We consider the truth in Genesis 2:22-24 again.

> 'Then the LORD God made a woman from the rib he had taken out of the man, and he brought her to the man. The man said, "This is now bone of my bones and flesh of my flesh; she shall be called 'woman,' for she was taken out of man." That is why a man leaves his father and mother and is united to his wife, and they become one flesh.'   Genesis 2:22-24. NIV.

These translations emphasise the truth being expressed:

NLT: 'This explains why …. the two are united into one.'

ERV: 'That is why …. two people become one.'

Adam was correct when he said that Eve was "bone of my bones …. flesh of my flesh …. taken out of man." From one man, God made a second human being, a woman. Adam's bone became a woman. One became two but, 'when a man …. is united to his wife,'

- 'they become one flesh.' NIV.
- 'the two are united into one.' NLT.
- 'two people become one.' ERV.

Question: Why did Paul mention marriage when he disclosed the truth revealed to him about The Church?

Answer: The oneness of the union of Adam and Eve aptly described the relationship of Christ and His Church.

Ephesians 5:25-28

There are various translations of these verses that require careful consideration and to assist readers we quote three, the NIV, GNB, and ERV:

> NIV: Ephesians 5:25. 'Husbands, love your wives, just as Christ loved the church and gave himself up for her 26 to make her holy, cleansing her by the washing with water through the word, 27 and to present her to himself as a radiant church, without stain or wrinkle or any other blemish, but holy and blameless. 28 In this same way, husbands ought to love their wives as their own bodies. He who loves his wife loves himself.'
>
> GNB: Ephesians 5:25. 'Husbands, love your wives just as Christ loved the church and gave his life for it. 26 He did this to dedicate the church to God by his word, after making it clean by washing it in water, 27 in order to present the church to himself in all its beauty---pure and faultless, without spot or wrinkle or any other imperfection. 28 Men ought to love their wives just as

> they love their own bodies. A man who loves his wife loves himself.'
>
> ERV: Ephesians 5:25. 'Husbands, love your wives the same as Christ loved the church and gave his life for it. 26 He died to make the church holy. He used the telling of the Good News to make the church clean by washing it with water. 27 Christ died so that he could give the church to himself like a bride in all her beauty. He died so that the church could be holy and without fault, with no evil or sin or any other thing wrong in it. 28 And husbands should love their wives like that. They should love their wives as they love their own bodies. The man who loves his wife loves himself.'

Those who have translated these verses into English that we can understand have tried to make sense of, and link Paul's words in Ephesians 5:27, with his references to husbands and wives in Ephesians 5:25 and 28. To make our point clear, we itemise the verses from the NIV:

- Ephesians 5:25. Refers to husbands and wives.
- Ephesians 5:27. Does not refer to husbands and wives.
- Ephesians 5:28. Refers to husbands and wives.

However, Ephesians 5:27 was written in the context of references to husbands and wives. Ephesians 5:28 begins, 'In this same way.' It seems clear that Paul referred to a bride being presented to her husband, and the unique features of this bride, obviously, The Church, are stated:

- 'radiant,'
- 'without stain or wrinkle or any other blemish'
- 'holy and blameless.'

These features should not surprise us as The Church is only composed of believers and we read what Paul wrote about them in Ephesians 1. Note carefully God's past, present and eternal view of believers.

> Ephesians 1:3-8. NIV. 'Praise be to the God and Father of our Lord Jesus Christ, who has blessed us in the heavenly realms with every spiritual blessing in Christ. For he chose us in him before the creation of the world to be holy and blameless in his sight. In love he predestined us for adoption to sonship through Jesus Christ, in accordance with his pleasure and will--to the praise of his glorious grace, which he has freely given us in the One he loves. In him we have redemption through his blood, the forgiveness of sins, in accordance with the riches of God's grace that he lavished on us.' Ephesians 1:3-8. NIV.

You might not realise that God does not share your view of believers. You see believers who are not 'holy and blameless,' but it is God's view of them that counts and He sees them as holy and blameless as Jesus, their Saviour. If you are not yet a believer, you might consider your life as good as, or even better than, the lives of the believers you know. From a human standpoint, your view might be correct, but the vital issue is whether your view counts with God. Ephesians 1:3-8 teaches us that it does not.

The vital difference between unbelievers and believers is clearly stated in the words of Ephesians 1:7. To prove this to you, we quote the words we refer to in two translations, the NIV and the NLT. A believer can read these words knowing that they refer to them. They are one of the 'we' and the 'our,' two extremely important pronouns in the text:

> NIV. Ephesians 1:7. 'we have redemption through his blood, the forgiveness of sins.'
>
> NLT. Ephesians 1:7. he purchased our freedom with

the blood of his Son and forgave our sins.

Believers can honestly say to Jesus, "All my sins have been forgiven because you shed Your blood for me."

Forgiveness is available to everyone everywhere willing to repent and ask Jesus to be their Saviour. Jesus has done everything that God required Him to do so that repentant sinners, who realise they need a Saviour, can ask Jesus to save them. When Jesus died, His blood was shed so that sinners could be forgiven but, as you have just read, only believers have been forgiven. This is not our opinion. You read it in Ephesians 1:7. Sadly, many have their own, or their churches view of how their sins can be forgiven:

- Many are taught that forgiveness must be earned by good works, self-punishment, pilgrimages, and the like.
- Many think it is obtained from their church or its priests.
- Some have been taught that it must be paid for.

All sorts of beliefs are preached. Much of it has become dogma. But The Bible remains unambiguous. God has provided Jesus. He is the only Saviour. He shed His precious blood on the Cross. It was the price God willingly paid so that, if you repent and accept Jesus as your Saviour, you can have your sins forgiven.

The Forgiveness of Sins

Whoever you are, wherever you are, and whatever you have done, you could have your sins forgiven now. The Gospel is a solemn warning that you need to repent, and believe in The Lord Jesus Christ.

Ephesians 1:13 is the key verse of this book. The title is taken from it. Its words could apply to you. They have to all believers for the last 2000 years and will to all who become believers before Jesus comes again to take every believer, whether they are living or have died, to Heaven.

> Ephesians 1:13. NIV. 'You also were included in Christ when you heard the message of truth, the gospel of your salvation.' Ephesians 1:13. NIV.

If you are not yet a believer, we earnestly ask you to read what we have written. You might assume that you know what you are going to read because we have made the same request before. Your assumption is correct because it will always be the same Gospel that we mention.

We try to present The Gospel from different angles. Experience proves that some earnestly want to be saved and they hear or read something in The Bible that The Holy Spirit can use to remove their spiritual blindness. They can then see why they need Jesus to be their Saviour.

Like all the Gospel preachers whose messages we can read in The New Testament, we believe that repenting and accepting Jesus as Saviour, enables sinners to obtain God's Salvation. Experience teaches that believers never weary of hearing or reading about Jesus and The Gospel.

We ask you to reflect on your personal standing in the sight of a holy God. These two questions might assist you:

1. Does a holy God see you as 'holy and blameless?'

2. Are you relying on the precious blood that Jesus shed on the Cross for the forgiveness of your sins?

We quote our key verse, Ephesians 1:13 again.

> Ephesians 1:13. NIV. 'You also were included in Christ when you heard the message of truth, the gospel of your salvation.'

As you reflect on your personal standing in the sight of a

holy God, note that in Ephesians 1:13 The Gospel is called 'the message of truth.' So, other messages that contradict The Gospel must be false. Sadly, experience teaches that there is no lack of:

- lies and false ideas preached.

- those who listen to the lies and false ideas because it makes them feel good about the way they live and they can forget about God until the next Sunday.

So, we state again, if you hear and obey The Gospel, it will become 'the gospel of your salvation.' Those are Paul's words in Ephesians 1:13. If you become a believer, how thankful to God you will always be that you personally are 'included in Christ,' because you heard 'the message of truth,' The Gospel.

As Ephesians 5 concludes, we must mention the standard of behaviour that God requires from The Church in this present day. Attaining this standard will not result in anyone receiving God's Salvation as The Church is only composed of believers. But it will result in obedient believers receiving the rewards that God has for them. You would be surprised if God rewarded disobedient believers. As you read the following verses, you will either be doing, or not doing what God requires of you and hence, you will either be an obedient or a disobedient believer. There is no third category.

Submission, Reverence, Love and Respect

Ephesians 5:21-33.

These verses relate to three instructions that need to be carefully considered. Consider Paul's initial instructions. They are printed first. We will comment on the additional words that Paul clearly considered he needed to mention after you have considered his initial instructions:

1. Ephesians 5:21. NIV. 'Submit to one another out of reverence for Christ.'
2. Ephesians 5:22-24. NIV. 'Wives, submit yourselves to your own husbands

   as you do to the Lord. For the husband is the head of the wife as Christ is the head of the church, his body, of which he is the Saviour. Now as the church submits to Christ, so also wives should submit to their husbands in everything.'
3. Ephesians 5:25-33. NIV. 'Husbands, love your wives

   just as Christ loved the church and gave himself up for her to make her holy, cleansing her by the washing with water through the word, and to present her to himself as a radiant church, without stain or wrinkle or any other blemish, but holy and blameless. In this same way, husbands ought to love their wives as their own bodies. He who loves his wife loves himself. After all, no one ever hated their own body, but they feed and care for their body, just as Christ does the church—for we are members of his body. "For this reason a man will leave his father and mother and be united to his wife, and the two will become one flesh." This is a profound mystery—but I am talking about Christ and the church. However, each one of you also must love his wife as he loves himself, and the wife must respect her husband.'

Comments on Ephesians 5:21-33.

The first and foremost matter that applies to all three instructions is Paul's reference to either 'the Lord' or 'Christ.' It will not be long before readers realise that they are learning truths that are based on God's wisdom, and not a man-made religion based upon 'man's wisdom.'

Readers will also realise that believers have no option but to do as Paul instructs them to do if they want to be obedient to God. So, in respect of the first two instructions:

1. Ephesians 5:21. 'believers must submit to one another.'
2. Ephesians 5:22. 'wives must submit to their husbands.'

What does 'submit' mean? The GODS WORD translation states what God requires:

1. 'Place yourselves under each other's authority out of respect for Christ.' Ephesians 5:21. GW.
2. 'Wives, place yourselves under your husbands' authority as you have placed yourselves under the Lord's authority.' Ephesians 5:22. GW.

We ask three questions, the third one applies to wives:

1. Do you try to get your own way, or are you doing what God requires?
2. Will you change and adopt a submissive attitude to other believers because you want to be obedient and respect Christ?
3. Are you willing to place yourself under your husband's authority?

Ephesians 5:22. The Instruction to Wives.

This instruction is skilfully worded. No wife could think it did not apply to her. Paul's example, 'as you do to the Lord,' must apply to every Christian wife, as does his statement, 'the husband is the head of the wife.' The additional words, 'as Christ is the head of the church,' aptly make Paul's statement unarguable.

Wives can choose to be disobedient. This choice is often based on the incorrect view that all Paul's instructions about women in his letters are out of date and can now be ignored in this so-called enlightened world of equality. But this view only considers Ephesians 5:22, and ignores the two quotations in Ephesians 5:21 and Ephesians 5:25.

The three quotations are:

1. Ephesians 5:21. 'Submit to one another.'

2. Ephesians 5:22. 'Wives, submit yourselves to your own husbands.'

3. Ephesians 5:25. 'Husbands, love your wives.'

The instruction to submit applied to wives and the instruction to love applied to husbands. Hence, it really is foolish to conclude that Paul, 'disliked or hated,' women. That foolish conclusion also ignores the wonderful truths that Paul taught all the Ephesian believers in Ephesians 5 about Christ and The Church.

EPHESIANS 6. NIV.

Children, obey your parents in the Lord, for this is right. "Honor your father and mother"--which is the first commandment with a promise- "so that it may go well with you and that you may enjoy long life on the earth." Fathers, do not exasperate your children; instead, bring them up in the training and instruction of the Lord. Slaves, obey your earthly masters with respect and fear, and with sincerity of heart, just as you would obey Christ. Obey them not only to win their favor when their eye is on you, but as slaves of Christ, doing the will of God from your heart. Serve wholeheartedly, as if you were serving the Lord, not people, because you know that the Lord will reward each one for whatever good they do, whether they are slave or free. And masters, treat your slaves in the same way. Do not threaten them, since you know that he who is both their Master and yours is in heaven, and there is no favoritism with him. Finally, be strong in the Lord and in his mighty power. Put on the full armor of God, so that you can take your stand against the devil's schemes. For our struggle is not against flesh and blood, but against the rulers, against the authorities, against the powers of this dark world and against the spiritual forces of evil in the heavenly realms. Therefore put on the full armor of God, so that when the day of evil comes, you may be able to stand your ground, and after you have done everything, to stand. Stand firm then, with the belt of truth buckled around your waist, with the breastplate of righteousness in place, 15. and with your feet fitted with the readiness that comes from the gospel of peace. In addition to all this, take up the shield of faith, with which you can extinguish all the flaming arrows of the evil one. Take the helmet of salvation and the sword of the

Spirit, which is the word of God. And pray in the Spirit on all occasions with all kinds of prayers and requests. With this in mind, be alert and always keep on praying for all the Lord's people. Pray also for me, that whenever I speak, words may be given me so that I will fearlessly make known the mystery of the gospel, for which I am an ambassador in chains. Pray that I may declare it fearlessly, as I should. Tychicus, the dear brother and faithful servant in the Lord, will tell you everything, so that you also may know how I am and what I am doing. I am sending him to you for this very purpose, that you may know how we are, and that he may encourage you. Peace to the brothers and sisters, and love with faith from God the Father and the Lord Jesus Christ. Grace to all who love our Lord Jesus Christ with an undying love. Ephesians 6. NIV.

Commentary: Ephesians 6.

Ephesians 6:1-4. Children, Parents and Fathers

> Ephesians 6:1-4. NIV. 'Children, obey your parents in the Lord, for this is right. "Honor your father and mother"--which is the first commandment with a promise--"so that it may go well with you and that you may enjoy long life on the earth." Fathers, do not exasperate your children; instead, bring them up in the training and instruction of the Lord.'

This is Paul's third reference to 'children.' Paul used this word in both its natural and figurative senses. It is a word that emphasises birth. It is easy to understand that Paul used its natural meaning in Ephesians 6:1, as he referred to both children and parents. However, we have read Paul's figurative use of the word twice in previous chapters and readers should consider which of two specific families they now belong to. We write 'now belong to' because when we were born, we were all born into the same family. However, those 'born again' belong to a new family. Put very simply, which family you now belong to depends upon the number of your birthdays. Those only born once belong to their original family. Those born twice have two birthdays and belong to a new family. As your eternal destiny depends upon whether you have or have not been born again, we quote from the two verses that distinguish the two families:

1. Ephesians 2:3. '... we all .... were by nature the children of wrath, even as others.'
2. Ephesians 5:8. '... children of light.'

Basically, the two families are distinguished by the two words 'wrath' and 'light.' But there is more. Paul wrote about divine wrath and divine light. If you consider the context of these two verses, one notable difference is the way the two families live. Put simply, the first family that we were all born into please themselves how they live. The second family live to please God because they are the children of light.

Note that in Ephesians 2:3 Paul includes himself. His words could not be clearer. He wrote, 'we all.' Paul knew that when he was born, he was one of the children of wrath. His words, '... we all... were by nature the children of wrath, even as others,' tell us why no one needs to be taught how to sin. Sin comes naturally to us. It is part of our nature.

Hence, despite what you might hear preached today, when Paul was instructing the Ephesians to 'live as children of light' he clearly distinguished between those who had been born once, and those who had been born again. Only the children of light could live as God required them to live. It was not possible for the children of wrath to live as God required. So, Paul did not waste his time asking them to do the impossible. If you doubt what we have written, read Ephesians 5 again. Note the pronouns, 'you and them.'

If at this moment you belong to the family that Paul referred to as 'them,' re-read the first nine verses of Ephesians 2 and you will realise that although by nature we were all deserving of God's wrath, you can be saved. God's gift of Salvation can be yours. You can personally experience God's love, mercy and grace when, but only when, in the words of the song we referred to earlier, 'you come as a sinner to Jesus.'

We always refer to God's Word, The Bible, to prove what we write. Before we leave the subject of 'being born again,' you might find it useful to learn the following. It is not a quotation from The Bible, but it does sum up our natural and spiritual births and deaths. It is this:

'Born once, die twice, born twice, die once.

Those familiar with John 3 and John 11 will realise that this short ditty, refers to what the Lord Jesus said when he spoke to Nicodemus about the new birth, and Martha about the resurrection of those who believed in Him.

Children and Parents

These four verses in the ERV could hardly be more simply expressed. In view of the importance of them in the world in which we live we ask you to carefully consider them:

> Ephesians 6:1-4. ERV. 'Children, obey your parents the way the Lord wants, because this is the right thing to do. The command says, "You must respect your father and mother." This is the first command that has a promise with it. And this is the promise: "Then all will go well with you, and you will have a long life on the earth." Fathers, don't make your children angry, but raise them with the kind of teaching and training you learn from the Lord.'   Ephesians 6:1-4. ERV.

The instruction in Ephesians 6:1 is to obey 'your parents.' This includes obedience to the mother. Note that Ephesians 6:5 refers only to 'fathers' as they, rather than mothers, are responsible for discipline.

An interesting matter that we could easily miss is that alongside a quotation from what we know as 'The Ten Commandments' Paul adds an instruction to believers who are fathers. So, we have an instruction from God Himself addressed to Jews and an instruction from Paul addressed to Gentile believers. Paul added to what God said to the Jews. This is not uncommon in The New

Testament. We do not have the space to show you that The Gospel that was so readily rejected by the majority of Jews, found acceptance with a minority of Gentiles. Paul's ministry was primarily to the Gentiles although he sought to preach The Gospel to the Jews whenever he could.

Think carefully before you decide only to read The New Testament. Remember that The Gospel was being preached from The Old Testament long before there was a New Testament. But we do caution against those who teach believers that the blessings God intended for the Jews, His earthly people, are also appropriate for believers. Ephesians 6:3 is a good example of a promise that was only appropriate for the Jews. We quote the actual commandment and the promise:

> Exodus 20:12. NIV. 'Honor your father and your mother, so that you may live long in the land the LORD your God is giving you.' Exodus 20:12. NIV.

God had promised the Jews that they would be given their own land, Canaan, often referred to as 'The Promised Land.' In Exodus 20:12 we read that God added the promise 'so that you may live long in the land the LORD your God is giving you.' The Jews had left Egypt. When God spoke, they were in the Sinai Desert. God's promise would have had great relevance. God's promise had no relevance at all to Gentile believers living in Ephesus, the most important city in present day Turkey. We ask and answer two simple question:

1. When God gave the Jews 'The Ten Commandments,' did obedient Jewish children live longer than disobedient Jewish children? 'Yes.' The penalty for disobedience was death. Read Deuteronomy 21:18-21.

2. Could believing Ephesian children who were obedient to their believing parents expect to live a long life? "No."

The wonderful promise of 'The Gospel of God' is forgiveness for sin, power over sin, absence from the presence of sin in Heaven, eternal life, a new spiritual nature and the indwelling of God's Holy Spirit. Sinners receive these blessings immediately they accept the gift of God's Salvation. But, there are no promises in, 'The Gospel of God,' relating to material benefits. Jesus set out the consequences of discipleship. Read Luke 14:27. ERV.

> "Whoever will not carry the cross that is given to them when they follow me cannot be my follower."

When some have a problem they say, 'This is the cross I have to bear.' The people listening to Jesus knew what He meant. A man carrying a cross was walking to the place where the Romans would crucify him.

Jesus never promised a long, healthy and successful life. Then as now, the political and religious world had no time for Jesus, His followers or The Gospel. The Jewish religious rulers were determined to eradicate anything connected with Jesus. Read Acts to ascertain the extent of their hatred and the problems they caused believers.

Hence, we repeat our caution against those teachers who refer to God's promises to His earthly people and teach that they are available to believers. Experience teaches that many believers have backslidden because they think that God has let them down. They did not receive the material blessings they were taught to expect. God has not let them down. They believed false and silly teaching.

'Fathers, stop provoking your children to anger ...'

Ephesians 6:4

Our heading is from Wuest's translation. The NIV states, 'Fathers, do not exasperate your children ...' Paul gave no examples but it would be foolish to think that he referred to the rare behaviour of one or two fathers. Although we have no examples of what should not happen, we have positive instructions as to what should happen. Ephesians 6:1 and Ephesians 6:4 refer to 'the Lord.' We like the ERV translation of these verses because it stresses the importance of relying upon the Lord for guidance:

Ephesians 6:1. ERV. 'Children, obey your parents the way the Lord wants, because this is the right thing to do.'

Ephesians 6:4. ERV. 'Fathers, don't make your children angry, but raise them with the kind of teaching and training you learn from the Lord.'

These verses do not suggest that believers should read a book on how families should behave, even one written by a believer. We see the connection between these verses. It is for the parents to learn 'what the Lord wants,' and for the parents to teach the children what they themselves, 'learn from the Lord.' Hence, 'training' follows 'teaching.' The Lord wants to be involved in believers' family lives.

Slaves and Masters

We know from Acts 20 that Paul spent three years in Ephesus preaching and teaching. As you can read in 1Corinthians 19:5-9, it was during his time in Ephesus that he wrote to the Corinthians. Historians tell us that Corinth was the chief city in Greece with an estimated population of 650,000 and almost two-thirds were slaves. We do not know how many slaves there were in the Corinthian Church, but from what Paul wrote in 1Corinthians, it seems that many were slaves.

> 1Corinthians 1:26-29. ERV. 'Brothers and sisters, God chose you to be his. Think about that! Not many of you were wise in the way the world judges wisdom. Not

> many of you had great influence, and not many of you came from important families. But God chose the foolish things of the world to shame the wise. He chose the weak things of the world to shame the strong. And God chose what the world thinks is not important--what the world hates and thinks is nothing. He chose these to destroy what the world thinks is important. God did this so that no one can stand before him and boast about anything.'   1Corinthians 1:26-29. ERV.

Instructions for Slaves

We know from history that slavery was customary in Paul's day. It had existed for centuries. Whatever their awful plight, Paul had instructions for believers who were slaves.

> Ephesians 6:5-7. ERV. 'Slaves, obey your masters here on earth with fear and respect. And do this with a heart that is true, just as you obey Christ. You must do this not just to please your masters while they are watching, but all the time. Since you are really slaves of Christ, you must do with all your heart what God wants. Do your work, and be happy to do it. Work as though it is the Lord you are serving, not just an earthly master.'   Ephesians 6:5-7. ERV.

If you saw slaves and knew that only two were believers, you should be able to identify them. When we read Ephesians 6:5-7 we note that these principles apply to all employed believers. So, if you are the only believer in your place of work, it should be easy to identify you.

The Christian Principle of, 'Doing Good Works.'

We have been considering the obligations of believing slaves. We shall shortly consider the obligations of believing masters. Humanly speaking, an irreconcilable gulf separated slaves and masters. Only God's Gospel and Salvation dealt with slaves and masters on equal terms. It appears from 1Corinthians 1:26-29 that those who responded to The Gospel and received God's Salvation were more likely to be slaves than masters.

Ephesians 6:8 not only separates God's instructions to slaves and masters, but if taken out of context, it could be completely misunderstood. It is a good example of:

- the necessity of reading verses in their context.
- the foolishness of taking verses out of their context to prove this or that alleged truth or doctrine.

We quote the verse in isolation so that you will understand the reason for our caution:

> Ephesians 6:8. NIV. 'because you know that the Lord will reward each one for whatever good they do, whether they are slave or free.'   Ephesians 6:8. NIV.

Ephesians 6:8 begins with the word 'because.' What follows must relate to what has been written and so, the words 'each one' can only apply to believers. Space limits a full discussion of this but it is clear in Ephesians 6:5 that the words 'earthly masters' tell us that the slaves also had a 'Heavenly Master.' Hence, in Ephesians 6:5-7 we read:

- 'just as you would obey Christ.'
- 'as slaves of Christ, doing the will of God …'
- 'as if you were serving the Lord, not people.'

Paul had already made it crystal clear that:

- we cannot do good works to be saved.
- God's rewards are only for believers' good works.

Read Ephesians 2:8-10 and you will understand why God takes no account of the good works that unbelievers do.

> Ephesians 2:8-9. NIV. 'For it is by grace you have been saved, through faith--and this is not from yourselves, it is the gift of God--not by works, so that no one can boast. Ephesians 2:8-9. NIV.

Introduction to Instructions for Masters

Did you note that in the verses quoted from 1Corinthians we read the words 'not many' three times?

How many high-ranking and educated believers must have been thankful to God for their Salvation. It might be true that 'not many' were saved, but it does not say 'not any.' The Gospel is for anyone and everyone everywhere. God's Salvation is available to all. Hence, the repeated word, 'whoever,' in The Gospel of John. Sadly, few receive God's Salvation. Paul wrote more of 'The New Testament' than any other writer, but he was not the first to tell us that The Gospel will always have a better reception among those regarded as 'the nobodies,' the people who are:

- regarded as unimportant.
- overlooked.
- exploited.
- abused.

The Gospel will always have a worse reception among 'the somebodies.'

- The rich and famous.
- Those considered well-educated.
- The high and mighty.

We have used modern expressions to prepare you for the following verses. Read Jesus' words about two groups of people. Note that only one group willingly listened to John the Baptist and Jesus as they preached The Gospel.

And because we know that many people rely upon their religion for God's Salvation, we suggest that while you are reading Jesus' words, you also consider what John the Baptist and Jesus thought about their religious rulers.

It never ceases to amaze us that so many people ignore God's Word, The Bible, but are willing to rely for their eternal futures upon what churchmen say.

> Luke 16:13-15. GNB: "You cannot serve both God and money." When the Pharisees heard all this, they made fun of Jesus, because they loved money. Jesus said to them, "You are the ones who make yourselves look right in other people's sight, but God knows your hearts. For the things that are considered of great value by people are worth nothing in God's sight."
>
> Matthew 11:2-5. GNB: 'John heard about the things that Christ was doing, he sent some of his disciples to him. "Tell us," they asked Jesus, "are you the one John said was going to come, or should we expect someone else?" Jesus answered, "Go back and tell John what you are hearing and seeing: the blind can see, the lame can walk, those who suffer from dreaded skin diseases are made clean, the deaf hear, the dead are brought back to life, and the Good News is preached to the poor." Matthew 11:2-5. GNB.
>
> Luke 4:16-19. GNB: 'Jesus .... unrolled the scroll and found the place where it is written, "The Spirit of the Lord is upon me, because he has chosen me to bring good news to the poor. He has sent me to proclaim

liberty to the captives and recovery of sight to the blind, to set free the oppressed and announce that the time has come when the Lord will save his people."'

Mark 12:37-40. NIV: 'A large crowd was listening to Jesus gladly. As he taught them, he said, "Watch out for the teachers of the Law, who like to walk around in their long robes and be greeted with respect in the marketplace, who choose the reserved seats in the synagogues and the best places at feasts. They take advantage of widows and rob them of their homes, and then make a show of saying long prayers. Their punishment will be all the worse!"'

Matthew 21:23-32. NIV: 'Jesus entered the temple courts, and, while he was teaching, the chief priests and the elders of the people came to him. "By what authority are you doing these things?" they asked. "And who gave you this authority?" Jesus replied, "I will also ask you one question. If you answer me, I will tell you by what authority I am doing these things. John's baptism--where did it come from? Was it from heaven, or of human origin?" They discussed it among themselves and said, "If we say, 'From heaven,' he will ask, 'Then why didn't you believe him?' But if we say, 'Of human origin'--we are afraid of the people, for they all hold that John was a prophet." So they answered Jesus, "We don't know." Then he said, "Neither will I tell you by what authority I am doing these things. For John came to you to show you the way of righteousness, and you did not believe him, but the tax collectors and the prostitutes did. And even after you saw this, you did not repent and believe him.'

Experience teaches that the important truths mentioned in the above verses are not well-known, even by those who are regarded as 'churchgoers.' May we ask you to re-read these verses and familiarise yourself with them before reading on. The last six lines are especially important as they show both the inherent power in The Gospel to change lives and the division that occurs whenever The Gospel is preached. Note this division carefully.

We quote the words that Jesus said the chief priests and the elders of the people:

- "you did not believe him, but the tax collectors and the prostitutes did."
- "even after you saw this, you did not repent and believe him.'

We emphasise Jesus vital words:

- "you did not believe."
- "you did not repent and believe."
- "the tax collectors and the prostitutes did."

This division, 'did not' and 'did,' results in an eternity in either Heaven or an eternity in The Lake of Fire. Can you think of anything that is more important to you than your eternal bliss or eternal punishment? And it all depends on whether or not you repented and believed The Gospel.

God's Salvation - A Special Request

This special request is for readers who are either:

1. relying for Salvation on their religion and its teaching.
2. rejecting Salvation because they want God to prove that The Gospel is the only way to Heaven.

Over many years of being involved in the preaching of The Gospel we have personally experienced those who have rejected it, and even seen those who have joked and laughed about it. We are aware of some of the reasons for these negative responses. In this section of the book we request those who have rejected The Gospel for any reason to reread the verses we have quoted above.

How sad it is that people hear The Gospel, but reject it for this or that reason. If only they realised that in rejecting The Gospel, they choose to spend eternity in Hell.

If you are not yet a believer, we request that you re-read the verses we have quoted above.

1. If you are relying on religion for your Salvation, we are sure you will agree with us that Jesus was scathing of the Pharisees and the religious hierarchy of His day. Maybe it is the first time that you have read about the contemptuous way Jesus spoke to religious people. He certainly did not equate them with 'the truth.' Hence, in reading this book, you will have noted that we have not asked you to become religious, or to change your religion. To be blunt, we are not interested in religion. We only want to present you with God's Word, The Bible, and give you suggestions for your thoughtful consideration of The Gospel, the only way to Heaven.

2. If you are waiting for a miracle, one thing you might have missed in the above verses is this. The religious people saw a miracle but they still rejected The Gospel. The miracle involved two groups who heard The Gospel:

    (i) The tax collectors were treacherous Jews who had agreed to work for the occupying Romans. They collected taxes from their own people and paid them to the occupying enemy.

    (ii) The prostitutes. You can imagine what the religious people thought about them.

The tax collectors and the prostitutes heard The Gospel preached by John the Baptist. They believed it. It totally changed their lives. That was the miracle the Pharisees saw. They ignored it. That same miracle occurs whenever 'a Hell deserving sinner' becomes a child of God. Being born again is a miracle. Unbelievers see the changes that occur in the lifestyles of those who are saved. Regrettably, unbelievers still prefer their existing lifestyle. They do not want to repent and be born again into God's family.

Ephesians 6:9. Instructions for Masters

> Ephesians 6:9. NIV. 'And masters, treat your slaves in the same way. Do not threaten them, since you know that he who is both their Master and yours is in heaven, and there is no favoritism with him.' Ephesians 6:9. NIV.

A point worth considering. Unbelievers can be reformed by various means, but only God's Salvation changes lives. God's Salvation changes unbelievers. Only by repenting and believing The Gospel can unbelievers become believers who are indwelt by The Holy Spirit. Hence, being reformed and becoming a believer are totally different.

When Paul used the word 'master' he did not refer to the owners of businesses that had employees. Paul was referring to slave owners. However, you will find nothing in The New Testament to suggest that believing slave owners should release their slaves, or that believing slaves join with unbelieving slaves and start a political campaign for freedom. But what you do find is the instructions in Ephesians 6:8-9. Can you imagine the change that would take place in the slave owner's household when he became a believer?

The words 'in the same way' connect the last instruction in Ephesians 6:8 to Ephesians 6:9.

'The Lord will reward everyone for whatever good he does whether he is slave or free.' Ephesians 6:9. NIV.

There is no partiality with God. He looks only at our hearts.

We judge that there would be fewer masters than slaves in the Ephesian Church, but there were obviously some masters as Paul wrote instructions to them.

You know your own character and how you deal with people. If you were a slave master in Roman times, would:

- it make you proud that you were of a superior class?
- you be harsh with your slaves?

Many readers will be either employers or employees. If we apply what we have read about masters and slaves to ourselves, do 'our good deeds' mark us out as believers?

Ephesians 6:10-17. God's Armour

> Ephesians: 6:10-17. KJV/AV. 'Finally, my brethren, be strong in the Lord, and in the power of his might. Put on the whole armour of God, that ye may be able to stand against the wiles of the devil. For we wrestle not against flesh and blood, but against principalities, against powers, against the rulers of the darkness of this world, against spiritual wickedness in high places. Wherefore take unto you the whole armour of God, that ye may be able to withstand in the evil day, and having done all, to stand. Stand therefore, having your loins girt about with truth, and having on the breastplate of righteousness; And your feet shod with the preparation of the gospel of peace; Above all, taking the shield of faith, wherewith ye shall be able to quench all the fiery darts of the wicked. And take the helmet of salvation, and the sword of the Spirit, which is the word of God.'   Ephesians: 6:10-17. AV/KJV.

We have quoted from the King James Version, known to most of us as the Authorised Version, as this translation will be familiar to many.

To bring Paul's words up-to-date, we also quote the Good News Bible. In view of the importance of this matter, reading both translations will emphasise how essential it is for believers to be prepared for the Devil's attacks upon them. The GNB states:

Ephesians 6:10-17. GNB. '... Build up your strength in union with the Lord and by means of his mighty power. Put on all the armor that God gives you, so that you will be able to stand up against the Devil's evil tricks. For we are not fighting against human beings but against the wicked spiritual forces in the heavenly world, the rulers, authorities, and cosmic powers of this dark age. So put on God's armor now! Then when the evil day comes, you will be able to resist the enemy's attacks; and after fighting to the end, you will still hold your ground. So stand ready, with truth as a belt tight around your waist, with righteousness as your breastplate, and as your shoes the readiness to announce the Good News of peace. At all times carry faith as a shield; for with it you will be able to put out all the burning arrows shot by the Evil One. And accept salvation as a helmet, and the word of God as the sword which the Spirit gives you.'

For the sake of completion, we also quote Ephesians 6:18 from the GNB. It puts Ephesians 6:10-17 in its context:

Ephesians 6:18. GNB: 'Do all this in prayer, asking for God's help. Pray on every occasion, as the Spirit leads. For this reason keep alert and never give up; pray always for all God's people.'

It is essential that we emphasise that we are reading about the protection that God provides for every believer. God does not expect (so neither should we) believers to provide their own protection against both evil, and the evil beings that want to see believers defeated. Regrettably, for one reason or another, some believers have surrendered to evil and this should be a warning to us.

Paul did not write these words of warning because he thought that every now and again believers would be under attack. Read the verses again and you will realise that believers must always be on their guard. So, believers have been supplied with all they need to defend themselves continuously.

Note that believers must defend themselves. They must not expect God, their local church, or other believers to defend them. Some believers appear to be strong and others weak, but these words were written to all believers.

We repeat that God provides every believer with all they need to successfully defeat sin and Satan. In the AV, Ephesians 6:10 reads,

'be strong in the Lord, and in the power of his might.'

We know that you will agree with us that there is nothing that suggests weakness in these words. There can be no ambiguity as to the meaning of, 'strong, power and might.' We state without hesitation that you will:

- never fail if you do what Ephesians 6:10-17 teaches.
- fail if you do not do what Ephesians 6:10-17 teaches.

Ephesians 6:11 tells us why God has provided believers with all the protection they need. Paul referred to it as 'the whole armour of God.' God wants you personally to be able to 'stand.' If you do not use the protection provided by God, you will be defeated. You will 'fall over.' Whatever your own view of yourself is, you will not be able to defeat evil in your own strength. You are dealing with a crafty Devil who knows how to bring believers down and ruin their testimonies. We have known believers we regarded as strong brought down by evil. Their ruined testimony ended their once valuable Christian service. The Devil hates believers and wants to destroy their testimonies. It makes sense to take out those who are the strongest first because, humanly speaking, only taking out the weak will make no difference.

We now consider the armour that God provides to all believers. Paul does not write about it sequentially and we comment on what he wrote in the order he chose to use. Note that you are reading about total protection, and that means protection without weaknesses. It is obvious that the Devil will attack your weaknesses first.

Belt

This belt refers to truth. Note that the belt had to be 'tight around your waist.' What was the 'truth' Paul referred to? Was it the opposite of deceit, or does it have another meaning? We have noted in Ephesians that Paul used the word 'truth' to mean 'doctrine.' We like to think of the 'belt that is tight around a believer's waist,' as both honesty and doctrine. We would not expect believers who made sure that the Christian doctrine was tight about their waist to be less than totally honest. Likewise, you would not expect a dishonest believer to care much about Christian doctrine.

Breastplate

This breastplate represents personal righteousness. Never confuse righteousness with Bible knowledge. The Lord Jesus Christ said,

"Now that you know this truth, how happy you will be if you put it into practice!" John 13:17.

It has been said before and it is true. The more you know of God and His Word, the more He will expect of you.

Shoes

Nothing in The New Testament suggests that believers should hide themselves away from the world. If they did, how could the world be evangelised? In Paul's day, believers travelled long distances to proclaim The Gospel and they needed good footwear. Paul mentioned 'shoes' as believers must always be ready to proclaim The Gospel. Paul described it as 'The Gospel of Peace.'

The Gospel of Peace

We need to be frank once again. If you are an unbeliever, there cannot be peace between God and you. Your sins have not been forgiven. God can only regard you as His enemy. We do not have the space to prove this to you from The Bible in this book, but we can tell you that until you become a believer you will never:

- have peace with God.
- know the peace of God in your life.

Because you belong to the Devil, you will, unlike believers, never experience his attacks.

If you are concluding that a believer's life is not as easy as an unbeliever's life, you are correct. But we can tell you that in well over half a century, we have met many believers from many countries, and however difficult a believer's life can be, we have never met a believer who wanted to revert to being an unbeliever. But it is not just our personal experience that we mention to you.

Even a cursory reading of The New Testament will prove to you that although unbelievers have an easier life now, their eternal future is awful. Believers, on the other hand, experience the Devil's attacks now, but their eternal future is in Heaven, God's Home. If you are not a believer, those responsible for this book tell you that they would not exchange places with you.

Shield

Unlike the other items mentioned, except a sword, a shield is carried and not worn. This shield represents faith. Re-read Ephesians 6:16 because we ask a question.

Question: Did Paul mean a believer's personal faith or The Christian Faith?

Answer: Some translators use the term 'The Christian Faith' but we support those translators who consider that Paul wrote about a believer's personal faith. Clearly that would also include their personal faith in 'The Christian Faith.' Hence, we would suggest that Paul referred to 'their personal faith, and their faith in The Christian Faith.'

There is no doubt that the tenor of The New Testament is that following their Salvation, believers need to be taught God's Word, The Bible. We do not have the space to elaborate on this but we doubt that any believers who read this book would disagree that only some believers have the gift of teaching. If some are teaching spiritual truths, others must need to learn them. Experience teaches that a working knowledge of The Bible is an excellent shield for warding off the Devil's attacks. The more you know of The Bible, the harder it will be for the Devil's servants to mislead you. You will instinctively know when you hear or read something that contradicts what The Bible teaches.

We have met unbelievers who believe religious myths that would embarrass the writers of children's fairy story books. If you are a believer, your best protection against the false doctrines that the Devil's servants preach, and doctrinal error in general, is to make time to study your Bible.

Helmet

It would be unusual for those engaged in warfare not to be wearing protective headwear. The translators vary as to how they describe a believer's headwear for instance:

GNB: 'accept salvation as a helmet ...'

NLT: 'put on salvation as your helmet ...'

We like the wording of the Contemporary English Version. It reads: 'let God's saving power be like a helmet ...'

Believers have accepted God's saving power, His Gift of Salvation. They must use 'God's saving power' to protect themselves from the Devil's attacks.

Sword

Regrettably, some believers reject the view that believers are engaged in warfare. They refuse to sing hymns such as, 'Onward Christian Soldiers,' and spiritual songs that refer to 'marching' and the like. Do they erroneously think that the hymns and spiritual songs refer to warfare with unbelievers? Why do they not sing hymns and spiritual songs that refer to warfare against evil forces?

Correctly reading God's Word, The Bible, eliminates silly notions. Paul could not have made it clearer. Read Ephesians 6:12. We quote the GNB:

'For we are not fighting against human beings but against the wicked spiritual forces in the heavenly world, the rulers, authorities, and cosmic powers of this dark age.'

Consider the word, 'sword.' Paul also used it in Romans 13 when he referred to the punishment of wrongdoers. He wrote that the one in authority does not bear the sword for nothing. It is obvious that a sword is an instrument of death. The sword in Romans 13 refers to the execution of wrongdoers. The sword in Ephesians 6 refers to God's Word. Use it to ensure that false doctrine, or anything else that would destroy your spiritual life is rendered 'lifeless.'

False doctrine often relates to Jesus:

- It demeans Jesus.
- It detracts from or adds to the Salvation that Jesus died to procure for undeserving sinners.

Whenever you come across those who believe and spread false doctrine, you should 'kill it' and instantly introduce them to Jesus and The Gospel. They might never have heard what you are able to tell them about Jesus and The Gospel. But if they will not accept what The Bible teaches, you will not be responsible for their eternal punishment.

Believers must be proactive. They cannot rely upon other believers to defend them or eliminate the false doctrine that an evil crafty Devil will use to defeat and overthrow every unprepared and unprotected believer.

Ephesians 6:12. Spiritual Wickedness In High Places

We mentioned earlier that we would consider 'the place' from where those who control wickedness govern the Earth, and in particular mankind. Unfortunately, many were brought up believing that Heaven, God's Home, is above us, and Hell, the Devil's home, is below us. We had no reason to question whether this was right or wrong.

As we are considering a specific letter that Paul wrote, we cannot mention what The Bible teaches about sin, evil, spiritual wickedness and the Devil, but as Ephesians 6:12 mentions 'spiritual wickedness in high places,' we need to spend time considering it.

Wuest gives us an accurate translation of Ephesians 6:12 but some of the words used are not in common use. Wuest's Expanded Translation is unlike other translations. They translate the original language into understandable English. To assist readers, we also quote GODS WORD:

Ephesians 6:12. Wuest. 'hold your ground against the strategems of the devil, because our wrestling is not against blood and flesh, but against the principalities, against the authorities, against the world rulers of this darkness, against spirit forces of perniciousness in the heavenly places.' Ephesians 6:12. Wuest.

Ephesians 6:12. GW: 'This is not a wrestling match against a human opponent. We are wrestling with

---

> rulers, authorities, the powers who govern this world of darkness, and spiritual forces that control evil in the heavenly world.' Ephesians 6:12. GW.

When we read Wuest, we realise the power and authority that evil has in this world. Without 'God's Armour' to protect them, believers would not stand a chance of surviving the onslaughts of the Devil and his evil servants.

'In The Heavenly Realms'

Translators use expressions such as 'heavenly places' and 'heavenly world' when translating Ephesians 6:12. We quote the NIV and use the world 'realms' as previously as we continue our commentary on 'the heavenly realms.'

> Ephesians 6:11-12. NIV. 'Put on the full armor of God, so that you can take your stand against the devil's schemes. For our struggle is not against flesh and blood, but against the rulers, against the authorities, against the powers of this dark world and against the spiritual forces of evil in the heavenly realms.'

'The heavenly realms' in Ephesians 6:12 is where the spiritual forces of evil implement the Devil's schemes against believers. This might surprise readers as this is Paul's fifth reference to 'the heavenly realms' in Ephesians and the only time 'evil' is mentioned.

The four previous references, quoted from the NIV, are:

1. Ephesians 1:3. 'Praise be to the God and Father of our Lord Jesus Christ, who has blessed us 'in the heavenly realms' with every spiritual blessing in Christ.'

2. Ephesians 1:20. 'he exerted when he raised Christ from the dead and seated him at his right hand 'in the heavenly realms.'

3. Ephesians 2:6. 'And God raised us up with Christ and seated us with him 'in the heavenly realms' in Christ Jesus.'

4. Ephesians 3:10. 'His intent was that now, through the church, the manifold wisdom of God should be made known to the rulers and authorities 'in the heavenly realms.''

Note that twice in Ephesians Paul mentioned 'heaven and earth.' We have already commented on these verses:

1. Ephesians 1:10. '... to bring unity to all things in heaven and on earth under Christ.'

2. Ephesians 3:15. '... from whom every family in heaven and on earth derives its name.'

When Paul did not also refer to Earth, he only once mentioned 'Heaven.' He wrote to the masters of slaves:

Ephesians 6:9. NIV. '... since you know that he who is both their Master and yours is in heaven ...'

We would not disagree with those who think that as 'in,' in the original language, denotes a 'fixed position in place, time, or state,' 'in Heaven' in Ephesians 6:9 is God's home.

Note that it is only in Ephesians that Paul referred to 'the heavenly realms,' and Ephesians is the only book in The Bible that mentions 'the heavenly realms.'

For the sake of completeness, we state that:

- 'Earth' is mentioned seven hundred and thirty-nine times in The Bible. Sixteen of these were written by Paul, including the three verses in Ephesians mentioned above.

- 'Heaven' is mentioned seven hundred and thirty-nine times in The Bible, sixteen were written by Paul, including the three in Ephesians mentioned above.

- 'World' is mentioned two hundred and sixty-one times in The Bible. Fifty-four were written by Paul, including the four in Ephesians that we have commented on.

We can calculate the usage of the names 'Earth,' 'Heaven' and 'world' in The Bible. Paul mentioned all three in his thirteen New Testament letters. Hence, we can state with certainty that Paul not only made a distinction between 'Earth,' 'Heaven' and 'world', he also made a distinction between them and 'the heavenly realms.' So, what did Paul refer to when he mentioned 'the heavenly realms?'

So readers will have some background knowledge about what The Bible says about Earth, Heaven and the world, we leave Ephesians 6 to provide a brief overview of them.

We read in Genesis1:1 that 'The Creation Story' begins:

'In the beginning God created the heavens and the earth.'

This story is uncomplicated so we can understand it, as no one could ever comprehend what God did to create what we can see, yet know little about, what we cannot see but know exists, and what we will never know anything about.

God existed before Creation. God is eternal. Genesis 2:4 refers to 'the Lord God.' 'Lord' means 'without beginning or end.' The Old Testament records God confirming that He speaks to His creatures from Heaven.

But we must never forget that The Bible only discloses what need to know, and little is disclosed about Heaven. The few disclosures that we do have indicate that until Satan is cast into The Lake of Fire, he has access to God. Consider what we learn about Satan in Job 1:6-7 and the references to Heaven and Satan and his angels in Revelations. We quote from the NIV:

- 'One day the angels came to present themselves before the LORD, and Satan also came with them. The LORD said to Satan, "Where have you come from?" Satan answered the LORD, "From roaming throughout the earth, going back and forth on it." Job 1:6-7.

- 'Then war broke out in heaven. Michael and his angels fought against the dragon, and the dragon and his angels fought back. Revelations 12:7.

- 'The great dragon was hurled down—that ancient serpent called the devil, or Satan, who leads the whole world astray. He was hurled to the earth, and his angels with him.' Revelations 12:9.

- 'And the devil, who deceived them, was thrown into the lake of burning sulfur, where the beast and the false prophet had been thrown. They will be tormented day and night for ever and ever.' Revelations 20:10.

In the original language, the expression 'in the heavenly realms' is 'in the heavenly.' The AMPC translation prints words in italics, brackets and fainter print if they are added:

- to make the original language lucid in English.
- inferred in the original language.

In Ephesians 1:20 in the AMPC Translation reads:

'Which He exerted in Christ when He raised Him from the dead and seated Him at His [own] right hand in the heavenly [places]' Ephesians 1:20. AMPC.

The more popular translations use 'heavenly' but add the words 'realms' 'world' and 'kingdom.' Unfortunately, if the plural is not used, readers could believe that 'the heavenlies' are an actual place such as 'Earth.' Hence 'realms,' and 'places,' are unlikely to mislead. 'World' and 'kingdom' are.

Paul wanted the Ephesian believers to know that there are realms where The Lord Jesus Christ and His Church are together. Because all believers are part of The Church, they were with The Lord Jesus Christ. Paul also wanted them to know that God had a purpose in The Lord Jesus Christ and His Church being in the heavenly realms.

God's Purpose and The Church

God wanted all the rulers and powers in the heavenly realms to know the many different ways He displayed His wisdom, and The Church would make His wisdom known. So, the Ephesian believers were informed by Paul that:

- they are in the heavenly realms, blessed with every spiritual blessing in Christ.
- God raised Christ from the dead, and seated Him at His own right hand in the heavenly realms.
- because they are a part of Christ, when God raised Him from death to life, He also raised them from death to life, and He seated them with Christ in the heavenly realms.
- they are The Church that is in the heavenly realms with Christ and, as The Church, they make God's wisdom known to the rulers and authorities there.

The Heavenly Realms and The Full Armour of God

The wonderful privilege of being in the heavenly realms with Christ still requires believers to put on the full armour of God or they will not be able to stand their ground against the Devil's evil schemes.

Believers have four evil opponents who are involved in the Devil's schemes. Three of them, the rulers, the authorities and the powers are in 'this dark world' and the fourth, 'the spiritual forces of evil.' operates in the heavenly realms. Paul clearly warns believers that only the full armour of God will protect them from the evil of their four opponents.

If you are not yet a believer, you might wonder if it is prudent being a believer because you conclude that if you become a believer, you will also become a target for the Devil's evil attacks. As your conclusion would be correct, we earnestly suggest that you spend time considering the first three references in Ephesians to 'the heavenly realms.' We also ask believers to do the same because as you read these three words in their context, you will discover wonderful divine truths:

1. Ephesians 1: 3-8.
2. Ephesians 1:19-20.
3. Ephesians 2:1-8.

You will discover that:

- believers have every spiritual blessing in Christ.
- God's incomparably great power is for believers.
- believers sit with Christ at God's right hand.

Reading these truths explains why believers praise and thank God for His wonderful Salvation, and for sending His One and Only Son, Jesus, to this world to make His Salvation possible for anyone and everyone, anywhere willing to repent and accept Jesus as their Saviour.

If you are not yet a believer, may we remind you of Jesus' own words. We hear them at some funeral services but they need to be heeded by those who are alive and want to know 'the way to Heaven.' Jesus' message is in the simplest of words. It is unambiguous and only a few words have more than four letters. Jesus said:

"'I am the way and the truth and the life. No one comes to the Father except through me.'" John 14:6. NIV.

Ephesians 6:12. (Continued)

Although The Bible mentions so little about Satan, the Devil, and the forces of evil, or where evil is controlled or operates from, Ephesians 6:12 lists believers' adversaries, states what or who they are, and names the places they control. The translators, although they use different words, seem agreed as to the meaning of this verse. We quote Ephesians 6:12 again, from the NIV and the NLT, so that you can compare the words used by the translators. Doing this will make you even more aware that believers must defend themselves from these powerful adversaries with all the armour that God has provided to all believers.

> Ephesians 6:12.
>
> NIV: 'For our struggle is not against flesh and blood, but against the rulers, against the authorities, against the powers of this dark world and against the spiritual forces of evil in the heavenly realms.'
>
> NLT: 'For we are not fighting against flesh-and-blood enemies, but against evil rulers and authorities of the unseen world, against mighty powers in this dark world, and against evil spirits in the heavenly places.'

What do we know about a believer's enemies? They:

- are spirits, powerful rulers, authorities and powers.
- operate is the dark, unseen world.

Although we might not know where the heavenly places are, we are warned that a believer's enemies are:

- 'the spiritual forces of evil in the heavenly realms.' NIV.
- 'evil spirits in the heavenly places.' NLT.

Satan, also known as The Devil, and Evil

When you become a believer, you are immediately aware of the evil that exists all around you and the Devil appears to be in total control of everything. This was not obvious when you were an unbeliever but when you became a believer, you were instantly indwelt by The Holy Spirit. So:

- You instinctively knew right from wrong.
- What you once did instinctively you stopped doing.
- God's Salvation gave you power over sin.

Before you became a believer:

- sin had power over you.
- you did the Devil's bidding. He was your master.

You did not know it, but you were the Devil's slave, a slave to sin. Read Wuest's translation of Ephesians 6:12 again:

'our wrestling is not against blood and flesh, but against the principalities, against the authorities, against the world rulers of this darkness, against spirit forces of perniciousness in the heavenly places.' Ephesians 6:12.

The world's evil is not controlled by human beings, no matter how evil they and their organisations are.

God's armour can repel the Devil and evil. The Ephesian believers were taught the necessity of putting on all the armour that had God supplied. We need to emphasise that God did not put His armour on them. They had a choice. Then, as now, it would be a very foolish believer who failed to put on all God's armour.

Do you want to stand your ground when the Devil chooses to attack you, and with whatever scheme he has devised to get you to sin and ruin your testimony?

- Believers must constantly wear all of God's armour to repel evil. Evil will choose when to attack. God's armour is for putting on and keeping on.
- All believers must wear God's armour. It is not for a specially selected few that we might consider will be prone to attack. The elders wear the same armour as the newly saved.

Experience teaches that the world of evil is exceptionally

well organised and successful. We are reading words written 2000 years ago, but they are still valid and wise.

Believers never forget that the day is coming when the Devil and his associates will be cast into The Lake of Fire. Evils end gets closer every day. We ask a question.

Question: As the end of evil gets closer every day, is that the reason why evil works so hard against believers?

Answer: We cannot give a positive answer but we do know that The Bible teaches that the Devil was eternally defeated at Calvary when Jesus died so that all who repent and accept Him as their Saviour can be saved from the penalty, the power, and the presence of sin.

Further, Jesus' resurrection justified believer. God sees them 'just as if they had never sinned.' Jesus' resurrection also destroyed Satan's power over death. Because Jesus died and was resurrected, believers who die before Jesus comes again will also be resurrected. The Holy Spirit indwells believers and He can never die. His presence within believers guarantees that they have eternal life and they will live again for eternity.

Believers who have been saved for many years will probably agree with us that evil is more evident today than when we first believed but believers know that they have been saved from the power and the penalty of sin, but not from the presence of sin. This will not happen until believers are in Heaven where there is no sin. Until then, they have God's armour to ward off the attacks that Satan and evil have strategically planned for them. We ask an important question because it will make every believer consider the provision that God has for each one of them.

Question: When God has provided all believers needs to 'stand firm' and stay faithful to Him, why would they seek to fight evil with their own resources?

God's Five Pieces Of Armour for The Believer

Because of its importance, we list God's armour for the believer. If you are a believer, it is God's protection for you.

1. Belt of Truth - Ephesians 6:14.
2. Breastplate of Faith - Ephesians 6:14.
3. Shoes - Ephesians 6:15.
4. Shield of Faith - Ephesians 6:16.
5. Helmet of Salvation - Ephesians 6:17.

Ephesians 6:18. Pray, Watch, and Persevere.

Ephesians 6:18 mentioned these three practices that will also protect believers from the Devil's onslaughts. When you consider them, only the second one related solely to a time of warfare. So that an enemy did not take an army by surprise, lookouts were a 'must have.'

Paul mentioned prayer before lookouts and perseverance. Consider Matthew 26:36-45. It records Jesus' words when He knew that His enemies would soon arrive to arrest Him. In the context of a believer's enemies at a time of danger, Jesus' words are so meaningful:

'Then Jesus went with His disciples to a place called Gethsemane .... He said to them .... "Stay here and keep watch with Me" .... Then He returned to His disciples and found them sleeping. "Could you men not keep watch with me for one hour?" .... Watch and pray so that you will not fall into temptation. The spirit is willing, but the body is weak." .... "Rise, let us go! Here comes my betrayer!"

Instead of keeping watch and praying, the disciples fell asleep. Jesus associated their failure with the danger of falling into temptation. The disciples were tired, and you might think justly so, but they failed to persevere and stay awake at a time of danger. Jesus required them to watch and pray. His words, "The spirit is willing, but the body is weak," prove that believers are weak. Believers must admit this. They must realise that they are indwelt by God the Holy Spirit and that prayer makes weak believers strong. Praying would also have kept the disciples awake.

Believers need to pray and persevere in keeping a constant lookout for a tireless enemy who will strike at any time to destroy them. He will know when they are not wearing God's armour or praying.

Ephesians 6:18-19. Paul's Closing Requests

> Ephesians 6:18-24. NIV. 'And pray in the Spirit on all occasions with all kinds of prayers and requests. With this in mind, be alert and always keep on praying for all the Lord's people. Pray also for me, that whenever I speak, words may be given me so that I will fearlessly make known the mystery of the gospel, for which I am an ambassador in chains. Pray that I may declare it fearlessly, as I should. Tychicus, the dear brother and faithful servant in the Lord, will tell you everything, so that you also may know how I am and what I am doing. I am sending him to you for this very purpose, that you may know how we are, and that he may encourage you. Peace to the brothers and sisters, and love with faith from God the Father and the Lord Jesus Christ. Grace to all who love our Lord Jesus Christ with an undying love.' Ephesians 6:18-24. NIV.

It is possible for us to be selfish and pray only for ourselves. Paul made it clear that believers should pray for all the Lord's people.

In the context of the Devil's attacks, as no believers are

exempt, all will be attacked.

The Lord's People

You might only have read a few pages of this book and not be aware that only a small minority can be referred to as 'The Lord's People.' They have repented of their sins and accepted The Lord Jesus Christ as their Saviour. If that does not describe what you have done, you are not one of 'The Lord's People.'

If Ephesians 6 has bewildered you, is it because you know nothing about evil and the Devil's attacks that 'The Lord's People' experience? The Devil does not attack his own people. Why should he? They already do his evil bidding.

Note in Ephesians 6:18 that Paul encourages 'The Lord's People' 'to pray on all occasions with all kinds of prayers and requests.' Although many religions rely on prayer books that contain set prayers for different occasions, 'The Lord's People' are not so restricted. To put it bluntly, 'The Lord's People' can pray at any time and wherever they are. They are speaking to their Heavenly Father and He listens to His children's prayers however they express their prayers. The Holy Spirit within them assists them to pray. Hence, Paul's words, 'Pray in the Spirit.' This is how Paul told the believers in Rome The Holy Spirit assists them with their prayers. We quote Romans 8:26 from the CEV:

'In certain ways we are weak, but the Spirit is here to help us. For example, when we don't know what to pray for, the Spirit prays for us in ways that cannot be put into words.'

Believers are not limited to praying on a Sunday and they do not need a priest to be present or to pray for them. Consider Ephesians 6:18 carefully. We are sure you will agree that what we write is true. It might contradict what religions teach, and what churchgoers believe and do, but it is what The Bible unambiguously asserts.

Paul was not selfish asking for the Ephesian believers' prayers. He was in prison. He had travelled thousands of miles preaching The Gospel. This made him unpopular with the Jews and those who opposed what in Romans 1.1 Paul called 'The Gospel of God.' His future was uncertain, but he wanted prayer so that wherever he was, he would continue to proclaim The Gospel without fear.

Paul had been entrusted by God to disclose The Gospel to both Jews and Gentiles. The Gospel troubled the Jews. It proclaimed that Jesus, the One they conspired with the Romans to have killed, was 'The Christ of God.' He died for our sins, but He came back to life and returned to Heaven. This meant that the Jews had been responsible for their Messiah being crucified.

Rather than take responsibility for their dreadful mistake, the Jews persecuted their own people who believed and preached this new message, The Gospel. More Gentiles than Jews believed it, although The Gospel did not distinguish between them. Hence Paul wanted to preach The Gospel in his prison in Rome, and wherever he was sent or allowed to be.

Paul was not a criminal awaiting trial. Although we do not have precise details of Paul's situation in Rome, we do know that Tychicus was with him when he was writing this letter, and he delivered it to the Ephesian believers. He also had the responsibility of encouraging them. Paul obviously considered that encouraging them was necessary. Regrettably, there seem to be few believers who take the trouble to encourage other believers today. Encouragement is as essential today as Paul thought it was so long ago.

You only have to read The Gospels, to know that Jesus never pretended that becoming one of 'His People' would result in an easy life. The opposite is true. Accepting Jesus

as your personal Saviour makes you a target for the:
- Devil's onslaughts. We have read these about above.
- Devil's people. Those who do not belong to Jesus will consider that mocking you and snubbing you is what you deserve for being a believer.

We ask you to reflect on the closing verses of Ephesians. We trust that they will challenge you to think about the Lord's People and your own spiritual condition.

Read in Ephesians 6:20 'The Gospel Preacher's Prayer,'

'Pray that I may declare it fearlessly, as I should.'

God disclosed The Gospel to Paul. Without modern means of transport, Paul travelled thousands of miles to preach The Gospel message he received from God.

Question: What is so special about Paul's words, 'Pray that I may declare it fearlessly, as I should?'

We abridge our Answer into one sentence. Paul suffered dreadful maltreatment for preaching The Gospel, as his testimony in 2Corinthians 11 so clearly indicates.

Gospel preachers may not be maltreated today, but if you want to be laughed at, shunned, and unpopular, preach The Gospel to unbelievers without their consent. Why?

- The Gospel shows God's, not man's, wisdom.
- The vast majority consider The Gospel is foolishness. They ignore it.

Believers today preach the same Gospel that Paul preached, and although statistically few seem to believe it, it is still, in the words Paul used in Romans 1:16. NLT:

'the power of God at work, saving everyone who believes.'

Hence, believers are not ashamed of it, and not ashamed to preach it. The words quoted above were written 2000 years ago by Paul and remain true today. In a way that we cannot explain to you, The Gospel contains God's power to save. We personally know this to be true:

- It saved us.
- For over 60 years we have witnessed it saving others and we assert that it still saves those who believed it.

The Gospel will save you, but only if you believe it. Experience teaches that few are prepared to believe it. The majority will not repent of their sin. We have seen some 'almost saved' but we have seen far more reject The Gospel. They choose to spend eternity in The Lake of Fire.

Fearless

Remember Paul's request. 'Pray that I may declare it fearlessly, as I should.' Preaching The Gospel requires a fearless preacher, one who will not, 'change The Gospel,' to be popular, or to 'be more acceptable' to the congregation. The wonderful truth about The Gospel is that no one is excluded from being saved. But no one will be saved if they do not hear it faithfully preached.

Peace, Love, Faith and Grace

Paul used these very special words to conclude his letter. They are associated with The Gospel and God's Salvation. We could write another book about these four words and their divine association. However, the following four questions should have your thoughtful consideration:

1: Are you are at peace with God?

2: Do you experience God's peace day by day?

If you cannot answer, "Yes," to the first two questions, we recommend The Gospel and God's Salvation to you. Why be excluded from God's blessings, when, like the Ephesian believers, you could be included in Christ? This is what Paul wrote to them. It is the key verse of this book, and the verse we used to choose the title of this book:

> Ephesians 1:13. NIV. 'And you also were included in Christ when you heard the message of truth, the gospel of your salvation. When you believed, you were marked in him with a seal, the promised Holy Spirit ...'

3: Can you think of anything better than being 'included in Christ?'

4: When you hear The Gospel being preached, do you think of it as 'the gospel of your salvation?'

Only you can answer these vitally important questions. We again ask you to consider them carefully. They refer to spiritual matters that will have both present and eternal consequences for you.

God The Father and The Lord Jesus Christ

We cannot conclude Ephesians without listing the words Paul wrote to remind the Ephesian believers of their divine relationship to God The Father and The Lord Jesus Christ. We quote seven verses we read in Ephesians. Time spent musing on them will be time well spent:

1. Ephesians 1:2. NLT. May God our Father and the Lord Jesus Christ give you grace and peace.

2. Ephesians 1:3. NLT. All praise to God, the Father of our Lord Jesus Christ, who has blessed us with every spiritual blessing in the heavenly realms because we are united with Christ.

3. Ephesians 1:17. NLT. Asking God, the glorious Father of our Lord Jesus Christ, to give you spiritual wisdom and insight so that you might grow in your knowledge of God.

4. Ephesians 3:11. NLT. This was His eternal plan, which He carried out through Christ Jesus our Lord.
5. Ephesians 5:20. NLT. And give thanks for everything to God the Father in the name of our Lord Jesus Christ.
6. Ephesians 6:23. NLT. Peace be with you, dear brothers and sisters, and may God the Father and the Lord Jesus Christ give you love with faithfulness.
7. Ephesians 6:24. NLT. May God's grace be eternally upon all who love our Lord Jesus Christ.

Ephesians 1:13.

We again ask you to read our key verse, Ephesians 1:13. Consider thoughtfully what Paul wrote. It applied to every believer in Ephesus. It could apply to you.

> 'And you also were included in Christ when you heard the message of truth, the gospel of your salvation. When you believed, you were marked in him with a seal, the promised Holy Spirit ...' Ephesians 1:13. NIV.

A charity was set up in the Greater Manchester (UK) area by believers. The charity assists offenders who have been released from the prison which is located in Manchester. The charity has this statement printed on its notepaper:

'You cannot change your past, but you can change your future.'

We are sure that every Ephesian believer would have agreed with that statement, as would every unbeliever who has become a believer.

We have sought to tell you from Paul's letter to the Ephesian believers that you can be 'included in Christ.'

After out commentary on Ephesians 6 is concluded, we print in note form our 'Notes on Becoming a Believer.' If you are asked to preach The Gospel, you are at liberty to use these notes to prepare your 'Gospel message.' You can copy these notes without permission, provided that you do not alter them, omit any part of them, or add to them. If you are not yet a believer, these notes might assist to bring together matters relating to The Gospel and God's Salvation so that you can decide to be 'Included in Christ.'

'Included in Christ'

We conclude our commentary with these words:

There is nothing more important and no greater privilege than being 'included in Christ.'

Be wise and ensure that you are 'included in Christ.'

Notes on Becoming a Believer.

1. Paul wrote what unbelievers need to become believers:
   1) Unbelievers must hear, 'a message.'
   2) Paul called it 'the message of truth.'
2. This 'message' is The Gospel.
3. If unbelievers do not hear, or will not hear, The Gospel, or if they hear it, but do not believe it, then:
   1) there can be no spiritual change in their lives.
   2) they were born sinners, and they will remain as they were born.
   3) they will die unforgiven sinners.
4. The Gospel 'the message of truth' requires a response from unbelievers who hear it. There are two options:
   1) believe it.
   2) reject it.
5. Unbelievers who hear The Gospel and believe it:
   1) are included in Christ.
   2) receive God's forgiveness for their sins.
   3) receive God's eternal life.
   4) are indwelt by The Holy Spirit.
   5) will know it is 'The Gospel of their Salvation.'
6. Because God hates sin, The Bible warns of the eternal consequences for those who die unforgiven sinners:
   1) God's wrath remains forever on unforgiven sinners.
   2) Unforgiven sinners will be cast into The Lake of Fire.

ABOUT THE AUTHOR

The author was born during World War II in Prestbury, Cheshire, England, UK. He has lived and worked in and about the Greater Manchester area.

He attended the local Gospel Hall Sunday School from childhood. He was taught stories and truths from the Bible. His parents read and respected The Bible. They accepted it as God's Word.

His childhood abilities to read and memorise and his inclination to discuss, argue and debate with his peers and those of senior years enabled him to investigate, analyse and evaluate what he had read and been taught. These skills were also invaluable to him in his career as a litigation lawyer.

When he was young, he realised that what The Bible taught about sin was correct. Knowing that he was a sinner, and that on a Cross at Calvary, The Lord Jesus Christ died having been punished for sinners, he accepted God's offer of Salvation. That was well over sixty years ago but he remains convinced today that:

- The Bible is God's Word.
- All have sinned against God.
- God requires all to repent.
- Jesus died to save sinners.

God's Salvation is for all who will repent and accept Jesus as their Saviour. This is the Good News, The Gospel. It has the inherent ability to change the lives of those who believe it.

From Genesis, the first book of The Bible, to Revelation, the last book, God has made His way of Salvation unambiguous.

God's Salvation is available to you and to everyone today.

These verses, quoted from The Bible, should be carefully considered by those do not possess God's Salvation.

Jesus said:

"I am the way, the truth and the life. No man cometh unto the Father but by me." John 14:6.

The following verse has aptly been referred to as:

'The Gospel in a nutshell.'

'For God so loved the world that He gave His only begotten Son, that whosoever believeth in Him should not perish, but have everlasting life.' John 3:16.

ACKNOWLEDGEMENTS AND NOTICES

ACKNOWLEDGEMENTS

The following Bible translations have assisted the author:

- Contemporary English Version
- God's Word
- Good News Bible
- King James Version
- New International Version
- Revised Standard Version
- The Living Bible
- The Message
- Today's New International Version
- Wuest Expanded Translation

These translations and others can be downloaded from www.e-sword.net. The author is grateful to the website owner for the use of the Bibles, Dictionaries and Maps that have greatly assisted him.

NOTICES

The views and opinions expressed within this book are those of the author.

COPYRIGHT NOTICE

COPYRIGHT

© Harold J Booth 2019

OTHER BOOKS BY THE AUTHOR

GENESIS

This book contains comments that should provoke all who read it to consider the events recorded and their own relationship to the God who created the world and yet wishes to be involved in and bless the daily lives of His creatures.

In Genesis, God reveals the beginnings of His Plan of Salvation and tells us that although man sinned and continues to sin, God has always desired that man should repent of sin, be forgiven and return to Him. God has always offered man the opportunity to have, 'a new start,' and God's offer is available today.

Reading this Book will not only increase your knowledge of Genesis. It will challenge your attitude to God and to sin. It will teach you that you are special to God and that God wants you to live to please Him in a world that is hostile to Him and to those who have accepted His Son, the Lord Jesus Christ as their Saviour.

IS YOUR NAME IN THE BOOK OF LIFE?

Dr Derek Stringer, who before he retired was the National Director, Good News Broadcasting Association (UK) writes,

'The author believes that The Book of Life has become a forgotten truth and he desires to make it a primary truth again. This book sets out to help people understand that their names could be written in Heaven and why without God's Salvation, their eternal future is bleak.

This down to earth book is written in a clear and direct style. It does not duck difficult issues and it would be a very useful tool to those who wish to live wisely and well in this life because their eternal future in Heaven is assured. This book will also be of value to those who want to share their Christian faith but struggle to present the Gospel.'

This book examines:

- How Jesus dealt with those who believed that their lives were good enough for God and who thought that they had no need to repent.
- The Gospel's requirement of repentance and faith in The Lord Jesus Christ.' The true meaning of, 'repentance.'
- The visible evidence that distinguishes those who believe The Gospel from those who do not.
  - A different lifestyle.
  - A different attitude to sin.
- God's hatred of sin, His love for sinners and His eternal Judgment for those who do not accept Jesus as their personal Saviour and Lord.

THE WORD FROM JOHN

John's Gospel Chapters 1-4.

Dr Derek Stringer, who before he retired was the National Director, Good News Broadcasting Association (UK) writes,

'The Gospel of John is one of the greatest books of all time. We owe so much to the insights of John in giving us a clearer picture of Jesus Christ. It is no small accomplishment to present time-honoured truth in a fresh way. But this is what Harold Booth accomplishes with distinction. With a lucid style, Harold takes us into the opening chapters. There are no cliché bromides here, but rather rigorous Biblical truth presented with eyes wide open to contemporary life and practical application. Read it because it is worth it.'

PAUL'S LETTER TO THE ROMANS

A Verse-by-Verse Commentary

Paul had a very privileged background and education.

Paul was a distinguished lawyer in Jewish and Roman Law and an expert in The Old Testament, to name just two of his renown abilities.

Paul wrote the majority of the letters in The New Testament. However, he wrote his letter to the Romans in a legal style that you would anticipate from a distinguished lawyer. You must therefore expect Paul to introduce facts and evidence, and argue the case for the truth he presented. Paul used legal words such as case, judge, judgment, defence, proof, evidence, sentence and witnesses.

Those who read The Bible soon realise that it is no ordinary book. That is because it is God's Word. Those who never read it are the ones who criticise it most. Some unwisely think that it contains myth and stories suitable only for children. The letter to the Romans was written by a lawyer. It would persuade anyone prepared to read it that no one need lower their intellect to find God's Truth.

But there is more. Paul's letter was intended to deal with the fundamental doctrines of 'The Christian Faith' that were under attack and being undermined. Even the truths of The Gospel and God's Salvation were being challenged. So, if you are a believer in The Lord Jesus Christ, you can expect to read wonderful truths about why:

- only Jesus is able to be your Saviour.
- God is able to forgive your sin that He hates, and give you the eternal blessings He has prepared for you.

Those not yet believers will discover in Romans why they need God's Salvation, and why only The Gospel can deal with the problem of sin.

THE ACTS OF THE APOSTLES

The One And Only Church

Who would have guessed that from the small group who followed Jesus, a worldwide Church would have emerged?

Although so diverse, the members of this worldwide Church are all cleansed by the precious blood that Jesus shed when He suffered and died at Calvary for the sins of the world. They are forgiven because they have believed The Gospel, the good news from God that Christ died for our sins, was buried but came back to life.

The members of this worldwide Church have their own story to tell as to how they were saved, but when they were, they were built into 'The Christian Church.' It began at Pentecost when The Holy Spirit indwelt those who were saved.

Down the centuries for two thousand years, those who are saved have preached The Gospel so it would not be easy today to name places where The Gospel is unknown. As technology develops, broadcasts will reach wider areas and as people hear The Gospel and accept the Lord Jesus Christ as their Saviour, The Church will continue to grow.

This book looks at the early days of The Church recorded in Acts. Every event is considered and any changes that took place are studied to see if there are lessons to be learnt.

This book considers if The Church that began two thousand years ago is relevant today and if it will survive.

Good News Broadcasting Association

Tom Ward, the Director of GNBA, states that GNBA is a Christian charity that has been teaching the Bible through radio for over 60 years. He said:

- We create and distribute a number of different programmes to challenge and encourage believers while also trying to engage non-Christians who are exploring faith.
- We broadcast on local and national Christian stations in the UK as well as in Indonesia, the Philippines and the southern regions of Africa.
- We also broadcast on secular radio.

To find out more about what we do or to listen to any of our programmes, our website is www.gnba.net

If you would like to join our mailing list or contribute to our work, please:

- email:
  info@gnba.net
- write:
  Good News Broadcasting,
  Unit 27, Wilsons Park, Monsall Road,
  Manchester, M40 8WN